Christ
20

Lincoln's
Final Hours

LINCOLN'S
FINAL HOURS

Conspiracy, Terror, and
the Assassination of America's
Greatest President

KATHRYN CANAVAN

UNIVERSITY PRESS OF KENTUCKY

Scholarly publisher for the Commonwealth,
serving Bellarmine University, Berea College, Centre College of Kentucky,
Eastern Kentucky University, The Filson Historical Society, Georgetown College,
Kentucky Historical Society, Kentucky State University, Morehead State
University, Murray State University, Northern Kentucky University, Transylvania
University, University of Kentucky, University of Louisville, and Western
Kentucky University.
All rights reserved.

Editorial and Sales Offices: The University Press of Kentucky
663 South Limestone Street, Lexington, Kentucky 40508-4008
www.kentuckypress.com

Library of Congress Cataloging-in-Publication Data

Canavan, Kathryn.
  Lincoln's final hours : conspiracy, terror, and the assassination of America's
greatest president / Kathryn Canavan.
      pages cm
  Includes bibliographical references and index.
  ISBN 978-0-8131-6608-7 (hardcover : alk. paper) —
  ISBN 978-0-8131-6610-0 (pdf) — ISBN 978-0-8131-6609-4 (epub)
  1. Lincoln, Abraham, 1809-1865—Assassination. I. Title.
  E457.5.C25 2015
  973.7092—dc23   2015018012

For John, Matt, and Greg,
three marvelous writers
with unlimited stories inside them.

The life of the dead is placed in the memory of the living.

—Cicero

Contents

Preface

History burst through the front door of one Washington home on April 14, 1865. The Petersens, who owned a boardinghouse across the street from Ford's Theatre, were scarcely aware the president had been shot when doctors carried him to their front door.

Unbeknownst to them, one of their boarders was standing in a second-story window watching the commotion across the street. It was he who made the split-second decision to run outside with a lighted candle and beckon the doctors to their door.

Imagine how you might feel if there were a knock at your door this Friday evening and, without a word of warning, soldiers rushed the fatally wounded president of the United States into your bedroom, followed by the first lady, cabinet members, and a bevy of socialites. Now imagine you have no electricity, no hot water, and no bathrooms, just gas lamps, a stove to boil water on, and chamber pots that you must empty.

Ordinary people like the Petersens and their boarders were thrust into an extraordinary circumstance.

Some handled it better than others.

Until now, most of their stories were untold.

Although some of the events that took place that night startle, every detail and quotation in this book is true, actual and documented.

Petersen House, where President Lincoln died, shown on a 1907 picture postcard. The house originally had light green shutters.
Credit: The Collection of Jim Garrett

1

The Secret about Booth

Fred Petersen heard the clatter of a carriage pulling up at Ford's Theatre. The green, monogrammed carriage itself, with its solid silver hubcaps, was enough to merit a second look, but this night, one of the passengers inside was the most celebrated man in Washington.

Fred watched as the footman tugged the silver door handle, and a set of stairs automatically sprang forward. President and Mrs. Abraham Lincoln and their guests stepped out in silks and satins, the president carrying a monogrammed silver and ebony cane.[1] One of the happiest days of Mr. Lincoln's life was proceeding, just a little behind schedule.

Already late for the show, the party of four descended the carriage steps directly onto the wooden platform that led to the theater's five arched entrances, bypassing the dusty, rutted, sand street.[2] It was the tail end of the most exciting week in Washington history, one that had begun with General Robert E. Lee's surrender on Sunday and would end in an uproar.

While others gaped at the Lincolns, Fred sprinted down the street to make the curtain at Grover's National Theatre, four blocks away.[3] At fifteen, he already knew more celebrities than most adults. Three members of Congress had lived at his family's boardinghouse directly across the street from Ford's, and comedian John Mathews was a current resident.[4] Why, even the actor John Wilkes Booth, called the handsomest man in America, sometimes napped in a small back bedroom on the first floor.[5] Perhaps Fred would have stayed if he had known what was about to happen inside Ford's. Only a handful of conspirators knew that though. And even the conspirators didn't have an inkling of what the distant future held for the four members of the presidential party who were, right then, being greeted with five solid minutes of applause.[6] Before two decades had passed, two of them would be murdered by madmen. The other two would be committed to insane asylums.

Grover's National Theatre had illuminated its Pennsylvania Avenue entrance to mark the Union victory. Two oversized transparencies shone in

the light. The one on the left side of the doors read, "April 1861, the cradle."
On the right: "April 1865, the grave." The signs had been hung to celebrate
the birth and death of the Confederacy, but in a few hours, everything
would change, and passersby would view them as omens of evil.[7]

Inside Grover's, audience members, many hoarse from cheering and
singing all week, took their red, white, and blue programs and settled into
their seats to watch *Aladdin!*[8] The production was well under way when
the theater doors banged open and a man shouted, "President Lincoln has
been shot in his private box at Ford's! Turn out!"[9] The audience, thrown
into confusion, stirred, until a calm voice called out, "Sit down. It is a ruse
of the pickpockets." It was James Tanner, a War Department clerk who had
lost both his legs at the Second Battle of Bull Run.[10] As the evening unfolded, the twenty-one-year-old would play a key role in the assassination
investigation, but for now, the crowd sat.

The play went on.

Few people noticed the man who whisked twelve-year-old Tad Lincoln
from the theater. Even fewer could hear the messenger who slipped around
to Helen Moss's seat during a scene shift and whispered instructions from
her brother-in-law, theater manager C. D. Hess: "Leave your seats quietly,
and stand by the back door. President Lincoln has been shot at Ford's Theatre. Mr. Hess is going before the curtain to announce it and close the theater at once." Before the man walked off, he warned her, "Stand back, lest
there be a rush for the door."[11]

Moss couldn't believe her own ears. Just that afternoon, Mr. Lincoln
had welcomed her and her sister-in-law Julia Hess to the Executive Mansion conservancy. April 14, 1865, was a memorable day for Hess and Moss.
They had shaken the hand of wavy-haired actor John Wilkes Booth in front
of Grover's. Then they had walked two blocks to the Executive Mansion,
where they had shaken President Lincoln's hand, too. The president, who
knew Julia Hess's husband, had given the women a tour of his conservancy,
where they breathed the mild bouquet of his prize lemon tree. Moss was
wearing flowers from that tree as she hurried from her seat to Grover's back
door.[12]

An acrobat was scheduled to tumble from a balloon to the stage some
time after ten thirty. Instead, the balding twenty-seven-year-old theater
manager stepped through the curtain. With the footlights shining on his
stocky frame, Hess said he had a very grave announcement. Then he repeated the intruder's words: "President Lincoln has been shot in his private box at Ford's." The house became still as death, Moss noticed. So still

that she was sure she could have heard a pin drop. Patrons seemed glued to their spots. Then, the audience rose almost as one body, dazed looks on their faces. Soldiers armed with bayonets were on hand in case the crowd rushed the exits—but there was no rush. Cheerless patrons silently filed out onto Pennsylvania Avenue, Washington's widest commercial street. Illuminated for the war's end, it was so bright that you could see for blocks in either direction. The only sound was horses' hooves striking the cobblestones as the cavalry made for Tenth Street and Ford's.

James Tanner, on his wooden legs, headed one block over to Willard's Hotel to learn what he could.[13] Fred Petersen tried to go home. Theatergoers, speaking in hushed tones, formed an impromptu procession headed for Ford's. And, as soon as he could, the young manager Hess wired theater owner Leonard Grover at his New York hotel: "President Lincoln shot tonight at Ford's Theatre. Thank God it wasn't ours. C. D. Hess."[14]

As Fred ran east to his house directly across from Ford's Theatre, the mood shifted. Word had filtered out from Willard's that Secretary of State William Seward's throat had been slit in his own home. Men shouted that the rebels surrounded the city. "They have begun their raid," one cried.[15] In the space of two blocks, as if someone had flipped a switch, bewilderment became hysteria. As Fred rounded the corner to Tenth Street, running as fast as he could, he heard some men yelling, "Hang him. Hang him." He turned just in time to see a knot of rowdies crowded under a sycamore tree. They had caught hold of a poor man they had decided to string up. Fred pushed his way past them and ran uphill toward home. As he reached his block, he eyed one solid mass of men waving knives and revolvers and denouncing the assassins.[16] Like Pearl Harbor in the twentieth century and September 11 in the twenty-first, no one knew what would happen next.

Word spread of the assassinations of Seward, General U. S. Grant, Vice President Andrew Johnson, Secretary of War Edwin M. Stanton, and Chief Justice Salmon P. Chase. It would be daylight before anyone really knew who had been assassinated and who had been spared.

The news passed from lip to lip that actor John Wilkes Booth was the president's shooter. Nonsensical! Everyone knew the president had come out to see Booth play in *Richard III* and *The Marble Heart*. The president had even asked to meet the actor; few knew that Booth had purposely evaded meeting Lincoln.

When Fred Petersen approached his curving brownstone porch, he found two soldiers blocking his door. "You can't go in," one said. "The president is lying in there." "But I live here," Fred said. And he heard back, "No difference, you can't go in." "I will see if I can't get in," Fred muttered to himself.[17]

After a kitchen fire in 1863, the Petersens had built an addition to their home, separated from the original structure by a brick walkway.[18] The president had been carried to a small slope-roofed bedroom in that back portion. The lot was just one hundred feet long, but a web of alleys and walkways crisscrossed it, and of course, Fred knew them all. Searching for an unguarded window, he spotted his chum Billy Ferguson, also rebuffed by the guards. The wiry, shiny-haired callboy at Ford's had just rung down the curtain for the last time.[19] Together, they pulled off a shutter, wriggled in a window, and climbed the crooked back steps to the floor where President Lincoln lay dying.[20]

The first man Fred saw inside his house was his father, a stern tailor with swept-back dark hair, thick eyebrows, and a square face framed by untamed muttonchop sideburns and a short, trim beard.[21] William Petersen made a good living sewing high-quality military uniforms at his shop at 442 Eighth Street West, good enough to send his oldest daughter to Moravian Seminary for Young Ladies, the Pennsylvania boarding school that had graduated George Washington's niece and John Jay's daughter.[22] Petersen, a cruel, oft-drunken German immigrant who had become an American citizen twenty-one years earlier, was fixing to pass the care of his president to his children, his boarders, and his live-in servant so that he could leave the house. His much-abused wife was out of town.[23]

He told Fred that President Lincoln was lying in the small room above the kitchen and instructed him to see what he could do to help the doctors. As he neared the room, the boy's stomach turned. Bandages stained with President Lincoln's brain matter were already piled in the hallway. The stench took his breath away.[24] The narrow bedroom was swollen with doctors, family, friends, members of the cabinet, and boarders enlisted to fetch hot water bottles. It was so jammed that Fred couldn't see more than an inch or two of the olive green and beige wallpaper with orange and mustard accents, except near the ceiling and behind the walnut bed where President Lincoln lay gasping on a corn-husk mattress topped with a softer cotton shoddy one.[25]

The president's face looked ghastly in the dim gaslight. His rigid lips never parted, but his face twitched. His right hand, the one that had signed the Emancipation Proclamation, jerked involuntarily.[26] The president's blood penetrated the feather pillows. His brain matter dotted the red, white, and blue Irish wool quilt. With each rise and fall of his chest, there issued a bleak, unforgettable moan. Senator Charles Sumner was sitting on the bed, holding the president's hand and sobbing like a child. The grim scene would have saddened anyone, but it jolted Fred and Ferguson. The boys knew something the sobbing cabinet members probably never imagined. They had both seen John Wilkes Booth lying on the same dark wood bed where Lincoln now lay unconscious. And they knew the assassin had cuddled up under the same quilt that now draped the dying president's nude body. Booth's convivial laughter had echoed through the small room then, just as the president's doleful moans did now.[27]

Billy Ferguson recalled hearing that lilting laughter three months earlier when he visited Petersen's boardinghouse to deliver scripts to comedian John Mathews, who was renting the room with the sloping ceiling that week. About a half dozen actors were horsing around inside the comedian's room when the boy entered. One of them was "Johnnie Booth," a childhood friend of Mathews. Uncommonly handsome, Booth was always impeccably dressed save one peculiarity—his necktie was usually a little askew.[28]

Ferguson's esteem for Booth was nothing short of hero worship prior to the assassination, so much so that, even decades later, he could describe what the dashing actor did in the tight confines of Mathews's room. Booth had been stretched out on the bed, his luxuriant black hair disheveled and a pipe hooked in his mouth. His gentle laughs made him seem even more attractive. Ferguson thought the inexpensive carte de visite photographs of Booth made him appear sullen, while the three-dimensional Booth was more joyous. The photographs could not capture his quick excitability and his unbridled love of fun.[29]

Fred's memory of Booth in the bed was even more recent than his chum's. He had seen the actor napping under the same checked-and-flowered quilt just one week earlier.[30] Fred probably knew it would come out that the president and his slayer had occupied the same six-dollar bed.[31] Mathews and the other actors all knew. And Harry Clay Ford, the treasurer of Ford's Theatre, had gotten into a heated political row with Booth in the room two months earlier.[32] Fred didn't have much time to think about any of that. The doctors asked him to find more bottles to fill with hot water so they could pack them around the president's stiff limbs to keep his circulation flowing. He walked downstairs to the kitchen, where the servant already had a fire going. He ordered her to fill the bottles and carry them to the bedroom.[33]

Then Fred's father approached. William Petersen told Fred he was returning to work at his shop until after the president had died. As the president gasped for breath, Petersen told his son to fetch him when it was all over. At least one of the lodgers was miffed that Petersen ducked out while he and the others trudged up and down the thirteen curving steps to the kitchen most of the night, filling hot water bottles. If his boarders were rattled about that, then they must have been outraged by what Petersen did three weeks later, before the president's body was even in the ground.[34]

2

Washington City Then

The city directory listed 111 boardinghouses in 1865, but nearly every home in Washington had a sign in the window welcoming those willing to pay three to ten dollars a week for a room.[1] Boarders were treated like family—and subjected to all the drama and dilemmas and confidences of the household.[2] Some families rented out one room. Some catered to a specific clientele, like Mrs. Beveridge's at 224 Third Street West, where Indian chiefs stayed while negotiating treaties.[3] And some houses, like the Petersens', rented every available space, even the 6.5 x 10-foot second-floor staircase landing.[4]

It was a simple matter for a homeowner to rent out a space, no matter how small, during the war. The city's population tripled to almost two hundred thousand, and prices rose too, so much that some foreign governments moved their embassies to Baltimore.[5]

Because Petersen's boardinghouse stood just one and a half squares uphill from Pennsylvania Avenue, its roster of past tenants included at least three members of Congress—William A. Newell and Andrew K. Hay of New Jersey and John C. Breckinridge of Kentucky, who went on to serve as vice president under James Buchanan and later switched sides and served as a Confederate general.[6]

In 1865, Washington was not the marble-faced, manicured capital it would become.[7] The Washington Monument stood temporarily abandoned at 156 feet—less than a third of its eventual height. Cows, sheep, goats, and poultry grazed around its stump. Pavement was uncommon. Drainage was unheard of. Pigs rooted for garbage in city streets. Rubbish and sediment swept out of shops and homes washed into intersections.[8] After a steady rain, the city's unpaved streets of clay and loam were mired in mud, one to three feet of it, so much that carriages would get swamped, and their occupants would have to dismount.[9] When a foreign delegation's coach sank up to its axles near the Treasury Building, its occupants, in full diplomatic regalia, cried in vain for planks to be brought so they

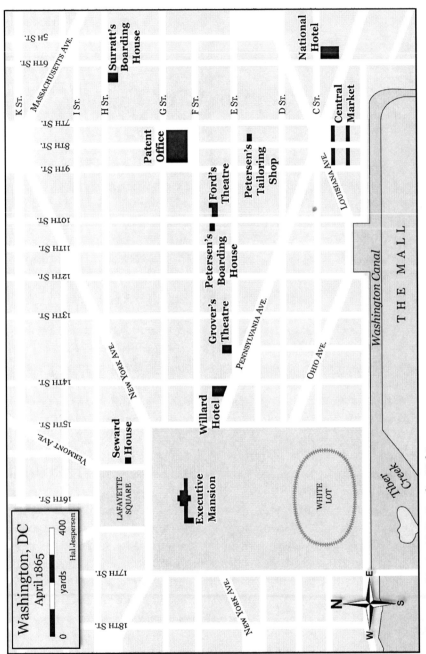

Washington City in 1865. Credit: Hal Jespersen

The Washington Monument stood unfinished as soldiers camped on the Washington Mall in 1865. Credit: Library of Congress

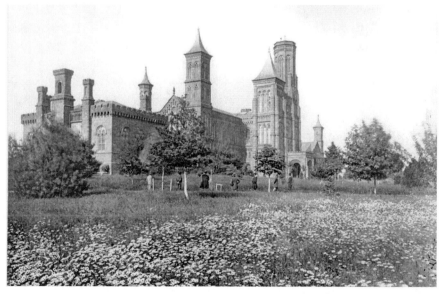

Smithsonian Castle in 1862, nine years before William Petersen died there. Credit: Library of Congress

could disembark without sinking into the sludge. Long after the sun dried the streets, deep washboard ruts remained. Men, even the president, wore shin-high boots with suits and formal wear, because shoes sometimes vanished in the paste-like muck.[10]

Dead dogs, cattle, and occasionally citizens drifted down the fetid Washington City Canal, along with most of the capital's sewage. The canal, eighty feet wide in some spots, was an unwholesome leftover from the early part of the century. Long since replaced by railroads as a mode of transportation, it still stretched across the city from the front of the Capitol to the back of the Executive Mansion, reeking of rotted produce, discarded fish, and human excrement.[11] Adding to the stench were the stables and corrals that dotted the city. The largest, Giesboro Point Cavalry Depot, housed twenty-one thousand horses.[12]

Ears were assaulted with a constant din of voices, gunfire, bugle calls, and horses' hooves. Soldiers discharged their weapons daily, and cannon fire vaguely echoed from battlefields in nearby Virginia. On top of the stench and the racket, the putrid canal water carried malaria, cholera, and the typhoid that killed eleven-year-old Willie Lincoln in 1862.[13]

Saloons and at least eighty-five houses of prostitution peppered the city.[14] Gambling halls aplenty beckoned bettors, including members of Congress. "Murderer's Bay" was the name locals gave to the shanties and saloons and houses of ill repute that lined the blocks just east of the Executive Mansion. Mrs. Lincoln insisted her husband carry a wooden stick when he walked through the city alone. When he remembered it, the president carried a thick oak plank studded with two bolts, one from the USS *Monitor* and the other from the rebel *Merrimac*. He didn't really believe it would alter his fate. "I long ago made up my mind that if anybody wants to kill me, he will do it," he told reporter Noah Brooks.[15]

War had wholly enveloped the federal city by 1865. Churches had been converted into makeshift hospitals. Members of Congress could hear barrels of flour being rolled into storage beneath the stately Senate chamber. The smell of fresh bread wafted into congressional offices from the ovens installed in the Capitol basement to feed the troops. Soldiers, about a quarter million in all, made camp on the Mall, in the Treasury Building, even next to the inventions in the Patent Office.[16] The Capitol's gleaming new dome was still unfinished inside, and for the moment, it was shenanigans central for Union soldiers. The high-spirited New York Fire Zouaves, a regiment outfitted in colorful ballooned harem pants, dangled ropes from the rotunda walls and swung willy-nilly back and forth under the gaping dome.[17]

The Eighth Massachusetts held its own mock congress in the new Senate chamber. The chamber wasn't the only thing the soldiers appropriated for their own use. When they wrote home, they did so on official congressional stationery.[18]

Wounded soldiers arriving from battlefields by train were treated at fifty-six army hospitals, some makeshift, others state of the art like three-year-old Armory Square, where the most severely wounded were taken. Adjacent to the magnificent new Smithsonian building, it featured eleven long pavilions placed side by side. Before the war's end, 1,339 men had died there, but that didn't stop loved ones from hoping. Whenever wounded soldiers arrived from the front, anxious family members crowded the city's sixty-six hotels, awaiting news.[19]

Four theaters brought celebrated actors and musicians like Laura Keene to town.[20] They stayed in boardinghouses or booked hotels like the National or Willard's. Willard's Hotel was the city's grandest, two blocks from the Executive Mansion, close enough for the president to pop in to exchange nods with leaders from every state and many foreign countries. Northerners and southerners tended to use different doors. Willard's was especially popular with Unionists, so much so that some guests slept on cots in the hallways.[21] H. S. Benson's National Hotel, eight blocks east on Pennsylvania Avenue, catered to "secesh people," Mr. Lincoln's word for Confederate sympathizers.[22] A city block long, she was the largest in the city. What was found there in Room 228 would make headlines on April 17.

In 1865, Washington City was part world capital, part small southern town. The magnificent hotels and marble palaces of government were just one of its faces. Diplomats wouldn't have noticed the hidden alleys teeming with those who served and entertained them. Nonwhites lived in places like Goat Alley, almost invisible from the main streets and topfull of small wooden living quarters.[23] Actors took shortcuts through openings like Baptist Alley, which ran between the back door at Ford's and Ninth Street, with a leg out to F Street. It took its name from the denomination that occupied Ford's before it was converted from a church to a theater in 1861.[24]

Successful immigrants like the Italians and Germans who lived on Tenth Street built row houses a comfortable twenty-five feet wide and drank in taverns like the Dew Drop Inn and Charley Bennett's, uphill from Ford's. Financiers and cabinet members lived in the posh mansions lining Massachusetts Avenue or the stately townhouses belting Lafayette Square. The public buildings were grander yet. Forty-two scrolled columns graced the marble front of the post office. The Executive Mansion featured two

Maimed soldiers gather outside the headquarters of the US Christian Commission. Walt Whitman and Louisa May Alcott were among the thousands of commission volunteers. Credit: Library of Congress

imposing porticos. The Capitol Building, which then housed the congressional library and the Supreme Court, stretched 457 feet.[25]

The US Christian Commission set about its mission from a plain brick building at 500 H Street. Its goal was to counter war, drinking, and gambling with prayer, patience, and the occasional gift. Armed with hymnals, Bible tracts, and three million dollars' worth of supplies, the commission volunteers, including Walt Whitman and Louisa May Alcott, comforted soldiers and supported officers in the field, especially chaplains.[26] Although they gave away 1.5 million Bibles, George H. Stuart, the wealthy Presbyterian layman who led them, said, "There is a good deal of religion in a warm shirt and a good beefsteak."[27]

While the war went on around them, small businessmen like William Petersen thrived. The city directory for 1865 listed looking-glass makers, bill posters, cider makers, stencil cutters, stair builders, fancy-box makers, embalmers of the dead, and one matchmaker, Philip Alldorfer of Twenty-sixth Street West.[28]

The ordinary citizens of Washington treasured their newly built mar-

The members of the Megatherium Society—William Stimpson (front left), Rob Kennicott (back left), Henry Ulke (back right), and Henry Bryant. Credit: The Estate of Henry Ulke

ble halls of government, but few enjoyed a public building quite the way the members of the Megatherium Society did the showy red-sandstone Smithsonian Castle. The young club members, whose namesake was an extinct giant sloth, were a loose band of amateur and professional naturalists, astronomers, biologists, and entomologists. They rented one room under the turreted and spired roof of the new faux-Norman castle for their weekly meetings. When the last of the staff left for the day, though, some nights they spread out. It began during the meetings, when enthusiastic members downed two inexpensive repasts—ale and oysters. Soon they were loudly uttering the imaginary call of their sloth namesake—"How! How!" They sometimes concluded with sack races in the Great Hall.[29]

The club, which included at least one boarder from Petersen's boardinghouse, was led by twenty-five-year-old William Stimpson, a charismatic curly-haired and bespectacled marine biologist. Stimpson later rented a house directly across from the Smithsonian and took in boarders with a scientific bent. The place was quickly dubbed "The Stimpsonian." He went on to serve as director of the Chicago Academy of the Sciences, but the Great Chicago Fire consumed the "fireproof" building and its collections in 1871.[30]

The year of the assassination, the grandest commercial street in the city was Pennsylvania Avenue, one of the few streets paved with stone. Washingtonians routinely shortened its name to "the avenue." Commercial buildings spilled over from the avenue onto Tenth Street—bars, restaurants, rooming houses, and the magnificent renovated Ford's Theatre.

Many of Tenth Street's private homes had been converted into boardinghouses before the war. Conveniently located near government buildings, they became homes away from home for congressmen. The actors whose names filled the playbills at Ford's Theatre sought rooms too. They were considered less desirable tenants, but most families, like the Petersens, welcomed them as long as they had cash to pay the rent.

The Lincolns had the Executive Mansion all to themselves except for the president's two secretaries, John Hay and George Nicolay, who had bedrooms across the hall from each other. But almost every man who visited Washington stopped in to shake hands with Mr. Lincoln.[31] The president often had blisters on all four fingers of his large right hand to show for it.[32] Twice a week, anyone who wished to talk with him could wait his turn at the Executive Mansion. Mr. Lincoln called the occasions "public opinion baths."[33] People began showing up before breakfast. Although the War Department budget had ballooned to more than one billion dollars by 1865, and the pressure on the president had swelled too, the Lincolns never gave short shrift to the concerns of ordinary citizens.[34]

Living in the nation's capital, shoulder to shoulder with politicians, actors, musicians, and individuals like the Megatherium Society members, was entertaining, but never so much as during the week of the Great Illumination.

3

The Great Illumination

The week of April 9, 1865, was the happiest and the saddest one in Washington, DC, history. In the space of seven days, everything changed to its core. The city went wild when news of General Robert E. Lee's Palm Sunday surrender arrived via the morning papers on Monday, April 10. Men threw their hats—and other people's hats—in the air. Booming brass bands strutted down the dirt streets. Choruses sang "When Johnny Comes Marching Home Again." Shopkeepers sold out of flags and fireworks. It was as if the weather were in on the celebration too. The skies were blue, and temperatures veered toward spring.[1]

Church bells rang swiftly and cheerily, despite it being the most somber week on the church calendar. A five-hundred-gun salute broke windows in fashionable Lafayette Square, across Pennsylvania Avenue from the Executive Mansion.[2] And everywhere, throats were growing hoarse from singing and shouting.[3] Washington saw no end to the celebrating, and while John Wilkes Booth wasn't in a celebratory mood, he must have felt accomplished. Before he left Boston the first week of April, Booth had visited Floyd & Edward's Shooting Gallery.[4] A crack shot with either hand, the actor practiced firing his weapon under his leg, from behind his neck, and in other showy stances.[5] He thought he had left little to chance.

Throughout the war, Washington City had been mostly dark, but by Tuesday, April 11, houses, shops, and offices were candlelit from basement to roofline. Red, white, and blue bunting was everywhere. The skies were ablaze with fireworks. Even Confederate general Robert E. Lee's graceful white-columned mansion across the river in Virginia was illuminated. Now in Union hands, its gently sloping lawn was dotted with thousands of former slaves singing with joy under the waxing moon.

About ten p.m., throngs of well-wishers made their way down Washington streets to the Executive Mansion. After they assembled on the lawn in front of the portico, a jovial Mr. Lincoln appeared at a second-story window. People who had never heard the president speak took a few minutes

This photo of President Abraham Lincoln was taken about two months before he was shot. Credit: Library of Congress

to adjust to the unexpectedly shrill voice coming from a man who stood about nine inches taller than average. Mr. Lincoln also spoke with a peculiar fifty-fifty Kentucky-Indiana accent. Still, when his thick, droopy lower lip rose into a wide smile and his gray eyes twinkled in concert, crowds got caught up, hanging on his every word. It was his cadence that captivated. The rhythms of Shakespeare and the King James Bible permeated his speeches. This night the Great Emancipator called for reuniting the country and extending the vote to black people—at least those deemed very intelligent and those who had served in the Union army.[6]

In the spotty torchlight of the Executive Mansion lawn, two accomplished young men listened closely. One, the hot-headed actor John Wilkes Booth, was beside himself. The twenty-six-year-old had already hatched an unsuccessful plot to kidnap the president.[7] Now he was white-hot furious and steeled to go further. The other man, Dr. Charles Leale, a twenty-three-year-old army surgeon, hadn't even intended to come to the speech that night. He was out getting some fresh air when he was swept into a torchlight parade bound for the president's house. The thin, fair-skinned New Yorker had spent an arduous day treating soldiers' gunshot wounds at Armory Square Hospital.[8] He arrived at the Executive Mansion just as Mr. Lincoln began addressing the crowd. From where he stood, Leale could hear every word of what would be the president's last public address. To Leale, the president looked divine as he stood in the rays of light. He promised himself that he'd seek out another opportunity to study the characteristics of this man who had saved the Union.[9]

Although Booth and Leale were both in their twenties, both compactly built and of medium height, both from bookish families, the similarities between them ended there. Their reactions to Lincoln's last speech were as markedly different as the presidents they admired. Leale looked up to Lincoln. Booth favored Jefferson Davis, a man Sam Houston once described as "cold as a lizard and ambitious as Lucifer."[10]

By the week's end, Booth would keep his promise to harm the president, and Dr. Leale would do his best to stop him.

Thursday, April 13, was like no other night before or since in Washington, DC. Never mind that it was Maundy Thursday, one of the most sacred days of the Christian calendar. The war that had killed one out of every forty-one Americans was almost over.[11]

Mary Lincoln's own family was a microcosm of the war's ravages. The Todds already had lost three sons and a son-in-law to the war. Samuel Briggs Todd had been killed fighting for the Confederacy at the Battle

Dr. Charles A. Leale was twenty-three years old when he tried to save the president. Credit: Library of Congress

of Shiloh. David Todd had died of wounds he suffered while fighting for the South at Vicksburg. Alexander Humphreys Todd, also a Confederate, had died in a friendly-fire incident in Baton Rouge. Son-in-law Benjamin Hardin Helm, a West Point graduate who also fought with the rebels, had

John Wilkes Booth was twenty-six when he killed the president. Credit: National Archives

been mortally wounded at Chickamauga. And, within forty-eight hours, the family would lose a second son-in-law at Ford's Theatre.

But this night, the American flag was once again flying over Fort Sumter. Children sang. Men hallooed. Guns fired in the air.[12] Bonfires shimmered in the streets. The sky was ablaze with bursting rockets. Tar sticks burned in metal cans, casting a dancing yellow light.[13] Military bands and impromptu torchlight parades zigzagged through the city. Three-story-high letters of fire spelled out "Union" and "Sherman" and "Grant" across City Hall. Some thirty-five hundred candles shimmered in the windows of the post office.[14] Homes and businesses glowed top to bottom with gas and candles. From a distance, the Capitol building looked as if it were on fire. Ten thousand lights flickered in its windows, and its twenty-two-story dome blazed with 425 gas jets.[15] Other large buildings were bathed in intense calcium light, that blinding brightness produced by igniting caustic quicklime, a process similar to the much smaller limelights that theaters trained on their actors.[16] Pennsylvania Avenue was one wide ribbon of fire and light. As young theatergoer Julia Adeline Shepherd wrote to her father, the lights "made noon out of midnight."[17]

The streets began to fill up long before darkness fell, and the tide of people pushed toward Pennsylvania Avenue. By dark, the wide avenue was a noisy sea of life and animation that swallowed up endless streams of partiers as they poured in from smaller streets.[18] It was, a Philadelphia newspaper reported, a carnival of sound the likes of which no one had ever heard before—cheers, whistles, rifles, cannons, brass bands, singing, and the shrill jangle of hose companies' bells.

"It sounds like hell let loose," a newsman wrote, "but it feels like paradise regained."[19]

4

The Making of an Assassin

On the morning of April 14, there was no bad news on the front page of the *Washington Evening Star*. The next morning, there was no good news.[1]

High spirits abounded around Washington, DC. Even the solemnity of Good Friday could not tamp the merrymaking. After four grim years of civil war, jubilant citizens were out and about, getting a head start on a triumphal weekend.

Charles H. M. Wood operated the front chair at Booker & Stewart's Barber Shop on E Street. The shop, right next to the federal paymaster's office, was always bustling with walk-ins. This Friday morning, Wood was especially pressed. He had already ducked out to Lafayette Square to shave Secretary of State William Seward in his home. The secretary was bedridden, recuperating from a serious carriage accident nine days earlier. Wood had just returned to the shop and polished off his breakfast when John Wilkes Booth strolled in, three friends trailing him. Several chairs were open, but Booth slid into his. The two knew each other well. Wood had been a Baltimore barber when Booth was a schoolboy there. He shaved around Booth's trademark horseshoe mustache, applied some tonics, clipped his curly black hair around, and dressed it with pomade. Listening to Booth and his friends laughing as he cut, Wood couldn't have had a clue he was giving the actor the last trim of his life.[2]

Booth was a charmer and a hard man to figure. Those who understood him best had known him when he was a boy. This day, only a small knot of accomplices had any clue he was planning to kill the president that night.

Johnnie Booth had been dealt a bad hand in life—quite literally if you believed the palm reader he consulted when he was barely a teenager. She said she'd never in her life seen a worse hand. He'd been born under an unlucky star, she told the fourteen-year-old. Staring at the crisscrossed lines of his hand, she saw sorrow and trouble everywhere she looked. He was jinxed. He'd be rich and generous with his money, but he'd have a thundering crowd of enemies. His life would be grand, fast, and short. He'd meet a bad end. The words came from the mouth of a woman who read fortunes in a wood, but Booth was young and impressionable when he heard them, and they haunted him for the rest of his life.[3]

It's true his life started out on shaky ground, by the standards of his time. He was illegitimate. His parents, Junius Brutus Booth and Mary Ann Holmes, were unwed when all ten of their children were born. If they had married, Junius would have been a bigamist.

Junius Booth, a celebrated Shakespearian actor in his native London, was twenty-five, married, and the father of a toddler son when he met eighteen-year-old Mary Ann Holmes selling blooms outside the Royal Opera House in 1821. He convinced the beautiful flower girl to elope with him to America. Adelaide Delannoy Booth, Junius's Belgian wife, believed her husband had gone on an extended tour in America.[4] She wasn't the only one who missed one of the young lovers. Mary Ann's deeply religious father, a London florist, frantically combed the world's largest city for his daughter after she slipped out of her bedroom window and out of his life. All that was left of his runaway daughter was a bundle of love letters from the adulterous actor.[5]

Divorce and remarriage was not a workable option under British law, so Junius and his raven-haired lover set up housekeeping in Baltimore. An ocean away from London, Mary Ann thought it would be safe to call herself Mrs. Booth. She was wrong.

A year later, the couple moved to the relative anonymity of 150 acres outside rural Bel Air, Maryland. There, in a small log cabin surrounded by beech and walnut trees, the free-spirited actor and his bookish mistress conceived ten children without undue notice. They produced a bogus marriage certificate that fooled their children, but the couple knew that if they were found out, their offspring would be labeled bastards, and Mary Ann would be labeled worse. And they knew illegitimate children had no standing in society. Their sons would not even have been able to inherit their father's elaborate hand-sewn stage costumes. Junius and Mary Ann remained constantly on guard, especially after his conniving sister Jane Mitchell arrived from England with her surly and shiftless husband and eight urchins in tow. Despite the large sums Junius commanded on stage, the Booths had little money to feed ten additional mouths. Junius had to send support money to Adelaide, and he often squandered the rest in drunken sprees if Mary Ann didn't get to the theater paymasters before he did. Still, Mary Ann shared their meager rations with her sister-in-law's family because of the unspoken threat that they'd spread the word of Junius's adultery. If that happened, in addition to the social consequences, Junius's lucrative stage career might be upended. While her husband was on tour, most of each year, Mary Ann had to deal with the ten unwelcome houseguests and manage her own brood to boot. The ten Booth children were not father-less, but they might as well have been. Junius charmed them when he was home, but he was on the road more than he was off. He frequently missed their births, and he even missed the death of little Mary in 1833. He ar-rived home a full week after the six-year-old had been laid in the ground, but he ordered a handyman to open her grave so he could try to resuscitate her. He failed. Two more children, Elizabeth and Frederick, fell to cholera within weeks. The couple's favorite son, lively ten-year-old Henry Byron Booth, died of smallpox in 1836. The child who replaced Henry Byron in his mother's heart was their fifth son, high-spirited, disarmingly handsome John Wilkes. Born in 1838, he was named for the raffish and radical British politician, a distant relative.[6]

While Edwin, five, was logical and disciplined, and Junius Jr., seven-teen, was calm and deliberate, Johnnie was sweet and joyous. As he grew, his love of fun attracted everyone.[7] John Wilkes was the best looking of the children, with his luminous skin, his curly black hair, and his athletic form. He had his father's high forehead and delicate features and his moth-er's magnetic black eyes topped by thick upward-curling lashes. When he smiled, his eyes twinkled, and his white teeth flashed from behind his per-fectly formed lips. His lithe body, with its ample shoulders, sinewy arms, and cinched waist, grew as sculpted as a Greek bronze. Johnnie's skills swelled in all the directions they might in the forests and farm fields of Maryland. He was an avid horseman, an agile boxer, handy at billiards, a clever practical joker, a crack shot with both hands, and an exception-ally skilled swordsman. The last was thanks to his superbly athletic brother June, seventeen years his senior but always willing to instruct him with foils or broadswords on visits home.[8]

The family patriarch's hard drinking led to missed performances and missed paychecks until Mary Ann realized her husband needed a keeper on the road. Because June had left the nest years earlier, that charge would fall to Edwin, a quick-witted fourteen-year-old with a head for business. The frail boy, who loved school and excelled at it, was torn from the class-room and sent on the road. John Wilkes, with his adventurous nature and his disdain for schooling, would have been closer to the mark, but Mary Ann wouldn't give him up.[9]

While Junius Sr. and Edwin zigzagged from stage to stage, Mary Ann and the younger Booths remained out of the limelight, living, sometimes hand-to-mouth, on the sleepy farm. All that changed when Junius's son by his first marriage grew old enough to travel from England to Maryland in 1842. Richard Booth, twenty-five, was flabbergasted to learn his father had sired ten additional children in America. He and his mother in London had been totally in the dark about it. The Booth children in Maryland were floored by the news too. They had been shown a bogus marriage certificate indicating their mother and father were man and wife.[10]

Adelaide Delannoy Booth arrived in America in 1846, bent on exposing Mary Ann Booth as a poser and her children as illegitimate. She was certainly unwelcome, but there was an upside to Adelaide's arrival in America. Mary Ann and Junius Booth no longer had to feed, house, and clothe his sister's family to keep them mum. The cat was out of the bag.[11]

In 1846, the Booths bought a modest Baltimore home with store-bought furniture and a parlor decorated in the family's signature colors of gold and green. The ever-aspirational Mary Ann placed her children in all manner of lessons in Baltimore, hoping to rear them to work in a profession more respectable than stage acting. In the city, the biggest excitement for John was the clanging of the fire bells, signaling there was a fire wagon that he and his friends could chase to a blaze. Unless, that is, it was one of the days when Adelaide Booth was on a rampage. Whenever Junius was on the road, Adelaide made it her business to find Mary Ann shopping with her children or selling vegetables from their Maryland farm at a city market. She would upbraid the mother and children, screeching that Mary Ann's ten offspring were illegitimate. Johnnie, who often accompanied his mother to market, was humiliated by the outbursts.[12] Whether to defend his mother's honor or to stop other boys from calling him a bastard, he began fighting, bullying, and drinking. The sweet and loving child was becoming a troubled young man with a reputation as a skilled boxer and a bully who even belted his younger brother Joseph in the face. Perhaps to prove his lineage, he gave himself an amateurish India ink tattoo between the thumb and forefinger of his left hand—J.W.B. for John Wilkes Booth.[13]

In 1851, when John Wilkes was twelve, Adelaide Delannoy Booth won a divorce from Junius on the grounds of adultery. So John Wilkes's thirteenth birthday, on May 10, 1851, was a double celebration of sorts. It was also his parents' wedding day.

The next year, Junius Booth finished an engagement in New Orleans and boarded a steamboat bound upriver for Cincinnati. Before the boat passed Louisville, Kentucky, the patriarch became painfully ill, probably from drinking unclean water. There was no doctor aboard. Mary Ann Booth, who had been notified, arrived in Cincinnati expecting to nurse her husband back to health. Instead, she found a lead coffin and some costume trunks. Eighteen months to the day after her wedding, she was a widow. The coffin lid had a small window inset—just large enough for Mary Ann to know the body inside was that of the love of her life.[14]

John, who had always envied Edwin's chance to tour with his father, was devastated. Never privy to Junius's erratic, drunken behavior on the road, he felt shortchanged by his father's premature death at fifty-six. Always plodding at classroom work, he quit school after his father's death. At fourteen, John briefly farmed his father's acreage, reciting Shakespeare and Milton as he worked. With his older brothers out west, there was no one left on the farm to correct his pronunciation or inflection, no one to mentor him.[15]

After Junius died, money was short and tensions were high at Tudor Hall, the couple's dream home that had been completed while he was on his last tour. In the summer of 1854, John beat a saddle maker who had smirched his mother's name. As a result, he landed on probation, with a record for assault and battery. Bored and unemployed, John yearned for the stage more than ever. John Sleeper Clarke, a Baltimore friend who had a crush on Booth's pretty sister Asia, would be his vehicle. Clarke, an up-and-coming comedian, offered to arrange a stage debut for John at Baltimore's Charles Street Theatre in 1855. It was a drab second-story venue near the city docks. When the curtain was hoisted, John tried his best to become the Earl of Richmond, ironically a hero who slays a tyrant. The audience, who had paid to see a Booth, hissed him. He didn't measure up. And when John returned to Tudor Hall, his mother had cross words for him. Mary Ann was angry that he had squandered the Booth name, which she recognized as a valuable asset.[16] Mary Ann knew her husband's mantle as one of the country's greatest tragedians could translate into gold for at least one of her sons. Theater was highly lucrative, and audiences were wildly supportive of their favorite actors—supportive to the death. New York's infamous Astor Place Riot was proof of that. The deadly riot in 1849 had its roots in a simple stage spat. American actor Edwin Forrest accused British tragedian William Charles Macready of hissing during one of his performances. Forrest retaliated by hissing during Macready's Hamlet. When fans read about the feud, they fumed. The next time Macready visited New York, his admirers fought Forrest's fans on the streets surrounding Astor Place Opera House. Twenty-two people were killed; hundreds were injured.[17]

Edwin, armed with the Booth name, unusual drive, and a few well-placed friends, was having some success on the New York stage. In hard-scrabble Harford County, Maryland, though, John, unable to become the star he longed to be, whiled away the days at a local tavern. There, he bonded with men his father never would have abided—the Know-Nothings. The secret, often violent, anti-Catholic, anti-immigrant fraternal order comprised mostly powerless white Protestant men resentful of the millions of Irish laborers and German craftsmen flooding into the country in the 1850s. The group took its name from the words members were instructed to use when outsiders inquired about their activities: "I know nothing." John's association with the secret society was short-lived, but its effects may have been lingering.

In 1857, with Clarke's help once again, John signed on with a troupe in Philadelphia, billed as "J. B. Wilkes" this time, to save his family the embarrassment of any lackluster reviews. For an excruciating 165 performances, he was a handsome background player without a single line to speak. After six months with the troupe, John finally was assigned a speaking part in *Lucretia Borgia*. He had twelve lines as a cavalier. He flubbed them.[18]

Eventually, Edwin Booth intervened to help his younger brother. He arranged for John to join the stock company at the Marshall Theatre in Richmond, where his old friend John Ford was the manager. Edwin surely regretted it later. In fact, when a servant awakened Edwin in his Boston hotel room on April 15, 1865, with the news that his brother had just murdered the president, his mind accepted the fact immediately. That morning, Edwin, always logical and decisive, instantly calculated his younger brother was capable of such a wild and foolish act. Still, he told a friend that, when the servant uttered the words, it felt as if he had been struck on the forehead by a hammer.[19]

But in 1858, Edwin Booth not only gave his little brother his start in acting; he also tutored him on fashionable dress and comportment. He turned Johnnie into the dashing rising star Richmond couldn't get enough of. Edwin launched his brother on a five-year trajectory that would shoot him from an eight-dollar-a-week supporting player in Philadelphia to a twenty-thousand-dollar-a-year national star.[20] That was just five thousand dollars less than the annual salary of the president of the United States. Edwin ceded the less lucrative smaller southern cities to his younger, taller, and better-looking brother, while reserving the population centers of New

York, Boston, and Philadelphia for himself. Whether Edwin did it all out of brotherly love or out of sibling rivalry is uncertain. Two Booths on any playbill would have been unwieldy.[21]

The Marshall Theatre had a special significance to the Booth brothers. It was the stage where their father, Junius, had made his American debut. Unlike in Baltimore and Philadelphia, Johnnie did not wash out there. John Wilkes Booth, as he now billed himself, was an instant favorite in Richmond, on stage and off. Edward Alfriend, who knew him there, constantly spotted Booth among all the best men and the finest women. Always fashionably dressed, he had the polished manners and graceful moves of a second-generation entertainer. His conversation was brilliant, his charm abundant. The sole telltale signs that he hadn't been born into southern aristocracy were the three inky blue initials inexpertly tattooed on his left hand.[22]

His self-taught acting was uneven and sometimes wooden, but John Wilkes Booth was known as one of the best gymnasts in the country, able to leap over scenery five feet tall. Richmond audiences stamped their feet in appreciation. And with them cheering wildly, John probably saw no reason to take voice lessons or acting instruction. This Booth wasn't the sort of young actor whom older players took under their wings. His famous father had never taught him pronunciation or projection, but John Wilkes exhibited an inborn arrogance out of all proportion to his skills. That arrogance repelled older troupers who might have mentored a humbler young man. A Cleveland theater manager described him as an unharnessed young colt full of impulse, with his heels in the air.[23] However, the twenty-one-year-old did bond with the Virginia audiences that exalted him. He even wore the handsome caped overcoat of the Richmond Grays, the local militia group that served as bodyguards at the hanging of abolitionist John Brown in 1859.[24]

On the crisp December day Brown was hanged, when the militiamen lined up by height, Philip Whitlock, an enthusiastic theatergoer, realized the man standing next to him was the actor from Richmond. Booth, who had bribed some militia members to let him wear pieces of their uniforms, stood about forty feet from the gallows. As Brown's body crashed down, Whitlock watched Booth's face go pale, just as it would six years later at Ford's Theatre. When Whitlock called Booth's attention to his pasty skin, the actor allowed he did feel faint. He said he'd do anything for a drink of good whiskey.[25]

By the time Booth described the hanging to his boyhood friend comic

John Mathews, the queasiness apparently had passed. The kindly comedian was unnerved by the pride evident in his best chum's voice as he described the violent event.[26]

When Billy Ferguson recalled his memories of Booth years later, he conceded several things Booth said and did were wide departures from normal, but people accepted them without analysis as part and parcel of his dashing, high-spirited nature. For one, he said, the actor had no aversion to violence in support of his political sympathies.[27] Was this the same John Wilkes whose sister Asia said wouldn't harm even the animals the family trapped to eat? Was it the same man actress Clara Morris saw rescuing a small, dirty urchin he accidentally toppled when he was running to the telegraph office? Morris said Booth couldn't have known anyone was looking, but he stood the child on his little bandy legs and asked, "Good Lord, Baby. Are you hurt?" Then Booth took his handkerchief from his pocket and wiped the child's wet, dirty face. "Don't cry, little chap," he said. When the child managed a smile, Booth placed some coins in his little freckled hand and continued his run to the telegraph office.[28]

In a few short years, the name "John Wilkes Booth" topped playbills in Chicago, St. Louis, and Washington. He moved like a cat on stage. He once jumped ten or twelve feet to the stage during a performance of *Macbeth*. Lithe and agile, he could take on two swordsmen at once and win.[29]

In fact, Booth once fenced two actors just under Ford's presidential box. He struck one man's blade out of his hand with such force that it flew upward over the railing and landed in the upper box, the exact opposite trajectory to Booth's own on April 14.[30]

When he played Romeo at Ford's in November 1863, Booth cut himself on his own knife and fell on the green baize carpet stretched before the footlights. It was precisely the spot where he would stumble when he leaped from Lincoln's box sixteen months later.[31]

Although Booth weighed 160 pounds and stood five feet, eight inches tall, he always chided other actors to come on hard and hot in fight scenes.[32] One did. The much larger actor ran his sword clean through Booth's eyebrow. The bloody cut required stitches, but Booth laughed it off. When he saw the ice, cold oysters, and fat steak others brought to treat his cut, he joked that he had enough provisions to start a restaurant.[33]

While his movements were unpredictable and his elocution rough, he was, as a New York newspaper put it, "a rare specimen of manly beauty." His coloring was unusual—pale ivory skin and inky black hair, glowing black eyes under heavy pale lids, bright white teeth topped with a silky black mustache. Women crowded around him like doves at a grain basket. Married and single, they offered themselves to the actor with the magnetic, dark eyes. They blithely disregarded the low social status of the acting profession and, in some cases, all propriety. Socialites checked into hotels with him. Actresses followed him around the stage with their eyes. Waitresses overlooked their other tables and offered him free steaks. One theater manager's wife always fluffed her hair when he came into sight. Hotel maids made up his room even when it had already been made up. Star-struck fans mailed Booth hundreds of silly love letters. Other actors often passed around their fan letters for mutual amusement, but Booth cut the names off. "They are harmless now," he'd say. "The sting lies in the tail."[34]

Once he rose to stardom, Booth's clear favorite was a Yankee socialite whose father had not a single reason to like him. Lucy Lambert Hale took men's breath away. The stunningly built, flirtatious, socialite daughter of powerful abolitionist New Hampshire senator John Parker Hale was the kind of woman who had older men writing her love letters before she turned thirteen. Oliver Wendell Holmes, the future Supreme Court justice, was a former beau. Booth was utterly bewitched by her, the most ardent of all her admirers. A friend said that, whenever she accepted any attention from another man, he would act like a patient just out of Bedlam—the popular name for London's largest psychiatric hospital.[35]

Lucy fancied him so much that she gave him tickets to President Lincoln's second inauguration. One measure of his devotion to her became evident on February 13, 1865. Writing and spelling had never been easy for him growing up, and those memories came flooding back to his older brother June when John attempted to write a Valentine to his beloved Lucy. He wound up staying up until three thirty a.m. working on it, using June as his dictionary.[36]

Lucy's parents quickly calculated that their daughter's future would be more secure with any other of her many suitors, perhaps even the president's son, who reportedly was taken with her. A family friend said the Hales would have liked to see Lucy "queening it" at the Executive Mansion, the closest thing America had to royalty. The Booth name conferred royalty—but only on stage.[37]

John Ellsler, manager of the Cleveland Academy of Music, where Booth worked in the winter of 1863, said, "John has more of the old man's power in one performance than Edwin can show in a year. Wait a year or two, till he gets used to the harness and quiets down a bit, and you will see as great an actor as America can produce."[38]

At a time when the average carpenter worked for less than twenty-one dollars a week for an eleven-hour day, John Wilkes Booth was commanding five hundred dollars a week with nary an acting lesson. It was probably enough to make him forget the gypsy's prediction that he was star crossed. It was certainly enough for him to live lavishly, treat others generously, and still buy medical supplies for his beloved Confederates. All this less than a decade after he had to trap his own food on the farm. Reviewers said John had the spontaneous fire of his father, all the charms of Adonis, and almost the strength of Hercules.[39] He did have three professional weaknesses, any one of which would have been ruinous in his business. His voice was spotty and sometimes hoarse.[40] His acting was wooden. And of course, he was untamed, onstage and off. Newspaper reports chronicled stage accidents that vexed Booth. His movements were so unpredictable that fellow actors feared he would maim them. When the buttons on his sleeve became tangled in an actress's long hair in Boston, he yanked his arm loose with such force that he ripped her hair out by the roots.[41] He fell on his own dagger twice. His own agent accidentally shot him in Columbus, Georgia.[42] And, in Albany, New York, on April 26, 1861, four years to the day before his actual demise, a beautiful actress he had jilted rushed him with a dirk knife.[43]

Sometimes it seemed as if there were two distinct John Wilkes Booths. His friends described him as a polished, highly respectable gentleman—affable, fun loving, and generous to a fault. Even his family members admitted there was a darker side to Wilkes, though.

John Sleeper Clarke probably didn't know what hit him after he uttered some biting words about Jefferson Davis on a family train ride. Without warning, his brother-in-law lunged for his neck and dug his fingernails in. Booth once brandished a gun at a black man who did not automatically remove his hat in front of "gentlemen." And when a theater prompter missed his cue, leaving Booth waiting awkwardly on stage, the flustered actor hurled a heavy, sharpened wedge of wood within an inch of the man's face. Booth's politics, his hair-trigger temper, and his tendency toward throat infections were a money-losing combination. Theatrical managers began to view him as unreliable and inflammatory. A few were unwilling to book him.[44]

Booth's secesh leanings were an open secret. He was seconds away from revealing too much to a Union officer in Manhattan one day in March 1865. Booth was walking on Broadway when he ran into John Barron, an old friend from Baltimore who had acted with him in Richmond. Barron, wearing a borrowed overcoat against the cold March day, was pleased to see Booth. He always thought the Booths were generous and considerate but borderline insane. The two actors shook hands and chatted. As Barron turned to walk off, Booth called him back as if to confide something. As he turned toward Booth, Barron's overcoat blew open, revealing two rows of brass buttons and the gilt shoulder straps of a Union naval officer. Booth's face turned pale. His voice broke. He quickly recovered, though, and came up with a reason for calling Barron back. The two never met again.[45]

Booth's playbills usually hyped his family connections, as they did for his 1863 appearance in *The Marble Heart* at Ford's. The ad promised, "The gifted tragedian Mr. J. Wilkes Booth, the youngest star actor in the world, in a role in which he rivals the fame of his father, the great tragedian Junius Brutus Booth."[46] The family connections were fraying though. Edwin, who had voted for President Lincoln, had warned John in no uncertain terms to tone down his anti-Union rhetoric.[47] Edwin never quite broke the ties that bound them though. Even after the assassination, he kept his brother's photo on his bedroom wall.[48]

Losing his grip on the only profession he had ever fancied, John decided to try to strike it rich in the Pennsylvania oilfields. He went into business with two other theater men, starting an outfit aptly called the Dramatic Oil Company.[49] He invested with others as well. Eventually, he told playwright A. R. Cazauran he wouldn't touch theatricals again with a forty-foot pole. "I am now in the oil business," he said.[50] Booth's oil investment didn't pay off. And like a retiree who pines for the office, in the back of his mind, Booth probably still saw himself in the limelight. He did perform a benefit on Broadway in November 1864, but his brother Edwin was the real draw that night. Along with June, they performed *Julius Caesar* to raise money for a statue of a wistful William Shakespeare to be erected in Central Park. Mary Ann Booth sat proudly in the audience listening to the swells of applause for her three sons. After that taste of Broadway adulation, was it impossible for John to accept that the only Booth listed on the top of future playbills would be Edwin or perhaps June?

Joe Simonds, who acted as agent for Booth in the oil business, noticed a marked change in his good friend's behavior. In a letter to Booth that winter, Simonds wrote, "I hardly know what to make of you . . . so different from your usual self. Have you lost all your ambition . . . just what is the matter with you?"[51]

For the next few months, Booth turned to another of his passions—the Confederacy. John and his siblings viewed the war through entirely different lenses. Edwin and Asia, following Mary Ann's lead, were Unionists.

While the Lincolns enjoy the play, the devil sways John Wilkes Booth in this 1865 drawing. Credit: Library of Congress

Kindly June was devoted to his kid brother, but one evening in Washington, even he was given pause by John's anti-Union sentiments. If he had been present for John's early years, June might have put the pieces together. Young John was the only child to balk when the Irish field hands ate at the family table. He wore the banner of the Know-Nothings. And while northern audiences hissed John, Virginians applauded him. Even if he had known all that, it is doubtful June ever would have imagined his brother was scheming to abduct the president. Nor would he have thought that, when the kidnapping plot went haywire, John would mastermind an even more alarming plan. This one would put him back on stage, albeit for fewer than thirty seconds.[52]

When he left Booker & Stewart's Barber Shop on assassination day, Booth headed next door to Grover's Theatre, tarrying there just long enough to get wind of whether President Lincoln would attend *Aladdin!* there that night. He was one of the most recognizable actors in the country, so while he was waiting for the news, he shook hands with Helen Moss and her sister-in-law Julia Hess, the wife of theater manager C. D. Hess. The ladies, too, were all ears for news from the Executive Mansion. They were hoping that their "boys," as they called the management team, would have the honor of hosting the president.[53]

Leaving Grover's with no answer, Booth made several stops around town before he returned to his room on the fourth floor of the National Hotel. Henry Merrick, the desk clerk there, said the actor looked unusually pale when he saw him around eleven a.m. He noticed Booth was a tad agitated, but it wasn't until Booth asked another question that Merrick really thought something was queer. Booth asked him whether it was 1864 or 1865. "You are surely joking, John. You certainly know what year it is," Merrick answered. "Sincerely, I do not," Booth said.[54]

5

Plans and Dreams

Befuddled as he may have been that morning, it was a refreshed and freshly coiffed Booth who arrived at Ford's Theatre about noon. Faultlessly dressed in a dark suit of clothes, a tall silk hat, and kid gloves, and carrying a fashionable cane, Booth looked so superb that, when Harry Ford spotted him walking down Tenth Street, he called out, "Here comes the handsomest man in America."[1]

Booth was handsome, with such delicate beauty that one male actor said he would be in love with him if only he were a woman.[2] And lately, Booth had been doing physical training. Just a few days earlier, he had slipped off his coat to show a friend that he was honed to perfection, hard as iron, without an ounce of surplus flesh anywhere.[3]

An animated Booth walked directly into the theater to fetch his mail. One of the services the Fords provided for actors who played there was accepting letters addressed to itinerant players—even troupers like Booth who had only starred at Ford's an unlucky thirteen times, mostly in November 1863.[4] Booth may not have seen the notice posted inside: "His Excellency, the president of the United States, and family, together with Lt. Gen. Grant and staff, will visit the theater this evening." When Booth walked out the theater doors it was a pleasant 65 degrees with a few cloud ringlets in the sky. He strolled up to Harry Ford, probably inclining his head forward and looking slightly down, as he always did when he spoke to a close friend.[5] "What's on tonight?" he asked Ford. A presidential messenger had picked up show tickets about ten thirty a.m., so Ford told him Lincoln and General Ulysses S. Grant had taken a box for *Our American Cousin*. Knowing Booth was rabidly anti-Union, Ford jested that Jeff Davis and Bob Lee would also be attending—in handcuffs and shackles. "I hope they are not going to do like the Romans—parade their prisoner before the public to humiliate him," Booth answered bitterly. Ford told him he was only joshing.[6]

When Harry Hawk noticed Booth at about one p.m., he was standing on the steps of the theater, chuckling over a letter he was reading. Booth stopped reading and asked, "How are you, Hawk?" Almost ten hours and at least five drinks later would find Booth holding the horn handle of a bloody bowie knife and Hawk climbing a flight of stairs to escape him.[7] But no alarms were going off in anyone's head at one p.m. on that picture-perfect April day.

Perhaps Booth didn't seem capable of plotting. A better-than-fair billiards player, the actor liked to watch the matches at John Deery's Fourteenth Street parlor, but even a champion player like Deery couldn't hold Booth's attention for long. The actor would watch a short time, then insist everyone put down their cues and go out for a drink with him.[8]

Actor Ned Emerson, whose good looks and curly dark locks frequently got him mistaken for his good friend Booth, was at Ford's on April 14 rehearsing his part as Lord Dundreary in *Our American Cousin*. Emerson spotted Booth at the theater that afternoon, but he didn't approach him because he was still smarting from what had happened the previous day. On Thursday, Emerson was standing in front of the theater, holding a fashionable cane, when Booth, agitated over something President Lincoln had done, grabbed the cane out of Emerson's hands and said, "Ned, did you hear what that old scoundrel did the other day?" Emerson asked him whom he was talking about. Booth made it clear he meant President Lincoln and added, "Somebody ought to kill him." "For God's sake, John, stop where you are," Emerson said. "I am going to quit you." Booth responded by pulling the cane down over his friend's shoulders with such force that it broke into four pieces. Emerson had played with Booth in dozens of cities and always thought him genial and kindhearted, but he was so miffed about Booth's actions on April 13 that he avoided him at the theater the next afternoon.[9]

Before Booth left Ford's, he surveyed the ten-foot-wide box just off the dress circle and perhaps mentally rehearsed his exit strategy. No one thought anything was afoot. Any one of Booth's moves might have seemed revelatory in hindsight, but he was a national celebrity. Besides, there had only been one assassination attempt in American history, and it was a resounding failure. When a delusional house painter attempted to shoot President Andrew Jackson outside the House chamber in 1835, Jackson turned the tables on his would-be assassin. The sixty-seven-year-old president repeatedly clubbed the man with his cane.[10]

So Booth's actions went unnoticed, and soon Joe Simms, who worked for Ford's, was carrying an ornate button-backed crimson rocking chair on his head from Harry and James Ford's bedroom atop the Star Saloon to the presidential box. The Fords kept the roomy rocker in their apartment because, when it was in the theater, the ushers liked to nap in it, leaving telltale hair grease on the silk damask upholstery.[11]

Harry Clay Ford was decorating the presidential box with flags and a new addition—a large gilt-framed portrait of George Washington that had never been used in that spot before.[12]

Meanwhile, two blocks over, William Petersen was finishing up at his Eighth Street tailor shop, planning to take off early to have supper with his nine-year-old son Charles, his thirteen-year-old daughter Pauline, and fifteen-year-old Fred. His wife, Anna, was on Easter holiday in New York City visiting patent artist Gustave Dieterich, an old friend from Washington who had moved north two years earlier. Petersen had no idea that his wife had been on edge since she, her sixteen-year-old eldest daughter, and her sister checked into Jackel's Hotel and were handed the keys to Room 13. Anna Petersen was superstitious enough to regard the unlucky thirteen as a very bad omen. Her host, trying to persuade her to think no more of it, showed the ladies the splendid sights in America's largest city.[13] Dieterich had the money. In addition to his detailed patent work, he was becoming well known for his art and his wood engravings. Not one bit superstitious himself, Dieterich saw no reason why Anna Petersen should fret about what was happening on Tenth Street. After touring the city, Dieterich took the ladies across the Hudson River to Rommel & Leicht's Brewery in Union Hill, New Jersey, where they gazed at the Manhattan skyline as they lunched.[14]

Around the same time, John Wilkes Booth was leading his quick mare right past Anna's house in Washington. He was headed just uphill to James C. Ferguson's restaurant, where he ate almost every day when he was in town. Showing off his frisky steed in front of the establishment's two-story wooden porch, a tickled Booth told the restaurateur, "He [sic] can gallop and can almost kick me in the back."[15]

When Booth saw twelve-year-old Joseph Hazelton carrying his school books buckled in a strap over his shoulder, he lifted the boy's cap, ran his fingers through his dark curls, and asked him if he wanted to be an actor.[16] Booth seemed in excellent spirits, but when he chatted with Billy Ferguson, the theater callboy, he confided that he didn't feel too well. He said he might have pleurisy, an inflammation of the lungs that causes sharp pain whenever you take a deep breath.[17]

Across the street, Fred Petersen, carefree because he was on Easter vacation, took off to play ball on the lot next to the Executive Mansion.[18] It was called the White Lot because it was ringed by a white wooden fence.[19] He was not far from Willard's Hotel when he noticed Booth riding his copper-colored mare down Pennsylvania Avenue. Fred had always thought the actor was a strange man, nervous and erratic.[20]

The owner of Brady's Gymnasium watched Booth pull his horse up to the curbstone about four p.m. and buttonhole his old friend John Mathews. Mathews had the same jet-black hair and classic features as Booth but none of the style and charisma that made heads swivel to watch Booth. The two actors met across the wide avenue from the gym, so Brady wasn't close enough to tell, but Mathews saw that Booth was visibly nervous and pale as a ghost. He asked the actor what was the matter. "Nothing, Johnny, nothing," Booth said, shaking atop the small horse. Mathews asked if Booth had seen the line of shackled Confederate prisoners that had just been led up the broken cobblestone avenue. Placing his hand on his forehead, the pasty-faced Booth said, "Great God, I no longer have a country." Then, shifting both reins to his left hand, Booth leaned down over the horse's neck to his right and grasped Mathews's smaller hand tightly.[21] Booth's hand was trembling, but he squeezed Mathews's hand so strongly that his nails left marks. He said, "Johnny, I wish to ask you a favor. Will you do it for me?"[22]

Mathews would have done *almost* anything for Booth because the actor was generous and affable. In fact, Booth had helped Mathews get into acting. Still, Mathews knew his best friend was, in his words, "a little cracked in the upper story." Like many who had grown up on Baltimore's East Side, Mathews figured insanity ran in the Booth family. Junius Sr. was always reputed to be cracked.[23] Mathews would do *almost* anything because, months before, Booth had bugged him to join a numbskull plot to kidnap the president. Mathews flatly refused. The rebuff incensed Booth, who told character actor Samuel Knapp Chester that Mathews was a coward who was not even fit to live. Booth even confided that he wouldn't care much if Mathews were sacrificed for the cause. As Mathews looked up at Booth on the mare, though, he had no inkling that his old friend despised him. Anyway, this time, Booth just wanted him to deliver a letter. Simple enough.

Booth leaned down and handed Mathews a sealed envelope addressed to John F. Coyle, editor of the *National Intelligencer*. Mathews silently noted the oversized handwriting was identical to Booth's autograph on his publicity photos. His friend's handwriting was grand and impressive, not like Mathews's own hasty scrawl, with a letter *t* that looked more like a hastily drawn ship's mast.[24]

Booth asked him to deliver the letter the following morning. Mathews stuffed it into his overcoat pocket. As they talked, Mathews called Booth's attention to General and Mrs. Grant riding in an open carriage that had just rolled by. Suitcases were clearly visible in the rear. "I understood he was coming to the theater tonight with the president," the comedian said. Booth quickly grasped his friend's hand, mouthed, "Perhaps I will see you again," and galloped down the street after the carriage. It was the last time Mathews saw his boyhood friend, except for the instant when Booth barreled past him backstage that night.[25]

In New York City, Gustave Dieterich and his guests were enjoying a pleasant spring day, but Anna Petersen was still a tad uneasy. She asked if Dieterich would mind telegraphing her husband in Washington to inquire if everything was all right there.

He did so and got a prompt answer. Of course, everything was going well.[26]

Everything was very well at the Executive Mansion—or at least it seemed so. Actually, while Booth and the Fords prepared for him, President Lincoln was about to embark on his last round-trip carriage ride.

When the president walked out of the Executive Mansion sometime after three p.m., Mary was already waiting inside their dark green carriage with the rich maroon, gold, and white detailing.[27] It was a calm 68 degrees. The lilacs were in bloom, cloud tufts stippled the blue skies, and the hope of spring was in the air. It was the kind of weather you wouldn't monkey with if you could.[28]

In the twenty-two years since Abraham and Mary Lincoln had pronounced their wedding vows in Ninian Edward's Springfield parlor on another Friday, they had rarely felt this happy, certainly not since they lost eleven-year-old Willie thirty-eight months earlier.

He had had her wedding band engraved with the words "Love Is Eternal," but at first glance, they seemed an unlikely couple.[29] He was long and lean, with unruly black hair, dark weathered skin, and deep-set gray eyes under wayward brows. He had a large nose, with ears and a mouth to match. His left eye had a tendency to roll slightly. His hands were large, and he had a grip like a vise. Seated, he didn't look that tall, but he had unnaturally long arms and legs, so long that store-bought clothes could not be expected to cover them all the way.[30] Crowds hung on his every word as he seamlessly segued from some backwoods saw to a Robert Burns lyric

Mary Lincoln favored low-cut gowns with skirts so wide it was difficult to approach her. Credit: National Archives

delivered in a credible Scottish accent.[31] His habit of welcoming complete strangers with a warmth most men reserved for old friends charmed people wherever he went.

She was short and plump after bearing four children, soft where he was angular. Her sparkling blue eyes and creamy white skin were not as stunning as in her salad days in Springfield, where she was remembered as "a young woman who could make a bishop forget his prayers."[32] Mary was educated, curious, opinionated, and unorthodox at a time when women were expected to be none of those. She was so unpopular with her husband's staff that they dubbed her "the hellcat."[33] His old law partner said she was as cold as a chunk of ice.[34]

Much had been made of their differences, but the Lincolns' similarities were more telling. Both had lost their mothers before they reached ten years of age, and both their fathers had quickly remarried. Both cherished books and committed long poems to memory. Both had a little bit of the ham in them. Neither had grown up in poverty, although Robert Todd cared for his children in a way Thomas Lincoln never did.

By the time Abraham, Thomas's second child, was born on a cold Sunday in 1809, Thomas Lincoln owned two building lots in Elizabethtown, Kentucky, and two farms stretching over almost six hundred acres. He had more property than all but fourteen men in Hardin County.[35] Yet the rough-edged dirt farmer did nothing to make life easier for his son. He didn't put a floor in his house until his second wife demanded it. Until she arrived, the children ate without utensils.[36] Thomas Lincoln forced Abe into continual farm work, almost indentured servitude, and he required the boy to turn over any money he made working for neighbors. Young Lincoln's superior strength and good work ethic were legend in the corner of Indiana where they moved. One neighbor said he saw him pick up a six-hundred-pound chicken house and cart it away.[37] One said the future president could sink an ax deeper into wood than any man he ever saw. Whenever Abe and his friend Jack Kelso could, they would escape to the woods and recite Shakespeare from the creek rocks. This almost certainly would not have pleased Thomas Lincoln, who berated his boy for reading.[38]

Robert Todd, by contrast, applauded his daughter Mary's intellectual bent. Todd, a wealthy banker and cotton manufacturer, owned one of Kentucky's finest private libraries. Mary spent ten years at pricey academies, much longer than most girls in the early part of the nineteenth century and even longer than many boys. At Madam Mentelle's School, she earned the highest marks, became fluent in French, and developed a flair for acting. Her specialty was spot-on mimicry.[39] She spent her adolescent years in a mansion on Lexington's voguish Main Street, surrounded with fine china, gilded mirrors, crystal chandeliers, silk brocade wallpaper, and marble-mantled fireplaces.[40] But Mary Todd had her eye on an even more dazzling house. Her father's close friend Kentucky senator Henry Clay, a three-time candidate for president, promised little Mary that, if he were elected, she would be among his first guests at the Executive Mansion in Washington, DC.[41] Clay never was elected president, and she died before she could invite him to be her guest at the mansion. In all likelihood, she never forgot the goal. When the couple first toured the Executive Mansion, Mary stood in the doorway of the opulent Blue Room and exclaimed, "It's mine, my very own! At last, it's mine!"[42]

Mary moved with the confidence of a young woman whose family had enjoyed success for many generations. Her great-grandfather General Andrew Porter was a close friend of President Washington. When she moved to Springfield, Illinois, in 1839, both her figure and her intellect were ample, and she wasn't afraid to show either.

She moved in with her sister Elizabeth and her brother-in-law Ninian Edwards, son of a former governor. Soon, the most accomplished young men in the state capitol were driving their buggies up the Edwardses' curving driveway and crossing the columned front porch to court her. The grandson of Patrick Henry was smitten, as was the persistent Edwin Webb, a widowed state legislator. Stephen A. Douglas, the squat, tobacco-chewing, hard-drinking orator, was a suitor. At five foot, four inches, Mary stood eye-to-eye with Douglas. The man who caught her fancy was exactly a foot taller.[43]

Mary was keen on Abraham Lincoln, a backwoods lawyer with limbs so exceptionally long that Edwin Stanton once said he resembled a gawky, long-armed ape.[44] Mary's much younger half-sister Emilie thought he looked exactly like the hungry giant in "Jack and the Beanstalk"—until he smiled at her. Even his dress was not as fastidious as that of most of Mary Todd's suitors. Long after he ascended to the presidency, his horseback jaunts left shiny spots on the inside of his trousers.[45]

She was the reverse—impractically fashionable. Some of her hooped skirts were of such circumference that it was difficult to approach her.

Intellectually, though, Todd and Lincoln were as close as two bullets in the same bull's-eye. She was one of the best-educated women in most circles. He was an ambitious, self-taught attorney. They hashed over issues, reveled in politics, recited passages from literature, and surprised each other with expensive leather-bound books.

The only president ever to hold a patent, Lincoln invited inventors to the White Lot each week to demonstrate their newest contraptions.[46] His own patent was for a device to float a boat run aground in shallow water, but he was once spotted in the White Lot trying out a repeating rifle.[47]

The Lincolns were curious about the latest ideas—inventions, abolition, sociology, and phrenology, a crude precursor to neuroscience that held that character and emotions are dependent on the shape of the skull and the brain. So they were naturally interested in spiritualism, a trend that had been sweeping the country since the 1850s. It had its roots in the emotional needs of American women who were losing their babies to disease in stunning numbers. Spiritualists told mourners they could communicate with the dead, and mediums held séances and spirit circles to do just that. By 1862, the movement was on fire, stoked by thousands of battle casualties at places like Antietam and Fredericksburg. Mary Lincoln, with two sons and two brothers gone, visited a Georgetown medium. The president was wary, even asking Dr. Joseph Henry of the Smithsonian to investigate him. Mr. Lincoln went along with his wife's wishes and attended some spirit circles, but he brought his skepticism with him.[48]

Mary was highly superstitious. Although all misgivings were put aside for the victory celebration, she ordinarily considered Friday the unluckiest day of the week. Her sister Elizabeth joked that they shouldn't even bake a cake on that day because it would surely fall in the oven.[49]

The carriage ride was an impromptu postwar planning session for the Lincolns. The couple would finally have the time to indulge their mutual zeal for politics, poetry, travel, each other, and, of course, their two remaining sons.

Their enthusiasm for their children was always unbridled, even when others thought the boys were holy terrors. Twelve-year-old Tad thought nothing of interrupting cabinet meetings. He set up a lemonade stand in the Executive Mansion hallway. He once led a team of goats through a ladies luncheon in the East Room. He often inspected the troops with his father, wearing a tailored-to-fit Union uniform. Tad's toy theater was superior even to most wealthy children's. He played with real theatrical costumes and stage props supplied by Leonard Grover, proprietor of Grover's Theatre.[50] When Willie was alive, they held minstrel shows in the attic and turned some of Washington's most luxurious rooms into forts, ship decks, and circus grounds.[51]

When the boys' ponies were caught in an out-of-control stable blaze in 1864, the fifty-four-year-old president jumped some hedgerows, threw open the stable doors, and was about to rush into the roaring fire until soldiers restrained him. When he heard his deceased son Willie's favorite pony had perished, he collapsed his large frame into a chair and sobbed.[52]

Before Willie's death, Joseph Humphreys, a distant relative of Mary's, once traveled on a Kentucky-bound train with the Lincoln family without knowing who they were. Unbeknownst to either, both were headed for the Todd house when the train arrived in Lexington. Humphreys got there first. "Aunt Betsy," he fumed, "I was never so glad to get off a train in my life. There were two lively youngsters on board who kept the whole train in turmoil, and their long-legged father, instead of spanking the brats, looked pleased as punch, and aided and abetted the older one in his mischief." Just then, Humphreys glanced out the window and spotted the Lincolns arriving in the Todd carriage. Disbelieving, he said, "Good Lord, there they are now."[53]

This ride on April 14 was even more joyous. They could savor each other's company without the maelstrom of war. Both their surviving sons were snug and safe in the Executive Mansion, Tad and his older brother Captain Bob Lincoln, home free after serving fewer than seven weeks as aide-de-camp to General Ulysses S. Grant.

Their other two sons had gone to the angels. Eddy was nearly four when he died in 1850. With his full face, bright eyes, glossy hair, and pearly complexion, he resembled his mother. Willie was the breathing image of his father—lanky, sweet-tempered, and quite tall for his age. Willie's death was a loss so deep neither of them could refer to it. President Lincoln had convulsed in tears. He later asked his minister if he'd be able to talk to Willie in heaven. Mary was never again able to enter the room where Willie died or the one where he was embalmed. It was as if their lives were divided into before and after Willie's death.[54]

Despite their inmost sadness, the Lincolns were an entertaining team when it came to public events. When they visited army hospitals, she would distribute flowers and jellies and read to the troops. He'd look for any soldier of above-average height and ask him to measure their heights back to back. He never found one taller than he, but it was good for a laugh.[55]

Beginning this day, on this ride, the Lincolns could do something that had been impossible since the war had broken out almost exactly four years earlier. They could plan for their future as a couple. They finally had time to recall why they had taken a shine to each other back in Springfield.

As they rode along, he said, "We both must be more cheerful in the future. Between the war and the loss of our darling Willie, we have been very miserable."[56] It was as if someone had opened a seam in a garment to give them some room to relax.

There was no doubt they were in love. She still delighted in buying him books he cherished. His long, angular face still lit up when he saw her in one of her low-cut evening gowns.[57] They loved to travel with their children to places like the four-story Eagle Tavern at Niagara Falls. With its slogan "As famous as the falls," the luxury hotel jutted out into the mist hard by the 164-foot American falls. It had hosted Charles Dickens, Mark Twain, and nearly every American president.[58] This afternoon they discussed traveling, to Palestine perhaps, California definitely. After all, it was Mary's nephew William Todd who had drawn the grizzly on California's state flag.[59] The president said he wanted to cross the Rockies and see the Pacific Ocean. They talked about where they might settle in 1868—what if they moved to Chicago or Springfield or maybe even California, where there might be opportunities for their sons?

They had banked ninety thousand dollars, mainly from saving his twenty-five-thousand-dollar presidential salary, and he figured they could save more before the end of his term. He was careful with their money. When they left Springfield for Washington they had a six-hundred-dollar balance in their bank account plus some investments and their two-story Greek Revival house on a well-situated corner lot.[60] For a man whose stovepipe hat often served as his desk drawer—he kept his checkbook and papers in the wide inside band—Lincoln kept meticulous account of what was owed him. He sued at least six times to recover legal fees. He still held a sixty-dollar note for the 1859 defense of Thomas Patterson, who struck and killed a man with a two-pound scale weight. Patterson was convicted, but Lincoln secured a pardon for him.[61]

The Lincolns halted the carriage at the Navy Yard and talked with Ensign William Flood, whose grandfather had served in the Illinois Legislature with Mr. Lincoln. The president asked Flood which of the ships had been in the tightest spots during the fighting. Flood directed them to the USS *Montauk*. They met the crew, including Dr. George B. Todd, ship's surgeon. They spoke lightheartedly about the end of hostilities. Flood and Dr. Todd would see them again—in the theater that night.

For now, though, the elated Lincolns climbed back into their carriage. The president probably crossed his feet as soon as he sat down and then curled his right toe upward as if he were trying to wind it around his left leg. That was his habit when space was limited.[62] They rode along, perhaps imagining their future together. Their heads were filled with what-ifs.

After four bleak years of war, the Lincolns finally seemed like the Sunday's children they both were—bonny and blithe, happy and good.

6

Nothing Exactly According to Plan

Over at 453 Tenth Street, a graceful three-and-a-half-story Greek Revival brick row house directly across the street from Ford's Theatre, William Petersen was home for an early supper with his three youngest children. Anna Petersen had given birth to ten babies, but only five had made it to adulthood. Three were home that night. The couple's oldest daughter was on holiday with Anna in New York. Their twenty-year-old son, William Felix, worked as a drug clerk, and there is no record of his being at home on assassination night.[1] William Petersen had plans for the rest of the evening of April 14, 1865. He was going to leave the house after supper. He might have been rushing back to his shop to finish one of the military uniforms that had buoyed his business for the past four years. Or he might have already formed his eventual habit of mixing alcohol and laudanum for a Friday-night spree.[2] Either way, he was eager to leave.

Six blocks away, at the National Hotel, the pieces of Booth's plot to kill the president were coming together. Not eager to repeat that night in Philadelphia when he flubbed his first speaking part, Booth carefully wrote out his last. He asked a female friend who studied Latin, "Do you know if tyrannis is spelled with two ns or two rs?"[3] He did not want to bungle his last line, the one he would deliver as he alighted on the stage that night: "Sic semper tyrannis," or "Thus always tyrants." These were the words Brutus proclaimed after he slew Caesar—the same words immortalized in Shakespeare's play and imprinted on Virginia's state seal.

It would take surprisingly little time to kill the president. Booth would schmooze his way into the box, tiptoe up behind Mr. Lincoln's chair, aim his pocket-sized, silver-plated derringer, then squeeze the trigger, propelling a one-ounce lead ball through the president's brain. He would dash to the front of the box, vault over the railing, bask in the limelight, and deliver his line. Then Booth would make a beeline for the stage door.

Things didn't go exactly as planned.

Young Davy Herold walked into Taltavul's Star Saloon around five p.m.

William Petersen slipped out of his house after the president was carried in. Credit: Author's collection (public domain)

Davy Herold, Booth's companion on the run, was hanged. Credit: Library of Congress

George Atzerodt's last words before he was hanged were, "May we all meet in the other world. God take me now." Credit: Library of Congress

looking for John Wilkes Booth. Taltavul's, a dark, elegant bar with a wood-slat ceiling, shared a wall and an alley with Ford's. It was run by two musicians who lived near the Navy Yard—Scipione Grillo and Peter Taltavul, a former member of the US Marine Corp Band. Grillo told Herold he had served Booth a drink just before four p.m. but hadn't seen him since. Herold mentioned that General Robert E. Lee was in town, and he'd heard he might stop at Willard's. Grillo, hoping to glimpse the general, walked downhill to the avenue with Herold. As they walked, Grillo silently noted that something was amiss with Herold's gait.

They had walked only three blocks when they encountered George Atzerodt, a brawny man with tangled reddish-brown hair and cherry red cheeks. He was sitting on the steps of the Kirkwood House. The bartender waited on the corner for a few minutes while Herold and Atzerodt talked privately. He couldn't help noticing that Atzerodt's voice was surprisingly small and high for a man of his size. It seemed odd to Grillo that this ruffian had the ear of young Herold, a Georgetown-educated pharmacy assistant from a good family.[4]

Herold and Grillo had hardly walked into Willard's when Herold ran into two other men Grillo did not recognize. That trio talked in low tones, so Grillo didn't hear all of the conversation, but as they were leaving, Grillo heard Herold ask, "You are going tonight, ain't you?" It didn't seem cloak-and-dagger, at least until Grillo and Herold walked back onto the avenue. Then Grillo noticed Herold was still limping. "What's the matter?" he asked. "You are walking lame." Herold said his boot hurt him. He lifted his pant leg, revealing a large dagger tucked into his boot and protruding five or six inches above the top. "What do you want to carry that for?" Grillo asked him. "I'm going into the country tonight on horseback and it will be handy there," Herold said. "You ain't going to kill anyone with that?" Grillo asked, laughing.[5]

7

Shuffling History

After Booth took tea at the National Hotel around six thirty p.m., he went to his room, where he readied a dagger and a single-shot derringer to kill Abraham Lincoln. His hope was the hand-cast ball would proceed down the short barrel and, without interruption, into the president's head. The dagger was Plan B.

When he checked out of Room 228 around seven p.m., he left behind a broken comb, some other grooming aids, a pair of black cashmere pantaloons with his JWB monogram, a good-sized plug of Killikinick tobacco wrapped in brown paper, and a wardrobe trunk imprinted with his name and the word "theater." There was a blank space between the two, where the name of the theater had been rubbed out.[1] Later that night, a police lieutenant would open that trunk. His eyes would fall on a gag, a set of handcuffs, a colonel's military dress coat, and a pack of letters, including one from a woman who pleaded for Booth to forget his perilous plan.[2]

Before he left the hotel for the last time Booth ordered a brandy, but not in his usual genial manner. His charm not quite intact, he called out, "Brandy, brandy, brandy," and he rapped on the bar as if to say, "Make it snappy!"[3]

Booth spoke to room clerk George Bunker as he passed out of the hotel.[4] Colonel G. V. Rutherford was standing near the hotel counter when Booth walked by. His friend nudged him and said, "There goes J. Wilkes Booth," but by the time the colonel turned, the actor had passed, and he could only see his back.[5]

After almost a year of foment, one of Booth's schemes was about to be consummated. He was in the homestretch. The face is often not the best gauge of what is happening in the mind, but if Booth had any inkling his scheme could break badly, he certainly didn't let on. As he walked out from under the National's columned portico and into the night, Booth seemed cocksure he would soon be hailed as a patriot. He was so inexorably sure that he took his fat key ring with him on the run. If only he'd had a crystal

Booth's derringer pistol held only one round. If he had missed, he would have had to finish off the president with his knife. Credit: Carol M. Highsmith's America, Library of Congress

Booth's knife was inscribed with the words "Liberty" and "America." Credit: Carol M. Highsmith's America, Library of Congress

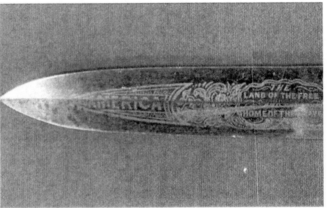

John Wilkes Booth walked out the National Hotel's front portico and turned right on his way to murder President Lincoln. Credit: Library of Congress

John Wilkes Booth took his keys with him on the run, but he never returned to the places the keys fit. Credit: Carol M. Highsmith's America, Library of Congress

ball, he would have seen that he would never again open the doors that his keys fit.[6]

He might have turned around if he could have just looked a few days into the future and seen himself labeled a "hellhound of treason" instead of a national hero. At seven p.m. on April 14, though, Booth was certain Lincoln was scheming to become king of America, and he was headed to Ford's Theatre to stop him.

While Booth was preparing for his final role on Tenth Street, his older brother Edwin was in Boston playing Sir Edward Mortimer in *The Iron Chest*. One of his lines was, "Where is my honor now? Mountains of shame are piled upon me." On Sunday, Edwin would write this to his old friend Adam Badeau: "I was not acting but uttering the fearful truth."[7]

As Booth walked along gas-lit Pennsylvania Avenue, another gaslight shone on the prominent Doric-pilastered entrance to Petersen's boardinghouse. Behind the thick wooden door, the inhabitants' weekly routines were being reshaped by end-of-war revelry. They must have sensed that they were living in a unique time and place in American history, but until later that night, they would have no idea how unique. When William, Fred, Pauline, and Charles Petersen ate an early dinner on Friday night, they could not have guessed that, within hours, they would be pulled into the orbit of the most powerful men and women in the country.[8] William Petersen sent thirteen-year-old Pauline to bed around eight p.m., but she tossed as hundreds of playgoers clustered in front of Ford's Theatre a few yards away.[9] It would not have been easy to sleep in her basement room facing Ford's Theatre, not with the lusty celebration going on outside the street-level windows just above her head.

One floor up, George and Huldah Francis occupied a handsome double parlor, that two-room configuration common to Greek Revival row houses. The rooms mirrored each other. Each featured a dark marble fireplace on the south wall and two large double-hung, leaded-glass windows to the outside. The Francises, an attractive couple, both forty years old, slept together in a double bed pushed against the north wall of the back parlor. That left room for a round table and chairs in the center of the room. Baby-faced George, a dealer in home furnishings, cutlery, guns, baskets, and Willcox and Gibbs sewing machines, kept a shop at 490 Seventh Street West. It was just a three-block walk from the boardinghouse where he and Huldah had lived for half a decade. What was about to happen would cause them to move away in forty-seven days.[10]

On the next floor was the front room Henry Safford shared with his roommate, Thomas Proctor. Safford was settling in for the night.[11] The dark-haired, mustachioed, seventeen-year-old War Department clerk, tuckered out after five nights of revelry, had decided to stay in and read on this clammy, cloudy Friday night.[12] Safford told people that he felt comfortable boarding at the Petersens' because they were a worthy German family, not secesh like the families on either side of them. If anyone had thought to put the pieces of the assassination plot together before it fully took shape, Safford could have offered a key piece. He had overheard Booth talking to one of the actors who boarded at Petersen's, trying to embroil him in a plot to kill the president. Apparently Safford had sloughed it off.[13]

Unlike John Mathews and the others who lived at Petersen's and worked at Ford's, actor Charles Warwick would not see John Wilkes Booth jump to the stage that night. Warwick was recuperating from an illness. He had already seen Booth earlier that day, though, when he went out to get some fresh air in his lungs. Booth, who knew Warwick had been under the weather, shook his hand and wished him good health.[14]

Henry and Julius Ulke, two bearded and mustachioed brothers who boarded at Petersen's, could have been twins save that Henry, the older of

Boarder Henry Ulke married a German actress months after the assassination. This is his wedding photo. Credit: The Estate of Henry Ulke

the two, wore his salt-and-pepper hair combed back, and Julius, the younger, swept his brown hair to the right. They had emigrated from Germany thirteen years earlier, after they took part in the failed revolution there. Henry, forty-one, was a popular portrait artist and photographer with a studio at 278 Pennsylvania Avenue. He had the distinction of being the first photographer to use painted backgrounds in photo portraits. He was friendly with President Lincoln and a real favorite of Spencer Fullerton Baird, assistant secretary of the Smithsonian. He had met Baird through his membership in the Megatherium Society, that group of amateur naturalists named after the spectacular South American sloth.[15] In the upstairs room he shared with his brother, Ulke was painstakingly assembling one of the country's best collections of pinned beetles, which made it no place to bring a president.

At least one room at Petersen House was unoccupied that evening. William Tilton Clark, a Massachusetts infantryman whose outstanding handwriting had won him a spot in the quartermaster's office, was out celebrating. He had a right. Before being posted to his desk job, the handsome twenty-three-year-old had fought in thirteen battles. Clark's room, as meticulous as his handwriting, was swept clean.[16] Freshly laundered sheets covered the cornhusk mattress from J. M. Curran's Mattress Factory in Washington, DC.[17] Clark had just moved in that week, after actor John Mathews moved upstairs to a larger room with its own fireplace and a foot-deep closet.[18] Clark's narrow, slope-roofed room was really part of a hallway that stretched from the front stairs to the back stairs. With its worn Brussels carpet and its single gaslight, it wasn't exactly fit for a king, but it would have to do.[19]

8

The Turning of the Tide

Across the street, Ford's Theatre was aglow. A jovial atmosphere prevailed, not only because of the president's scheduled appearance but because Friday was pay night at Ford's.[1]

Ingénue May Hart, in her first season as an actress, was particularly looking forward to receiving her pay envelope with twenty dollars inside. She knew treasurer Harry Ford had a thick wad of envelopes in his coat pocket.[2]

Auburn-haired actress Laura Keene spread her diamonds and other jewels out on a table in her unlocked first-floor dressing room as she prepared to perform for the president.[3] Keene was feeling down, woeful over her waning popularity and weary after performing *Our American Cousin* for almost one thousand nights. At thirty-nine, she was legendary in theater circles, the first female to run a Broadway theater, a generous mentor to new stars, and a vigorous supporter of homegrown talent who once offered one thousand dollars for the best American play submitted to her.[4] Perhaps the president's imminent arrival reminded Keene that she had been performing the same tired farce for five years. After all, she had been doing it at McVickers Theatre in Chicago on May 18, 1860, the night Mr. Lincoln captured the Republican nomination at that city's massive wooden Wigwam convention hall a few blocks away. All evening, cast members talked about how off Keene seemed. Billy Ferguson, the callboy who practiced lines with her, said she'd been drinking. "Full as a tick" were his exact words.[5]

John Mathews, in a rush to prep for his role as the rascally attorney Coyle, absentmindedly parked his overcoat with Booth's letter in the pocket.

Orchestra leader William Withers was already in a tizzy as he approached the backstage door at about seven thirty p.m. A thin, balding man with a walrus mustache as wide as his face, Withers believed the greatest triumph of his career was just a few hours off. Laura Keene had promised a tune he had composed would be performed to a packed house, including the president, at the end of the first act. When the management learned President Lincoln would be attending Ford's that evening, they sent someone to the D Street offices of their portly, wiry-bearded printer Henry Polkinhorn to stop the steam-powered presses. They changed that night's playbill, shoehorning in eight lines from Withers's "Honor to Our Soldiers" near the bottom.[6] Keene had lent the Fords her personal Chickering piano so the composition could be played to best advantage, and the entire cast was going to sing the lyrics.[7] So when Withers bumped into John Booth in his shirtsleeves, with his coat hanging over his arm, in the doorway of Taltavul's Star Saloon, hard by the back entrance to the theater, and Booth said, "Hello, Billy. Come and have a drink," Withers quickly agreed. Both had reason to celebrate. At Taltavul's, Withers had just one drink with Booth, always given to sudden bursts of energy but more fidgety than usual that night.

Booth seemed so high-strung that, when Withers returned to Ford's, he asked a musician, "What's come over Booth tonight?"[8]

If she overheard it, the very name Booth must have rankled Laura Keene. Ten years earlier, she had fallen in love with Edwin Booth, eight years her junior, on a six-month voyage to Sydney, Australia. The talented couple had planned to present a lucrative series of plays, but when the boat docked in Sydney, Edwin went on a drinking spree. Liquored up, he loudly insulted the British and tried to plant an American flag in front of the city's playhouse. The Australians, loyal to the British colonial government, thus boycotted Keene's plays. Her troubles with the Booths didn't stop there. More recently, a slip of the tongue from Edwin had ended badly for Keene, divulging an explosive secret from their time as lovers. In a conversation with his ruthless brother-in-law comedian John Sleeper Clarke, Edwin had let it slip that Keene had never divorced the abusive first husband she left in London. That meant she was not legally wed to her second husband and business manager John Lutz. Ironically, Keene's situation was identical to the fix Edwin's father Junius Booth had found himself in four decades earlier. Clarke, however, used Keene's dirty linen to blackmail her into dropping a copyright lawsuit against him.[9]

John Wilkes Booth cared about none of that. While the actors and musicians at Ford's were prepping for their big night, he was headed to Tenth Street for his. He had a palm-sized, silver-clad derringer concealed on his person. The six-inch walnut pistol could fire only a single large shot, so Booth had left himself little room for error. If the .44-caliber ball did not put the president down, then the assassin would need to wield his horn-handled bowie knife to finish the job and fight his way out of the theater. The steel blade was adorned with the words "Liberty" and "America" and the phrase "The Land of the Free."[10]

Abraham Lincoln had achieved the American dream—rising from a dirt-floored cabin to the Executive Mansion. John Wilkes Booth was about to put an end to that.

9

Looking Forward to a Memorable Evening

At Armory Square Hospital, the eleven long pavilions that constituted the city's largest and most modern hospital, Dr. Charles A. Leale had just finished his shift treating the most critically wounded soldiers able to survive the train ride from the battlefields. Leale, an army captain, hastily changed into his civvies to walk to Ford's Theatre. Army officers needed a special pass to attend the theater, and the young surgeon didn't want to be stopped.[1]

He was eager to secure a one-dollar ticket that would admit him to an orchestra seat, the perch he thought would afford the best view of President Lincoln and General Grant. Waiting to purchase a gold ticket, he could see the beautifully decorated presidential box ahead. But when he reached the box office, the clerk told him that the only vacant seats were in the dress circle, a balcony on the same floor as the presidential box. The president's appearance had transformed *Our American Cousin* into a hot ticket.[2]

Disappointed, Dr. Leale purchased a seventy-five-cent ticket admitting him to a seat about forty feet from the presidential box, hoping he might at least spot the president at intermission or after the final curtain. The cheaper seat afforded an excellent view of the stage because all the chairs in the dress circle were arranged on steps. Dr. Leale wasn't thinking about the play as he clutched his beige ticket though. He had an intense desire to study the face of Mr. Lincoln, whom he considered the country's savior. That face had looked so divine in the rays of light emanating from the Executive Mansion window Tuesday night.[3]

As he settled into his cane-bottom chair, he had no idea he'd play a central role that night. Few surgeons had the very particular skill set he did. Although he was only twenty-three, Dr. Leale had begun studying anatomy, physiology, and chemistry at fourteen and entered medical school at eighteen. He had taken additional instruction in the latest surgery techniques and gunshot-wound treatments just before his March 1 commencement. For most of the forty-five days since then, he had been treating the worst head wounds in the country.[4]

When President Lincoln rose from the table to get ready for the theater, he left his fine gold-rimmed coffee cup with the purple-red border on a windowsill. He expected he'd be back at the table for a late supper after the performance.[5]

April 14 was a bustling evening at 1600 Pennsylvania Avenue. One of the president's good friends, former Illinois senator Orville Hickman Browning, sat upstairs in his room hoping to talk with him before he left for the theater, but the president was running so late that he never walked back up the stairs. The two old friends were temporarily reunited five days later when Browning served as one of the president's pallbearers.

The Lincolns were so pressed that Friday night that Senator William Stewart of Nevada and his friend were also turned away. An usher handed Stewart a note card penned by the president: "I am engaged to go to the theater with Mrs. Lincoln. It is the kind of engagement I never break. Come with your friend to-morrow at ten, and I shall be glad to see you. A Lincoln." It is not known whether the note was on one of the tiny 2.5-by-3.5-inch cards the president usually favored. Either way, Stewart ditched it on the floor on his way out. He had many notes from the president; this one did not seem exceptional.[6]

George Ashmun, a Massachusetts politician who had served in the Thirteenth Congress with Lincoln, also dropped by as the Lincolns were rushing around. Ashmun wanted to ask a favor of the president. With no time left to meet, Lincoln penned a brief note that read, "Allow Mr. Ashmun & friend to come in at 9:00 a.m. tomorrow." It was the last piece President Lincoln wrote.[7]

The Lincolns were late to pick up Major Henry R. Rathbone and his fiancée, Clara Harris, for the theater. Harris, a friend of Mary Lincoln, was the daughter of Senator Ira Harris of New York, one of the president's staunchest supporters. The couple was a last-minute replacement for General and Mrs. Grant. Although General Grant had accepted the Lincolns' invitation and the papers advertised that he and his wife were coming to Ford's, Mrs. Grant had vetoed the excursion. Julia Grant, a plain and friendly woman who put on no airs, found the first lady exasperating. She told her sister that Mary Lincoln wanted to be treated like royalty, even expecting visitors to back out of rooms where Mrs. Lincoln presided. While

Bob Lincoln was awakened with the news his father had been shot. Credit: Library of Congress

many people did refer to the president as "your excellency," Julia Grant was not about to kowtow to his wife. She asked the general to tell the Lincolns they already had plans to visit their children at boarding school in Burlington, New Jersey.[8]

Suitcases piled in the back of their carriage, the Grants headed for the train station about four p.m., unwittingly passing by a plotting John Wilkes Booth as they rode up the avenue. They were eager to get away to their graceful two-story home in Burlington, their refuge from Washington politics.

The president had also asked his son Bob to join them. When he made the invitation, Bob was sitting in a chair cocked back against the wall, puffing away on his first cigar in days. After thirty days in the field without a bath or a change of clothes, the new Captain Lincoln was in no mood. "I'm too tired," he told his father, after polishing off his first warm meal in a month. "I'll just finish this cigar, and then I'll go up to bed," he said.[9]

The president's oldest son, a Harvard man who looked and acted more like the aristocratic Todds, was never as close to his father as younger brothers Tad and Willie. He told a correspondent he had scarcely ten minutes of quiet talk with his father during the five busy presidential years.[10] Hardly able to keep his eyes open and fancying a set of clean sheets, Bob had every reason to believe this was the night when he would finally rest easily and wake up in the pink.[11] His military service, less than fifty days total, was winding down. The Lincoln scion had finally enlisted that January, after three million other young men had signed on for the North or South; after Senator Harris had blurted out, "Why isn't Robert in the army?"; and long after the newspapers had harped that the president's son was safe at Harvard.[12] He was actually safe in the army too, because his father had arranged a sheltered position for him as an aide-de-camp to General Grant.

When Mr. and Mrs. Lincoln set out for Ford's, the beautiful day had turned to fog, and northwesterly winds were beginning to blow, but the mood was still festive.[13] Parades were breaking out all over downtown. More than two hundred thousand revelers filled the streets. That exuberance would be fleeting.

At eight twenty, when the presidential carriage stopped in front of the Harris mansion, the Lincolns had no way of knowing that they were damning the others they pulled into their orbit that night.[14] The Lincolns were so tardy that twenty-seven-year-old Henry Rathbone and his fiancée, Clara, feared they'd been forgotten. Then they spotted the candlelit Lincoln carriage with its raised gold monogram on the door.[15] When Clara, in her white satin dress, was helped up the steps, the Lincolns welcomed her and her plainclothes military man in the gayest of spirits.[16]

Clara and Henry were charming and socially connected. They were also stepbrother and stepsister. The Harrises and the Rathbones were two of the most prominent families of Albany, New York. After his wife Clarissa died, Senator Harris wed Pauline Rathbone, wealthy widow of Albany mayor Jared Rathbone, and their children were raised as siblings. Clara, always impeccably dressed and fashionably coiffed, was a plain but polished young woman more than three years older than her fiancé. Her eyes were small, and she had inherited her father's prominent nose. She had the delicate look of a hothouse flower that might wither in the winter but was much stronger than it looked, as she would prove decades later when she faced down a madman to protect her children.

It was Clara's vivacious personality that drew Mary Lincoln to her. Just three nights earlier, when the Executive Mansion lawn swarmed with well-wishers gathered to hear the president, the crowd had to tell the two ladies to hush. As the president's high-pitched voice wafted from an upper-story window, his wife and Clara huddled near another open window talking. The ladies' chatter got so loud that those who came to listen to the president could not hear him. Anyone who had listened to the ladies would have heard Mary tell Clara the past few days had been the happiest of her life.[17]

Major Rathbone, a tall, lanky, athletic man with a hooked nose and thinning red hair and beard, was widely traveled and known as a brilliant conversationalist. His father, a well-to-do wholesale grocer turned politician, had left him a sizable fortune. He had trained as a lawyer at Union College in upstate New York, where he pledged Sigma Phi, the first intercollegiate fraternity. He entered the army at captain's rank and served in five battles before he was assigned to a desk job in Washington. He prided himself on his marksmanship, but apparently no one had instructed him to watch out for the president's safety that night, as he took a seat at the opposite end of the theater box.

The two couples often went for a drive or attended the opera and theater together, sometimes just to escape the crush of office seekers and status seekers at the Executive Mansion, the ones Clara called "the crows who constantly thronged to see them."[18] This night, they chatted gaily as the carriage made its way past a circus of parades, victory banners, and light displays. The president's movements suddenly were more elastic, and a long-absent light had returned to his eyes. No one was happier than the president this night.[19]

All over Washington City, homes and businesses glowed from top to bottom. Public buildings were bathed in blindingly intense calcium light. As the carriage neared the theater, flaming yellow tar torches perched in barrels filled the air with asphyxiating fumes. Their light illuminated the faces of barkers who shouted, "This way to Ford's."[20] Amid all the hoop skirts and military uniforms, the Lincolns may have spotted tall sandwich boards plugging the next night's performance of *Octoroon,* a benefit for actress Jennie Gourlay. Before that romantic tragedy about a Louisiana woman who carries one-eighth Negro blood had earned one cent for Gourlay, Ford's would be shuttered for good.

At that point in the evening, people whose lives would soon be inextricably altered were going about their humdrum duties along Tenth Street—a tailor, a photographer, a Catholic priest, a six-year-old girl, a bar owner, a bug collector, a theater treasurer, and sundry others. And in New York City,

Gustave Dieterich, Anna Petersen, and the others were off to the Bowery for some German theater.

Ford's Theatre, one and a half blocks uphill from the avenue, had started out life as a sacred building. Until 1861, the sign outside read "First Baptist Church of Washington." The sanctuary, abandoned as its congregation dwindled, had been sitting vacant for two years before it caught the eye of John T. Ford.

The arrival of German Lutherans and Irish and Italian Catholics on Tenth Street had made a Baptist church superfluous, but residents preferred a church to a theater. A theater could bring with it rowdy, itinerant actors as well as actresses, who were regarded with the same disdain as prostitutes. When Ford leased the place, wags warned it would come to no good, turning a house of worship into a palace of hedonism. One Baptist board member forecast a dire fate for anyone who tried it.[21] Ford, a well-liked and well-connected Presbyterian entrepreneur, moved slowly. At thirty-two, he'd been in show business seven years, long enough to recognize that the sanctuary's wide chancel, the raised platform that the minister and choir occupied, would make a pretty good stage without expensive renovations.[22] Ford leased the sacred space and sublet it to Christy's Minstrel Show, a blackface entertainment group, so he could gauge the public reaction. Newspaper ads called the place "The George Christy Opera House." Meanwhile, Ford ran his other Northeast properties—the elegant Academy of Music in Philadelphia and the popular Holliday Street Theatre in Baltimore, the city where he had once served as mayor. Within months, he opted to sink more than ten thousand dollars into renovating the Washington church.[23] Ford's Athenaeum opened for business on March 19, 1862. Before that year ended, it looked as if the naysayers were correct. A gas meter on the fritz had fueled a blaze that burned the building to the ground on December 30. Only part of the twenty thousand dollars' worth of damage was covered by insurance. The Fords' history of community involvement paid dividends though. The brothers were known as civic-minded businessmen, so honest that they routinely paid royalties to Gilbert and Sullivan, something no other American managers did because they knew it would be difficult for the British playwrights to track them an ocean away.[24] So it was only mildly surprising when Ford's chief rival came to his rescue after the fire. Players at Grover's Theatre staged a benefit performance for Ford and his actors. Ford declined the charity for himself, but he accepted for his players, who had lost costumes and instruments as well as bookings. Sidelined at a time when Washingtonians were clamoring for entertainment to help them forget the war, Ford had one thing on his mind—rebuilding bigger and better.[25]

His friends tried to push a bill through Congress to secure public backing for a theater for the federal city. When that failed, Ford sold stock to raise money. The five-hundred-dollar certificates carried a fringe benefit—investors were entitled to free admission to all performances.[26]

High labor costs, wartime supply shortages, and even quicksand did not stop Ford from building a theater one newspaper said had few equals, even in larger cities. The *Washington Sunday Chronicle* said the theater's ventilation system, with its three huge hoods atop the slate roof plus ten air hatches, kept a capacity crowd as comfortable as if they were in a drawing room. There was an embellished saucer-shaped inverted dome over the orchestra seats.[27] Ornate gas chandeliers called gasoliers provided soft light. The acoustics were stellar. Nine chimneys around the building suggest that strategically placed stoves may have warmed guests as they did in Ford's Holliday Street Theatre in Baltimore. Perhaps to absorb noise, the Fords used green baize, the same material used to cover billiard tables, to carpet the apron of the stage that jutted out in front of the drop curtain. Beyond the baize were seventeen footlights and an orchestra pit sunk eighteen inches below the main theater floor and connected with the stage manager's desk by a speaking tube.[28]

Washington's best artisans combined their talents to fashion an elegant gold and white interior for Ford's. From its Turkish carpets to its five-story-high central dome, the place was a stunner. Master plasterer Charles Stewart swathed surfaces with ornamental appliqués of cherubs, scrolls, and blossoms. The moldings that framed interior wall panels were installed by Foster and Sommergetz Moulding and Guilding, not merely painted on, as was often the case. The white and red brick exterior, more than twice as wide as any other building on the block, was illuminated by a gaslight.[29] It shone the way onto a wooden sidewalk that led to five arched entrance doorways. Ten casement windows above the arches emitted more light.

Ford's New Theatre opened on August 27, 1863, with *The Naiad Queen,* a large-scale romantic operatic spectacle often staged with a cast of three hundred. Guests entering the curving thirty-foot-long lobby via the arched doorways could check the time on a clock hung above their heads or, if they had not yet purchased tickets, turn right to the box office. A full house at Ford's meant about seventeen hundred people sitting in the eight plush private boxes that flanked the stage, in cane-bottomed chairs in the down-

John Surratt was tried two years after the other defendants. Unlike them, he was not convicted. Credit: James O. Hall Collection

stairs orchestra section or the horseshoe-shaped balcony dubbed the dress circle, and on high-backed wooden benches in the uppermost balcony, the one dubbed the family circle to discourage its use by prostitutes and their johns. Seats were arranged on steps to afford excellent views from any spot in the house.[30]

The facades of both balconies were trimmed in ornate plaster appliqués, and the family circle railing was dotted with elegant gas lighting fixtures spaced thirty inches apart. On gala occasions, birdcages holding canaries were suspended from them.

At ten dollars per ticket, the theater's eight private boxes were the most expensive and the worst seats in the house. They were slanted slightly away from the stage to afford the audience the chance to gaze at the bigwigs who filled them.

The best in the business played at Ford's, including Edwin Forrest, whose Othello was unparalleled, and James Henry Hackett, President Lincoln's favorite Shakespearean actor. Lincoln liked Hackett so much that he came to see him in *Henry IV* on Monday, December 14, 1863, and returned the next evening to see him again. Lincoln came to see John Wilkes Booth perform the dual roles of sculptors Phidias and Raphael Duchalet in *The Marble Heart* on November 9, 1863, but he did not return. Theater critic Stanley Kimmel called Booth's performance apathetic and indifferent. He said the actor seemed to be waiting for the play to end. When, for a few moments, Booth did display emotion, the president genially joined in a round of applause for him.

Lincoln came to Ford's ten times—five times in 1863, three in 1864, one in February 1865, and on the ill-fated evening of April 14, 1865. He came to see John Sleeper Clarke in the comedy *Love in Livery* on February 10, just nine weeks before Clarke's brother-in-law shot him. Although many cried conspiracy because the president was unguarded on April 14, there was a guard outside his box when he saw *Love in Livery* with Generals U. S. Grant and Ambrose Burnside.[31]

Booth himself occasionally sat on the other side of Ford's limelights, too. When the actor attended a performance, he was partial to the seats in box seven or eight, the same two combined to form the presidential box. In fact, he had given four free box-seat passes to John Surratt, who would later be tried as a coconspirator. One of Surratt's guests was Lewis Powell, a preacher's son who would slit Secretary of State William Seward's throat and beat Seward's son with the barrel of a three-pound revolver.[32]

10

Booth's End Game

When the green Lincoln carriage pulled up at Ford's, footman Charles Forbes swung down to the wooden carriage platform. He tugged at the door handle, causing a set of steps to spring forward. Fred Petersen watched from the other side of the street as Mr. Lincoln and Mary alighted first, then Miss Harris and Major Rathbone. There's no way of knowing whether neighbors on either side of Petersen's boardinghouse were also watching. The owners of both houses, like many of the actors and musicians at Ford's, were reportedly secesh.[1]

When the two couples walked through the fourth arched door at around nine p.m., the play was already in progress. The gilt braid and buttons of the army and navy filled the seats. Veterans of almost every major skirmish had come to Ford's to celebrate with President Lincoln and General Grant. As he walked past the lobby clock and ascended the stairs to the dress circle, Mr. Lincoln carried his size 7⅛ black silk top hat, made by local haberdasher J. Y. Davis, the one with the thin silk mourning band buckled over the standard hat band in remembrance of eleven-year-old Willie.[2] If the president put a hand in the pocket of his Brooks Brothers suit as he walked up the stairs, his fingers might have brushed any one of nine items he was carrying, including his ivory-handled pocketknife, an oversized monogrammed handkerchief, his soft brown leather wallet with a five-dollar Confederate note and nine newspaper clippings inside, and two pair of eyeglasses, one mended with a piece of string.[3] Mr. Lincoln had been wearing reading glasses for almost eight years. He was forty-eight when he bought his first pair at a jewelry store for 37½ cents. Mrs. Lincoln, whose cataracts may have already been affecting her sight, carried the small black leather case that held her opera glasses.[4]

Led by sixteen-year-old doorman Edmund Schreiner, the foursome probably crossed the dress circle as quietly as possible, but their arrival might have been broadcast by the metal hobnails in the heels of the president's black leather boots.[5] When the audience members, like dominoes

John Wilkes Booth's spur would catch on one of the flags that draped the presidential box. Credit: National Archives

first touching, each became aware that the Lincolns were heading for the presidential box, heads swiveled, and waving and howling broke out in every corner of the building. Then the blare and crash of the orchestra interrupted actress May Hart's lines.[6] Witnesses disagree whether the full orchestra broke into "Hail to the Chief" or Handel's more sedate "Hail the Conquering Hero Comes." Either way, the timbre of the orchestra was fully met by hundreds of war veterans cheering hysterically, letting out their pent-up feelings of admiration for the man who had led them through four harrowing years. With the trumpets still blaring and the drums sounding, Captain Joseph R. Findley thought that surely such a reception was rarely given to any man.[7] Cast members came out from the wings to watch the president. Rows of theatergoers glanced around for General Grant and were disappointed, but nonetheless, the hysteria didn't stop for five solid minutes.[8]

From his balcony seat, Captain Oliver Gatch noticed that Mr. Lincoln walked slowly, his great body bent forward and his shoulders wearing a noticeable stoop. His high silk hat was in his left hand.[9] In response to the deafening ovation coming from every part of the house, the president smiled a sad smile. His delighted wife curtsied several times.[10]

May Hart tried to remember her lines as she stood at the stage's edge with Laura Keene, staring over the footlights into the dress circle, where the Lincolns, Major Rathbone, and Miss Harris were proceeding to their box. Hart, like Captain Gatch, noticed that Mr. Lincoln's tall figure was bent, and the sadness on his face seemed out of place on such a gala evening.

The crowd continued its wild cheering as the Lincolns stepped into the box. President Lincoln leaned in front of the lace curtains that screened the box from audience view and acknowledged the applause with a dignified bow, bringing the fanfare to a hush. The president signaled Ned Emerson, who was on stage at that moment, to go on with the play. Then he stepped in back of the curtains and seated himself out of sight. "How sociable it seems, like one family sitting around their parlor fire," Miss Julia Shepherd thought to herself as she watched from her seat in the dress circle.[11]

At about the same time, Louis Carland walked through the side door from Ford's to Taltavul's. The costume maker looked to his right and caught a glimpse of John Wilkes Booth's back as the actor strolled out the canopied front door. He looked to his left and saw Taltavul wiping the lower end of the bar. He supposed Booth had just finished a drink.[12]

Booth's fateful end game had begun.

Several artists depicted Satan whispering to John Wilkes Booth during the play. Credit: Collection of Edward Steers Jr.

11

'Tis the Wink of an Eye

'Tis the wink of an eye
'Tis the draught of a breath
From the blossom of health to the paleness of death
From the gilded saloon to the bier and the shroud
Oh, why should the spirit of mortal be proud?
  —William Knox, "Mortality" (President Lincoln's favorite poem)

Over at Ford's, the president was folding his frame into the walnut rocker Joe Simms had carried through the alley on his head. With a twelve-button back and padded arms, the crimson-silk-upholstered chair was the most comfortable seat in the theater. Mrs. Lincoln took a cane-bottom chair next to her husband. On her opposite side sat Miss Harris on a red velvet armchair. Major Rathbone took a seat behind her on the edge of a crimson sofa, at least seven feet from the president. Mr. Lincoln propped his head on his hand, staring aimlessly toward the footlights. From the stage, actress May Hart could see that the president's eyes were wide open, but he didn't seem to notice the actors twelve feet beneath him.[1] He may have been mulling over an issue as great as Reconstruction of the South, or perhaps his feet just hurt. The president had foot problems, and that night, his square-toed, size-14 boots were a little tight, and the sole of the left one had an irksome crease running along one side and into the toe box.[2]

John Wilkes Booth, meanwhile, was on the move. As an old friend of the Fords, Booth had the run of the theater. That night, he popped in and out five times, but the only time he stopped at the ticket booth was to bum a plug of tobacco from Buck Buckingham. The last time Booth walked into Ford's, he was heard humming a tune as he walked up the stairs to the dress circle on his way to kill the president.[3]

A. M. Crawford and Captain Theodore McGowan, who had the seats closest to the president's box, had to move their chairs for him to pass. They were miffed because he took his good old time. Crawford turned to his friend to complain the man seemed intoxicated.[4]

Helen Truman, awaiting her cue to go on stage, kept her eyes on Mrs. Lincoln until she saw something unexpected. Truman was musing to herself that the first lady was not wearing an evening gown to match her husband's formal attire. Instead, she wore a gray-and-black spring dress in silk, with a bonnet to match. Miss Truman silently sized up Mrs. Lincoln as not really beautiful but good-looking, animated, and dignified, the kind of woman who would be distinguished in any company; plus, she had a million dollars' worth of that wonderful thing called personality. Truman kept sneaking peeks at the first lady. Mary Lincoln was a favorite with actresses because she was courteous enough to send flowers when she enjoyed a performance. With one peek, Truman saw something that would be a bright red flag in twenty-four hours but only seemed odd at that moment. She noticed John Wilkes Booth standing in the corner near the entrance to the president's box. The actor spotted her staring and, his charm intact, bowed to her.[5]

Before Booth entered the box, he showed a calling card to Charles Forbes, Lincoln's footman. Then, in what the president's secretaries later called "the blinding swiftness of enchantment," history was shuffled. Stealthily, Booth opened the door to the box.[6]

Suddenly, unbeknownst to the others in the softly lit room, an additional person was sharing the same air. The intruder had barred himself in with them. The split second that would change all of their lives forever was imminent. Catlike, Booth crossed the four or five feet between the door and the president's rocker. The president was a sitting duck.[7]

The box faced the audience, but the assassin's movements were shielded from view by the flag-draped railing, the yellow draperies, and the honeycomb-patterned lace curtains that fell from the ceiling to the floor.

At that moment, Harry Hawk had the stage to himself. The frail comic, playing the title role of a bumbling American backwoodsman, stood between the lowered limelights and a stage piece painted to look like a door hung with curtains. The assassin picked this moment to kill the president, maybe thinking that it would be child's play to push Hawk out of the way and dash the sixty-two feet across the backstage to the door where his quick mare was waiting. Booth, who knew the play by heart, stood in the maroon-wallpapered box, waiting for Hawk to deliver the one line that always brought down the house with thundering guffaws: "Don't know the manners of good society, eh? Well, I guess I know enough to turn you inside out, old gal. You sockdologizing old man trap."[8]

The assassin wormed forward in his black calfskin riding boots, his silver-clad pistol probably directly fixed on the president's head. Hawk said it: "You sockdologizing old man trap." Tragedy transected comedy.[9]

While the audience howled with delight twelve feet below, John Wilkes Booth squeezed the tiny trigger. There was no going back. The trigger released the hammer, and the internal mechanisms of the derringer performed exactly according to specifications, speeding the .44-caliber metal ball through the president's wiry black hair, piercing his scalp, and burrowing through the left side of his brain until it lodged itself behind his gray right eye.[10]

Major Rathbone, a battlefield veteran, instantly recognized the sound and turned toward the rocker, which was surrounded by gun smoke. He thought he could make out the form of a man inside the smoke cloud.[11]

Laughter was one of the last things President Lincoln ever heard. The other might have been his killer's voice mouthing the word "freedom." That's what Major Rathbone thought he heard as he dashed into the bluish-white cloud.[12]

Several people leaped from their seats at the sound of the shot, only to sit again when others cried out "Down in front!" because they thought the gunfire was part of the play. The musicians in the orchestra pit, who knew better, looked bewildered.

Mrs. Lincoln, holding her husband's long hand, was laughing at Hawk's line when she saw the flash and heard the report of a pistol. She thought it was in some way connected with the play. Suddenly, she felt the president, without a noise or a struggle, sinking his chair.[13]

His light was out. Only one man in the vast theater noticed the first lady leap from her chair. From his front-row seat in the balcony, bar owner James Ferguson, staring through opera glasses, watched her catch her husband around the neck and brace his long body so it wouldn't slide out of the rocker.[14]

Miss Harris, enjoying the play, heard the pistol's snap and looked around the box. Smoke blocked her view of the president's chair. At once, she felt her fiancé spring from his seat behind her and rush pell-mell toward the president. Seconds later, it sounded as if the major were struggling with someone, but she couldn't see through the haze that enveloped them.[15]

Meanwhile, all Mrs. Lincoln's attention was on her husband. She placed her hand on his forehead. He didn't stir. When she moved it to the back of his head, her fingertips became moist. Suddenly, she felt something move past her, disturbing her shawl.[16]

A moment later, Miss Harris watched a good-looking man materialize out of the cloud. He darted between the two women and placed the tapered fingers of his left hand on the cushy railing with the surety of a gymnast.[17] Major Rathbone tried to clutch him, stretching his long arms around him, but he thought he might as well have tried to hold a machine of iron.[18] Rathbone was no match for Booth. At five foot, eleven inches tall, he would have seemed to have the advantage over the much shorter killer, but Booth was almost twenty pounds heavier, all of it muscle.[19] The agile assassin suddenly twisted himself around in Rathbone's arms so the men were face to face, close enough so that Rathbone could hear Booth's teeth grinding.[20]

Booth then pulled a Bowie knife from his coat. From her seat in the audience, Helen Du Barry thought it looked half as long as a man's arm.[21] Booth lunged for the major's heart with the power of an exceptionally skilled swordsman. Rathbone deflected the blow with his left arm, but the steel blade sliced the flesh open to the bone, from his elbow almost to his shoulder. The bloody arm fell, powerless.[22] James Ferguson was still watching from his seat as the assassin hopped the railing, moving his arm as if he were striking back at someone. The bar owner noticed something gleaming in the man's right hand. Booth leaped almost twelve feet to the stage, his small right foot catching on the box decorations as he dropped. A severed tuft of blue affixed itself to his right spur and trailed him as he fell.[23] It happened in a whirlwind—fewer than thirty seconds from the shot to the leap. The audience sat spellbound.[24]

Dr. Leale saw a figure in midair. He watched the jumper fall crumpled to the stage. As he landed, his boot spur ripped the green baize carpeting at the front of the stage and nicked the narrow wood floorboard underneath, leaving a semicircular indentation.[25]

Edwin Bates had heard the shot and thought the fine-looking man crouching ten feet in front of him had jumped to the stage for his own safety after someone else fired.[26]

Billy Ferguson, the callboy, also heard the shot, just as the rest of the cast probably did, but it didn't faze him because the company's property man often discharged old firearms in the alley directly behind the stage. It was Booth's crash to the stage that probably put a knot in Ferguson's stomach. Ferguson was backstage when he heard the thud. He thought a desk he was assigned to prepare for the next scene had been upended. "More work for me," he murmured to himself.[27] Then he spotted Booth rising onstage. He looked to his left and saw three players standing beneath the presidential box, as motionless as if they were frozen to the floor.[28]

Ned Emerson, the actor whose cane Booth had snapped a day earlier, was standing below the presidential box reading his lines by the gas jet when Booth leaped onto the stage in front of him, his hair in such wild disorder that his friend didn't recognize him. Stunned, Emerson never moved toward the assassin.[29] Booth dropped within spitting distance of violinist Isaac Bradley and violoncellist William Musgine, but no one in the orchestra pit moved or shouted or gave chase.[30]

Seconds after he alighted on stage, Booth rose. He turned to the audience with a manic stare and raised his left hand above his head, revealing the bloody knife. It was an outlandish spectacle.[31] Dr. Leale said the blade glistened like a diamond in the bright limelight.[32] Some audience members thought Booth hissed the Virginia state motto, "Sic semper tyrannis"—"Thus always to tyrants." If Booth expected applause, he didn't get it.

Mrs. Nelson Todd, a tourist watching from the audience, thought she was watching him commit suicide.[33] Ensign William Flood, watching the jaw-dropping stunt from the third row, recognized Booth instantly. Then he heard women screaming in the presidential box. He didn't know Mr. Lincoln had been shot.[34] Five-year-old Samuel Seymour started crying. He wasn't concerned about the president either. He thought the man who had fallen from the box was hurt.[35]

Harry Hawk, alone on stage and lost in his role, had no idea Booth was escaping when he saw him running toward him brandishing a knife. Hawk, who had been dating a woman Booth fancied, assumed the knife was meant for him. He ran off the stage and kept running up a flight of stairs.[36]

Behind the scenes, Helen Truman had taken just a few steps toward her dressing room when she heard a pistol shot, followed by a woman's screams. Suddenly, she saw a man speeding toward her and actress Jennie Gourlay. In his haste to get around them, the assassin knocked Gourlay into the scenery with the back of his arm. His face was drawn, but both women instantly recognized him as John Wilkes Booth. Truman instinctively tried to run, but she was so terrified that her legs wouldn't budge. Gourlay's eyes followed Booth as he ran for the stage door. She, too, was unaware the president had been shot.[37]

Fewer than forty-five seconds after the shot rang out, Booth, moving like lightning, now passed so close to Billy Ferguson that the callboy felt the assassin's hot breath on his face. Ferguson, who had been busy memorizing the ten lines of a minor actor who had called in sick, was stunned to see his stage idol, his black eyes blazing and his lips drawn up tight against his teeth.[38]

May Hart was standing next to Laura Keene awaiting her cue when she heard a pop, like a cork being drawn from a bottle. Suddenly, things went sideways. Booth blew past Hart as he sprinted toward the stage door. He was within three feet of her, but she was stiff as a frightened cat.[39]

The actors who knew Booth best were baffled when they saw his trademark shiny locks in wild disarray and his face a bloodless white. Ferguson thought the lithe assassin ran about seventy-five feet across the stage in about thirty seconds. Hawk thought he was even more fleet.[40]

"It was all done so quick that everyone was so astounded they could hardly move," Lieutenant John Toffey wrote to his grandmother a few days later.[41]

When it dawned on Toffey what had happened right in front of his eyes, he wished to God that he had had the presence of mind to shoot Booth. Cowardice certainly wasn't a factor. The twenty-two-year-old's valor in leading a charge up steep and seemingly impregnable Missionary Ridge in 1863 would eventually earn him the Medal of Honor, the nation's highest military award. None of the armed men in the audience unholstered their guns at first. The reason was simple. As Lieutenant Toffey wrote, "The thing was done so quick that there was hardly time to draw them."[42] The cries that the president had been shot weren't heard until a few seconds after Booth vanished behind the scenery. Booth's dramatic plan had worked. He had relied on citizens' expectation that a killer would slip away after his work was done. No one would ever expect him to jump to the footlights and display his bloody weapon. Audience members were baffled when Booth interrupted the play, but few put two and two together.

It wasn't until Miss Harris heard her bloodied and winded fiancé shout, "Stop that man," that she leaned forward and repeated his cry: "Won't somebody stop that man."[43] By that time, Booth was approaching the rear stage door.

Billy Withers, the high-strung orchestra leader, spent ten seconds he never forgot between the desperado and that door. Withers, somewhat exercised because the stage manager had ordered his original composition postponed, was backstage fussing when Booth jumped to the stage. The full effect of the composition would be utterly lost, he griped. As Withers walked back through the wings, still in his own world, he unwittingly blocked Booth's path. The lights were low, but Withers recognized his friend Booth glaring at him like a wild beast. The actor's hair was standing on end. His coat was torn. His jaw was set tight, and his eyes seemed to pop from their sockets. His face was as pale as if all the blood had been drained from it. His arms were flying. Beads of sweat glistening among his curling black locks, Booth shrieked, "Out of the way. Let me pass, or I'll kill. Kill!" Withers, stupid with terror, froze. Lowering his head like an infuriated bull, Booth sprang at Withers with the bloody knife. One swipe caught the back of his tuxedo jacket but not his flesh. Although Booth's blade never broke Withers's skin, one of his blows hit the orchestra leader's shoulder with enough force to fell him. Booth looked down at Withers. At that instant, he seemed to recognize his old friend. "God! Billy Withers!" he cried. With that, he turned and shot off like an arrow. Later, Withers would cut pieces out of his coattails to distribute as souvenirs, but at that moment he was too startled to move.[44]

So were the stagehands. Backstage at that moment, there should have been a doorkeeper, a prompter, a property man, a gas man, two carpenters, four scene shifters, and nineteen actors, but none of them stopped Booth.[45] "No one seemed to know just what to do," Ned Emerson said.[46]

Booth leapt over Withers's supine form and disappeared through the door.

Mary Ann Turner, who lived in a small house bordering the alley, saw a man dash from the theater with something glittering in his hand. He was moving so fast that it seemed like he just touched his horse, and in a flash, it was gone.[47] Two little boys from Ninth Street, already wrapped up in bed blankets, watched from their back bedroom windows as the door opened at the back of Ford's. In the dim moonlight, they made out a horseman dashing down the alley. They heard the horse's hooves ringing out in the still night.[48]

Booth was scot-free—for now. He would return to Baptist Alley in a little less than four years.

12

Thunderstruck

Withers was still lying in the dark like a turned turtle. Harry Hawk had run off. Confusion reigned backstage. When Ned Emerson told Jennie Gourlay the president had been shot, she fainted. He caught her in his arms.[1]

If George Parkhurst saw Booth, he must have been perplexed. The part-time actor was planning to drop by Booth's room after the play to pick up some costumes and odds and ends Booth said he wouldn't need any longer.[2]

The audience, albeit almost seventeen hundred strong, sat thunderstruck for several seconds, as if they were all chained to their seats.[3] A deathly silence fell over the house. Just as at Grover's, you could have heard a pin drop. The only sound was Booth's horse's hooves rattling over the cobblestones of Baptist Alley and dying away in the distance. Coming out of the hush, theatergoers looked at one another and whispered, "What is it?" and "Who was it?"[4]

Dr. Leale, still sitting in his cane-bottomed chair, was surrounded by cries that the president had been murdered, followed by cries of "Kill the murderer!" and "Shoot him!" from different pockets of the audience.[5] One man, albeit belatedly, jumped up on a chair and shouted: "Take out the ladies, and hang him here on the spot!"[6] As if the cries, groans, seat-smashing, and shuffling of thousands of feet weren't enough, soon the bloodcurdling shrieks of Mrs. Lincoln added to the inferno of noise.[7] The actors taking their breaks in the second-floor green room were puzzled. If the time on the ornate gold French clock was correct, then they shouldn't be hearing such a racket. They straggled out to see what was up.[8]

By the time May Hart and Laura Keene heard the ruckus backstage, Booth had already made his escape. When they heard a man's voice shouting, "The president has been shot," the women rushed forward through the footlights and peered up into the presidential box. Mr. Lincoln's head, which had been resting on his hand, had fallen limp onto his bosom, but there was no sign of violence. He looked as if he had fallen asleep. "I expected to see him rise from his chair and quiet the raving crowd before him," Hart told a reporter.[9]

All eyes turned to the box. The president was nowhere in sight. From the waist down, Mrs. Lincoln was hidden from view by the flag-draped banister, but onlookers could see her arms outstretched above her head and waving to and fro.[10]

Then Dr. Leale heard a woman call for a doctor. Just days after his twenty-third birthday, he was nimble enough to vault over the seats between him and the president's box, forcing a path through the dense crowd. He was the first person admitted to the box.[11] Major Rathbone rushed to him, cradling his wounded arm with his good arm, beseeching him to attend to it. The doctor checked Rathbone's eyes, realized he was in no immediate danger, and walked past him to the president, who appeared to be dead. Mrs. Lincoln, sobbing at her slumping husband's feet, stretched her hand out to him and asked, "Oh, Doctor! Is he dead? Can he recover? Will you take charge of him? Do what you can for him!" He took her hand and vowed to do all that possibly could be done. That soothed her. The gentle doctor inspired trust, even in strangers, with his kind light brown eyes and his erect and confident carriage. He thought how courageous Mrs. Lincoln had been to throw her body over her husband the entire time Major Rathbone battled a knife-wielding fiend just inches away. Then he went to work. After six weeks of treating serious gunshot wounds daily, he was perfectly suited for the task at hand. The president's eyes were closed, and he was slumping forward. He would have fallen further, but he was being held upright by his wife, who had braced herself at his feet. The doctor lifted Mr. Lincoln's eyelids and saw evidence of a brain injury. The president was in a profound coma, almost dead. With each breath, he was panting and choking, and all attempts to find a pulse had failed.[12] Recalling the shining blade the assassin had displayed on stage and noticing that the left shoulder of the president's coat was saturated with blood, he supposed Mr. Lincoln had been stabbed. He loosened the president's slip-on tie. Then he asked Major William Kent to cut away the president's clothes with his pocketknife. No stab wound could be found.[13] With the help of some men who had entered the box, Dr. Leale laid the paralyzed president on the carpet, Mr. Lincoln's head resting on the doctor's spread handkerchief. Quickly passing the separated fingers of both his hands through Mr. Lincoln's coarse, blood-matted hair, Dr. Leale touched the mortal wound. It was no bigger than the head of a lead pencil. Dr. Leale easily removed a clot of blood from the blue wound to relieve the pressure on the brain. Then he inserted the little finger of his left hand to probe the wound. It was too short. He realized the bullet had burrowed straight through the brain. As he dislodged his pinky, he thought no one with such a severe injury could survive, not even for an hour. All the while, Mrs. Lincoln was crying out, "My husband, my husband, my God, my God, he is dead!" Major Kent tried to calm her, but he had no luck. The doctor knelt over the president, with one knee on each side of his pelvis. Leaning forward, he opened Mr. Lincoln's mouth and inserted two fingers of his right hand as far inside as possible, pressing the paralyzed tongue down so he could open the larynx and allow air to pass to the lungs.[14]

Meanwhile, Dr. Charles Sabin Taft, another twenty-three-year-old army surgeon, had made it to the stage below. He was eyeing the wall for a way to get a foothold to the box when Daniel Beekman spotted him. "Do you want to get up there?" Beekman asked. When Charlie Taft said yes, Beekman instructed him to place one foot in his interlaced fingers and then step onto his shoulder. Dr. Taft was soon in the box.[15] Dr. Leale asked him and some others to manipulate the president's arms to expand the thorax while he pressed on the diaphragm to draw air in and out of the lungs. Desperate to help the president, Dr. Leale pressed his thumb and fingers beneath the ribs and massaged the heart until some irregular but independent breathing followed.[16] Suddenly, he thought of his mother telling him a Bible story about a prophet who had breathed life into another.[17] He quickly placed a handkerchief over the president's mouth, leaned over him, and squeezed his nostrils shut. He drew in a long breath and forced it directly into Mr. Lincoln's mouth. The president's respiration improved. His heart began pumping. The doctor was relieved that death would not occur instantly, in the box, but he knew the wound was lethal.

"His wound is mortal," he said aloud. "It is impossible for him to recover." Within minutes, Dr. Leale's words were being telegraphed around the country. Mrs. Lincoln, who was sitting nearby, sank back in her chair and sobbed brokenly.[18]

With actor Thomas Gourlay as her guide, Laura Keene hurried through back passages to bring water to the box, but the president's lips were already set in death when she arrived.[19] When Keene first saw the long-limbed, muscular president lying on the carpet with his shirt cut open to waist and perhaps his arms raised, she thought how much he resembled Rembrandt's classic *The Lamentation over the Dead Christ*.[20]

Mr. Lincoln said nothing after he was shot, but he responded with a slight groan when someone touched his skin or took his hand.[21] Little blood escaped from his wound, not enough to soil his clothes before he was carried from the box. While Keene was cradling the president's head in her lap, her manager-husband John Lutz was headed straight for her first-floor dressing room.

Lutz found the door open and his wife's diamond jewelry scattered across a dressing table. He systematically gathered up the jewels and locked the door. Then, as the president gasped for air, Lutz stormed off through the roaring crowd to upbraid his wife for her carelessness.[22]

At the moment when Booth raised his bloody knife, two men in the audience had reacted as differently as night and day. Restaurateur James Ferguson, who often served Booth lunch, saw the actor look him right in the face and instinctively pulled the lady who was with him down behind the white balcony banister.[23] Colonel Pren Metham instinctively reached for his gun while Booth was still muttering, "Sic semper tyrannis." When Metham realized he wasn't armed, the veteran of Sherman's March tried to pick up his chair and hurl it at Booth in order to slow his escape. When he realized the chairs were strung together, Metham elbowed his way to the aisle to give chase. He spotted a side door he thought might lead to the alley. Instead, he found himself standing in an occupied ladies' dressing room. That ended his pursuit.[24]

The man who got closest to capturing Booth was Major Joseph Stewart, known as the tallest man in Washington, overtopping Mr. Lincoln by two inches. Stewart was sitting in the first row talking to his sister when he heard the shot, looked up, and saw Booth tumbling over the railing, a curl of gun smoke directly above him.[25] The Pennsylvania Avenue lawyer knew the play. Quickly grasping that Booth was not part of it, he sprang from his seat and clambered on stage in pursuit of the assassin. Unfamiliar with the backstage area, Stewart wandered through the scenery in the dark and then tried to open the stage door on the hinged side. He reached the alley about three seconds too late. He watched Booth ride off in the dim moonlight.[26] Stewart hotfooted it after him for forty or fifty yards, but as a New York newspaperman wrote later, the assassin was simply too fleet to catch.[27] Had he not fumbled with the door, Stewart just might have been able to grab Booth's horse by the reins.

As a *Chicago Tribune* reporter wrote three days later, Booth's mastery of the theater layout made all the difference. As Pren Metham's and Joseph Stewart's efforts proved, a person not as familiar could not possibly have made his escape as quickly and well.[28]

Actors who had been behind the scenes drifted on stage. Ned Emerson hurried up to the presidential box. Audience members clambered to the footlights. Annie Wright, wife of the stage manager, tried to use a bass viol as a step.[29]

There was no order in the house. Mrs. Lincoln's bloodcurdling shrieks set the tone. Women fainted. Men smashed seats. People who hadn't lifted a finger as Booth escaped now screamed, "Hang him!" and "Burn the theater!" and "Who was he?"[30] Someone said, "Booth!" Then the cry was taken up: "Booth, Booth, Booth!" Still louder: "Booth!" Pistols were drawn. The frustration was palpable. As the word spread that the president's wound was serious, men tore seats away from their metal fastenings to the floor. Congressman James R. Morris of Ohio jumped on his chair and cried, "Hang the—scoundrel," using salty language he later allowed he was not proud of.[31]

"The audience were so exasperated that they would have hung him on stage had he been caught," twenty-year-old George Dorrance wrote to his sister Hattie the next day.[32] Audience members moved aimlessly, knocking into one another. Someone yelled, "Clear the house!" Soon others were repeating, "Yes, clear the house."[33]

Above the stage, Clara Harris was busy extending her hand to doctors and soldiers scaling the box to aid Dr. Leale. Kitty Brink was in her dressing room when she heard shouts and footsteps clumping through the scenery. When she walked out to see what was happening, she saw men being lifted to the presidential box.[34]

It was as if each minute were overfilled.

Many audience members, veterans of Shiloh or Gettysburg or Missionary Ridge, had seen death close up before, but this was different. No one had ever killed a president. As Helen Du Barry wrote to her mother that weekend, "We could not anticipate that an assassin could be in the box with the president. His only danger seemed to be from a shot fired by one of the audience."[35] Charles Sanford said the audience could not persuade itself the president had been assassinated. W. Henry Pearce said the news came to all like a clap of thunder in a clear sky.[36]

Louis Carland, the costumer, was standing on the carriage platform outside the theater talking with James Gifford, the chief carpenter, when a man came running out the doors at 10:10 p.m., saying the president had been shot. At first, Gifford made a joke about it. Then an usher and two other men all ran out, telling anyone who would listen that a man had shot the president, jumped onto the stage, and escaped behind the scenes.[37]

When a man rushed into Taltavul's announcing, "The president is murdered," Peter Taltavul said, "Oh, pshaw!" He thought it was a tasteless joke.[38]

It was just a busy Friday night at the Metropolitan Police Headquarters on Tenth Street, until Major A. C. Richards rushed in, fresh from Ford's. The police administrator made a beeline for the telegraph machine. "Take the other instrument quick," he instructed Detective James McDevitt. "The president has been shot. We must send out a general alarm!" The second he swallowed the news, McDevitt bolted for the other machine. They soon had the news flashing in every direction.[39]

Captain Joseph Findley hightailed it from Ford's to military headquarters to notify authorities. He found the officer on duty taking a smoke. When he told him what had happened, the officer just laughed. He treated Findley like he was crazy or drunk—until a servant from Secretary Seward's home showed up to report the attack there.[40]

13

Their Precious Burden

Back at Ford's, Dr. Leale, certain that he did not want the president of the United States to die in a theater on Good Friday, was making plans to move him. Someone suggested carrying him next door to Taltavul's. Peter Taltavul was aware this would be the death knell for his business, and he knew he could not support his nine children with his side jobs as a musician. He quickly proffered that it shouldn't be said that the president of the United States died in a saloon on Good Friday.[1] Finally, Joe Sardo, a thirteen-year-old theater helper, was dispatched to ask his mother to prepare a room at their boardinghouse at 461 Tenth Street West, directly across the street from Ford's.[2] Coincidentally, Joe's nine-year-old neighbor Charles Petersen was also in the theater that night, and the president would actually land in his home.[3]

Mrs. Lincoln scurried around the box, picking up the papers that had fallen from her husband's hat. She turned to Captain Edwin Elzaphan Bedee, a New Hampshire volunteer, and said, "You are an officer. Won't you take charge of these papers?" He did.[4]

Dr. Leale assigned Dr. Charles Sabin Taft to lift the president's right shoulder and Dr. Albert Africanus King to carry his left. (Dr. King would later distinguish himself as one of the first physicians to recognize the link between mosquitoes and malaria.) Leale himself held the president's head steady. Nineteen-year-old Private Jacob Soles and his fellow Pennsylvania artillerymen moved in to help—John Corey, Jake Griffiths, and William Sample. As they gently lifted the president's body, Soles thought it felt limp in his hands.[5]

Onlookers kept asking if the president could be taken to the Executive Mansion, and Dr. Leale repeatedly advised that his patient could not survive the carriage ride over rutted mud streets or even over the uneven cobblestone pavement. Dr. Leale led the way down to Tenth Street in search of a place to make the savior of the country comfortable. The bearers moved slowly toward the stairs, then stopped and reversed directions so the president's feet would descend first.[6] Mr. Lincoln's face was as white as his shirt when he was carried past Sarah Eastman, a pretty brown-haired debutante standing at the head of the stairway.[7] His face had fallen toward his chest. When Al Daggett saw the president stripped to the waist and apparently dead, he thought he would lose his senses forever.[8] Just a short time after the president had walked triumphantly up the staircase, high hat in hand, he was now being carried down it, stripped to the waist. Playgoers who had waved their handkerchiefs to welcome him were using them to dry their tears.[9]

Major Rathbone sprang forward to escort Mrs. Lincoln to the top of the steps, but he couldn't walk any farther. He asked some soldiers to escort her and his fiancé. He followed them, but his blood dripped down the stairs, across the lobby, and onto the muddy street. Sergeant Charles Johnson, who was standing six feet from him, said it looked like Booth had nearly cut his arm off.[10]

Just when they reached the bottom of the winding stairs, a self-absorbed soldier squeezed by in the narrow lobby, swiping the president's head with his coat sleeve. John Ramsay had his own agenda: the teen was rushing headlong to the exit because he didn't have a pass to attend the theater. People who could see the bearers graciously stepped aside to let them pass through, but the crowd was so compressed that the entire process had to be repeated every few yards.[11]

Even after the president had been removed, most audience members were reluctant to leave Ford's. "They all seemed to be groping for a way to lend a helping hand," actress Helen Truman said.[12] News of the assassination spread, and soon more individuals swarmed toward the theater. The noise outside on Tenth Street was so ear-splittingly loud that six-year-old Annie Sardo would remember it for all her ninety-plus years.[13] At Petersen's boardinghouse, William Petersen got up from his card game to see what the cries and shouts were about.[14]

His boarder Huldah Francis had already climbed into her bed on the first floor. Her husband, George, was dressed for bed too, but he was shutting off the gas lamps. Suddenly, they heard such a terrible scream that they ran to the front windows. Dressed in her nightclothes, Huldah carefully lifted the wide wooden Venetian window blinds and saw some people running into the theater while others ran out. Her first thought was that there was a fire in the theater. Hundreds of voices mingled in the greatest confusion. Then she clearly heard, "The president is shot." At that point, George Francis hurried on his clothes and ran out the door onto the porch just as

Dr. Leale came out of the theater holding the president's head. In the gas-light, George Francis could see the president's face, blankly pale with the eyes closed.[15] Joe Sardo had found it impossible to make a hole in the rip-pling mob to alert his mother that the president was coming.[16] So, as Dr. Leale made his way onto jammed Tenth Street in the darkness, he looked left and right for a place where a president could die. At five feet, seven inches, he may not have been able to see over some heads in the dense crowd.[17] Luckily, Henry Safford had heard the news from his upstairs win-dow at Petersen's and run downstairs to help. Leale spotted Safford stand-ing on the curving brownstone porch at 453 Tenth Street West, struggling to keep a candle lit in the light southwesterly wind.[18]

The row house shared a wall with the Sardos'. The bearers forged a path directly across the street. To part the throbbing mob, military men went before them with bayonets, pistols, and daggers. The doctors and soldiers slowly headed toward Safford's flame with their tender burden, carefully avoiding the deep, muddy ruts. Those who weren't too shocked to notice must surely have been chilled, because the temperature had dropped al-most ten degrees since the show began.[19] Someone threw the president's coat across his bare arms and chest.[20]

Captain Oliver Gatch, one of the army men who had hold of the president, was surprised to hear the swarm fall silent as the bearers slow-ly crossed the street. The only sounds he heard were quiet sobbing and the approaching hoof beats of the cavalry. Gatch must have marveled at the happenstance that had led to his carrying the president of the United States. A prisoner of war for more than two years after being captured at Chickamauga, Gatch had come to Washington on April 14 expressly to collect his back pay. The paymaster was on his way out to an engagement, though, and he asked if the captain could come back the next morning. With his plans to leave the city dashed, Gatch had decided to go see the president at Ford's Theatre.[21]

Gatch and the other bearers moved so slowly and cautiously that artist Carl Bersch was able to sketch the entire scene from his Tenth Street balco-ny. His finished painting shows Mr. Lincoln's rumpled body illuminated in the light of the lamppost in front of Ford's as loving hands convey it across the wet, rutted street in the pitch-black night.

As Major Rathbone walked through Ford's lobby and over the sandy street, blood dripped from his gaping wound. Onlookers who saw this by the dim light of the gas lamps in front of Ford's and Petersen's supposed it was the blood of the martyred president.[22]

Not a single person in the packed street interrupted the procession up the nine curved steps to Petersen's—but several people tried to follow it into the house.

After they passed, onlookers inquired in low, agonized voices, "Can he live?" and "Is there hope?"

Inside the house, Huldah Francis watched from the front window until she realized the bearers were edging toward Petersen's. As they maneuvered to lift Mr. Lincoln up the curved steps, she ran to pull on her clothes.[23]

When William Petersen saw the procession headed toward the house, he shouted up the steps, "The president is coming." Then he made himself scarce. Henry Ulke didn't see him for the rest of the night.[24]

As the president was being carried into Petersen's front hall, panic ensued in Ford's dressing rooms, less than one hundred feet across the street. News of the assassination had spread down Pennsylvania Avenue like wildfire, and rumor had it that a mob had formed at Willard's to hotfoot it to Tenth Street and burn the theater. Even inside Ford's, there was no universal agreement about what had happened before almost seventeen hundred people's eyes. When a songwriter asked Harry Hawk who shot the president, he said, "Booth." John Mathews, who overheard this, shouted, "You are a liar."[25] Mathews, terrified by the rumor about his chum, searched frantically for stagehands to carry all his costumes back to his second-floor room at Petersen's boardinghouse. He'd heard actors were being stopped for questioning at the stage door, so he blended with the theatergoers exiting onto Tenth Street. Squeezing through the throngs outside, Mathews was blithely unaware that the letter Booth had handed him that afternoon was in danger of falling out of his overcoat pocket as he walked.[26] He managed to get by the double military guard at the door and walked directly up to his room, presumably heedless of the assassin's letter edging upward as he climbed the stairs. As he ascended, he could no doubt hear the president's labored breaths and the first lady's wailing.

Back at Ford's, several employees would be questioned and jailed, but William Withers was the first to get a serious once-over. A half dozen policemen came upon the semiconscious Withers lying backstage, bleeding and disheveled after his encounter with Booth. They thought he was the assassin. Detectives dragged him, faint and bloody, through the stage door into Baptist Alley. All the while, he was protesting, "No, no, no. You've got the wrong man. I am Billy Withers, leader of the orchestra! Does nobody know me?" A seething mob gathered around the orchestra leader. He was drifting in and out of consciousness, but he heard men shouting, "Hang him!" and "Ropes, ropes!" and "Lynch the damned dog!" He saw pistol handles glinting in the moonlight. Some friends who could have identified him passed by, but he was too weak to scream to them. It was Richard Wallach, the mayor of Washington, who happened up the alley and intervened. Recognizing Withers, the mayor told the detectives to jail him until it could all be sorted out.[27]

Everywhere, actors were wildly gathering all their belongings before police or a mob could get their hands on them. The cast was anxious for a more mundane reason as well. Even amid one of the most important events in history, individuals think of themselves. Friday night was pay night at Ford's, and the actors were wondering if they'd ever get their money. The pay envelopes were still in Harry Ford's overcoat. The twenty-one-year-old treasurer, discovering May Hart nearly hysterical after the shooting, had left the theater to escort her back to her hotel. As they walked through the throngs, Hart made a mental note to ask Mr. Ford for her twenty dollars before they reached her hotel, but in the excitement, she forgot. Ford was thrown into a bare cell before they met again, and Hart wasn't paid until almost two years later.[28]

Theater workers thought they were home free after they escaped Ford's Friday night, but some were sadly mistaken. On the Monday after the assassination, a Washington detective arrested May Hart at a Baltimore hotel. A witness in Washington claimed she had seen Hart talking to Booth in Baptist Alley on the day of the assassination. Although Hart thought Booth was the most magnetic man she'd ever been around, she had actually never met him. She was able to convince detectives she was talking to Ned Emerson, who had about the same build and hair color as Booth.[29]

Harry Ford wasn't so lucky. He was jailed. While he was sitting in his cell, Ford's mind may have rewound to the conversation he had had with Booth two months earlier in Mr. Potentine's saloon on the avenue. Booth had told him something was going to happen that would astonish the world.[30]

As the men carrying the president padded into Petersen's front hallway, several young boarders bounded down the stairs from the floors above to offer their help.[31] Behind the parlor doors, Huldah Francis moved so quickly that she left her bed unmade.[32] Possibly she locked the door momentarily while dressing, because the soldiers tried the lock, but it didn't give. Downstairs in the boardinghouse's English basement, fourteen-year-old Pauline awoke from her fitful sleep with a start. She heard a noise that caused her to sit up in bed, probably the same noise that made Huldah Francis rush to the window one floor above. In the fog of sleep, she thought she heard, "The president's been shot!" From her room behind the front porch, Pauline could see men carrying a person up the brownstone stairs into her house. His body was so long that it took longer than she expected for them to pass by. Seconds after she heard the front door being pulled open and footfalls in the main hallway, Pauline's door popped open. The family servant instructed her to get up and get dressed. Her help was needed in the kitchen to boil water and tear up sheets to make bandages for Mr. Lincoln.[33]

The muddy-footed bearers squeezed down a hallway barely wider than a yardstick and entered a back bedroom. The room was small, and its sloping roof and drab olive patterned wallpaper made it seem even tighter.[34] The bed was a problem. Tip to toe, the frame for the cornhusk mattress was 71 1/4 inches long, 4 3/4 inches shorter than the president.[35] The bearers placed him on the bed with his knees bent up. Looking at Mr. Lincoln in that impossible position, Dr. Leale first ordered soldiers to break off the foot of the inexpensive bed. When that proved impractical, he settled for placing his patient diagonally on the bed. He called for extra pillows to prop up the head and shoulders. To give the president some fresh air, the two small six-over-six double-hung windows were pushed open, the door to the back porch was left ajar, and an army captain cleared the tiny room of everyone but medical men and the many close friends of the president.[36] The bed, which may have still had its small wooden wheels, was pulled out from the wall so doctors could squeeze in to examine his right side.[37]

When she made her way upstairs, Pauline noticed soldiers guarding the front door. The gas lamps, which had been turned down for the night, were burning brightly. The house was filled with whispers and weeping. Wondering how the tall president could fit on her little bed, she peeked inside the room she used to share with her sister, but she couldn't see past all the adults.[38]

Suddenly, everyone could hear Mrs. Lincoln enter the front hallway, frantic. Wringing her hands in front of her, she cried out, "Where is my husband? Where is my husband!"[39] As she rushed through the door, the end of the lace she had wound in her hair caught in the door. When she kept going, a piece tore off and dropped to the floor. She ignored it. While the first lady rushed to her husband's bedside, Henry Safford, the candle bearer who had welcomed Dr. Leale to the house, bent over and picked up the torn lace. Recognizing its historic value, he kept it for the next thirty-

Secretary of the Navy Gideon Welles wrote details of assassination night in his diary. Credit: Library of Congress

Secretary of War Edwin Stanton made a queer gesture just after the president breathed his last. Credit: Library of Congress

eight years.[40] His move probably went unnoticed as Mrs. Lincoln made her first visit to the room straight down the hall. She bent over her husband and kissed his face, which was normally the color of parchment but was now a pasty white. "You speak to me!" she begged, but he never responded.[41]

Gideon Welles, the secretary of the navy, arrived in a guarded carriage with War Secretary Edwin Stanton. The vice president was nowhere to be found, so Stanton swiftly moved into the vacuum. He began running the country from the small back rooms of the boardinghouse. Meanwhile, Welles chatted up one of the doctors, pressing for the truth on his friend's condition. He was told the president had three hours to live—or perhaps just a little longer.[42]

Stanton, a tall, broad-shouldered man with shaggy gray hair and a long frazzled beard fringing his thick-set head, was pushy and prickly and so heartily disliked that other cabinet members had politicked the president to fire him.[43] The cantankerous secretary had actually called the president "an ape" and "a damned fool."[44] They had come to admire each other, though. And in the last jubilant week, they had given each other a bear hug at least twice.[45]

Stanton, a seasoned trial lawyer, was almost never at a loss for words. That all changed when the surgeon general told him the president could not recover. At first, Stanton just stared in disbelief. Then he cried, "Oh, no, General. Oh, no." He wept like a child, his broad shoulders collapsing and his tall form sinking into a chair beside the low bed. All the while, the president's loud, unnatural groans mingled with the sounds of Mrs. Lincoln weeping as though her heart would break.[46]

The Petersen children and the boarders were pressed into service filling bottles with hot water, running up and down the thirteen narrow curving steps to the kitchen so often that the back door to the death room was propped open. The doctors massaged the president's limbs to keep the blood circulating, and for a time, Fred Petersen took charge of President Lincoln's right leg.[47]

Maunsell Field of the Treasury Department, a fortyish Yalie, heard the improbable news in Willard's lobby and sprinted the four blocks to Ford's to see for himself. The street was already packed wall to wall when he arrived. He saw about one hundred people he knew. They huddled around him, each telling a different story. The first person he met upon gaining entrance to the house was Miss Harris. "Oh, Mr. Field, the president is dying," she said. "But, for heaven's sake, do not tell Mrs. Lincoln."[48]

Dr. Leale had already made it clear that the president could not recover, although this may not have sunk in for Mrs. Lincoln. When Field walked into the front parlor, he saw Mary Lincoln standing alone by a round marble-topped table with her bonnet and gloves still on, just as she had come from the theater. "Why didn't he shoot me?" she asked Field three times in quick succession.[49]

Nevada senator William Stewart, who had thrown away the president's note earlier that night, heard the news at California senator John Conness's home. Conness's manservant burst into the room where Stewart and Conness were sipping wine with Massachusetts senator Charles Sumner. "Mr. Lincoln is assassinated in the theater!" he shouted. "Mr. Seward is murdered in his bed! There's murder in the streets!"[50]

The three went directly to Petersen's to see the president, and there Surgeon General Joseph Barnes told them Mr. Lincoln was mortally wounded. Barnes warned the men the room was already full, but he said he could not refuse them admission if they insisted because they were senators. Conness and Stewart turned to leave, but Sumner rushed past Barnes, saying, "I will go in!" Stewart was stunned.[51]

Alarm spread around Washington. C. C. Bangs, an eighteen-year-old volunteer with the Christian Commission, pushed his way up the steps of Petersen House and saw Mrs. Lincoln in the doorway. She wanted someone to fetch her son Bob.[52]

"I'll go, Madam," he said.

"And who are you?" said an officer standing nearby.

"A member of the Christian Commission," Bangs said, throwing his coat open so the man could see the silver badge of the well-respected commission pinned to his lapel. Bangs ran four blocks to Willard's Hotel to get a carriage, not even stopping to tie his shoes. He told the driver to get to the Executive Mansion as quickly as possible and to turn the carriage around while he went inside so they could leave pronto.

The president's son heard the horses' hooves racing up the driveway about ten thirty p.m., but he was still partially undressed when an usher brought Bangs to his room.[53] As Bob Lincoln grasped the grim news, just a block away, on tree-lined Lafayette Square, another well-to-do son was reeling from a surprise attack on his own father.

Fred Seward was standing in his underwear in the ornate hall of his family mansion, covered in blood, which poured from two holes in his skull. Minutes earlier, the thirty-four-year-old bureaucrat had tried to stop Booth's coconspirator Lewis Powell from entering his father's bedroom. Secretary of State William Seward was recuperating from a serious car-

Secretary of State William Seward was bedridden when Lewis Powell attacked and beat him. Credit: Library of Congress

Guards admired Lewis Powell's courage as he faced death. Credit: Library of Congress

riage accident in his upstairs bedroom. Powell's assignment was to assure that he did not in fact recover.

Powell, a dark-haired giant of a man eight days shy of his twenty-first birthday, had battlefield instincts honed at places like Gettysburg. Not to be deterred from his mission, the Confederate veteran had aimed his long-barreled Whitney revolver at the secretary's son and yanked the trigger.

Click.

Fred Seward was still standing only because the revolver didn't fire. When he couldn't shoot Seward, Powell used the almost three-pound gun to pistol-whip him. Wielding his revolver like a hammer, he clubbed Fred Seward on the head repeatedly, with the strength of a gladiator. Powell only gave up when the gun's ramrod became dislodged. But before he left, Powell stabbed the bedridden William Seward in his face and neck, despite the best efforts of the secretary's servant, his male nurse, and two of his sons. In the struggle, his slouch hat dropped in the secretary's room. By the time he escaped the mansion, men were screaming, "Murder!" and "Stop, thief!" out the windows. Still, the tall, athletic attacker was able to mount his stout bay horse, round the corner, and gallop out of sight in his blood-stained, light-colored duster, even with fifteen or twenty men chasing him. When he ditched the duster along his route, there was a false mustache in one pocket.[54]

Alfred Cloughley was walking along the square when he heard the cries. He offered to run to Ford's Theatre and inform the president. When the auditing clerk reached an intersection about three blocks from the theater, he met two gentlemen running toward him. Supposing they had heard of the assassination attempt against Secretary Seward, he asked them if they had informed the president. One of them said, "The president is dying."[55]

Cloughley didn't understand. Then one man said the president had been shot. Horror-struck, Cloughley continued on his way to Ford's. The same exchange was repeated many times in the next hour. The masses sweeping down the avenue with news of the bloody attack on the Sewards met the flock running downhill from Ford's.

Then, just as citizens thought nothing more could chill their blood, a mob from the Baltimore and Ohio Railroad Station delivered the erroneous information that General Grant had been shot.[56]

Families who had been celebrating rushed about in the chill wind. Mounted patrols and messengers dashed around the city, announced by the clatter of horse hooves. Up to one hundred thousand armed soldiers back from war added to the mix.[57] Several hundred black people stood vigil in front of the Executive Mansion.[58] A newspaper dispatch described the mood: "The wildest excitement prevailed in all parts of the city. Men, women and children, old and young, rushed to and fro, and the rumors were magnified until we had nearly every member of the cabinet killed."[59]

Other generations have braved major wars and paralyzing presidential assassinations, but both these events occurred in the same week in 1865, looming even larger because the assassination was America's first and because the War Between the States had killed more Americans than any war before or since. Dr. L. P. Brockett described the effect of the two tangled events in his rushed-to-print 1865 history of the assassination: "The streets of Washington on that awful night present a scene of wild terror, passion and gloom, such as was never known before, and, we trust, will never again be."[60]

Edmund Schreiner had gone home after he escorted the presidential party to its box. He was sound asleep when his father woke him to say there was some kind of trouble at the theater.

Although they lived only a block from Ford's, it likely took the sixteen-year-old some time to squeeze through the immense crowd. He couldn't get in the door at Ford's, but he did hear that the president had been shot and carried across the street to his friend Fred Petersen's house. He crossed the wet, sandy street and walked right into the Petersen house. Schreiner couldn't get upstairs to where the president lay, but he did learn the suspect was Booth, whose bags he used to carry. Although Booth was drunk most of the time, he was always nice to Schreiner.[61]

Upstairs in the entrance hall, Rathbone's arm was bleeding freely under his formal jacket, but, probably remembering Dr. Leale's reaction to his pleas for help, he didn't draw attention to himself.[62] He must have attracted glances, though, because his beard and coat were smeared with blood.[63] More and more blood began to soak through his jacket, and shortly, he fell in a swoon to the floor. He took up much of the entryway with his long legs.[64] Until a carriage could be secured to take him back to his house, Rathbone's blood dripped on the floor, which was lined with oilcloth, a forerunner of linoleum that made it easy to clean up muck tracked in from the unpaved streets.[65] While surgeons swarmed around the president, it was Clara Harris who probably saved her fiancé's life when she wrapped a handkerchief around his wound to stay the flow of blood.[66]

After packing the major into a carriage for the ride home, Miss Harris headed into the front parlor to console Mrs. Lincoln, her face, hands, and gown still spattered with her fiancé's blood. Recoiling at the sight of her, Mrs. Lincoln screamed, "Oh, my husband's blood, my dear husband's blood!"[67]

Meanwhile, neighbors, loyal and secesh, kept showing up at the front door with pillows and sheets to make the president comfortable and maybe to sneak a peek. It was the biggest thing that had happened in most of their lives.[68] The Sardos next door, most likely secesh, provided the small blue-ticking pillow that would prop Mr. Lincoln's head when his soul took flight.[69] Mary Sardo, the same age as Pauline, peeked into the packed bedroom to catch a glimpse of the president. Decades later, she told a reporter she and her friend both felt sorry for Booth.[70]

Meanwhile, John Mathews locked himself in his room upstairs.[71] The rooms on Petersen's second and third floors were mostly high ceilinged and spacious, and each featured a fireplace and a shallow clothes closet.[72] As Mathews removed his overcoat, he heard the letter Booth had given him that afternoon drop out on the pinewood floor.[73] He had forgotten all about it. "Great God," he said to himself. "There is the letter John gave me in the afternoon."[74] While cabinet members gathered downstairs, Mathews ripped open the sealed envelope and hastily scanned the three pages. As he turned the pages to read the words Booth had scrawled on both sides, he realized his boyhood friend thought his actions were righteous. Booth had brooded over the war so much that he had reached the point where he looked upon assassination as a patriotic act. Mathews admired his courage.[75] The comic instantly calculated that the letter in his hands was all the evidence police needed to condemn his old friend to death.[76] Without re-reading it or making a copy, he lit Booth's manifesto afire and watched it shimmy in his brick fireplace until the handwriting on both sides turned black. When it was licked to ashes, Mathews mixed them with the coal ashes until they were indistinguishable.[77] His sole impulse was to erase any evidence against Booth. He hadn't yet realized what a slender thread his own life would hang by if anyone learned he'd had proof of the plot before it was carried out.[78]

Mathews almost got himself hanged twice that night, all over his friend Booth, who was already miles from downtown and reunited with Davy Herold across the Anacosta River in Maryland.

After fussing with the ashes, Mathews walked out Petersen's front door and made his way through the hordes to Charley Bennett's saloon at 497 Tenth Street North.[79] Harry Hawk, seated inside the taproom, spotted him scanning the room as if he were searching for one individual. One of Hawk's friends asked Mathews who he wanted. "I wanted to see if John Booth was here," he said, apparently still not realizing that the Booth name had slid from famous to infamous. A horrified Hawk watched his friends take hold of Mathews, threatening to hang him unless he told them everything he knew. Luckily, Mathews was able to slip away from them without mentioning the letter he had burned to a crisp.[80] When he showed up at Williamson's Theatrical Boardinghouse, where he took his meals, a group tried to hang him from a lamppost. The manhandlers already had the rope looped around his neck when some soldiers rescued him. For a brief time, Mathews was so frightened that he thought about changing his name. Even decades later, he said he got a touch of throat disease whenever he thought about it.[81]

He later told his priest about the letter. Father Francis Boyle, a politically savvy assistant pastor, advised him to skip to Canada immediately and to stay there.[82] Despite it all, Mathews was so faithful to Booth that, even in his sixties, he had a tendency toward understatement when he described his deed. Mathews referred to the country's first presidential assassination as "the great mistake."[83]

Back at Petersen's boardinghouse, the president was lying unconscious on the rough cornhusk mattress topped with a thinner tick filled with straw and shoddy, a rough, inexpensive, recycled wool.[84] It was a far cry from the bed he'd awakened on at the Executive Mansion that morning, with its modern metal-spring mattress topped with a second mattress of soft hair.[85] The only light in this bedroom flowed from a small gas lamp attached to the wall and covered with a hand-decorated shade.[86] The surgeons had to stick a candle in a ruby red cologne bottle to probe the president's wound.[87]

President Lincoln's friends stood helplessly by while the leading medical men in the city massaged his limbs, applied hot mustard plasters to his midriff, and placed jugs of hot water under the covers next to his nude body to keep his blood circulating.[88]

Each time they turned down the sheets, they revealed a brawny chest and the immensely muscular arms expected of a much younger man, in unbelievably perfect proportions. Several visitors gasped in surprise the first time they saw the doctors turn down the covers. It was hard to believe the president was in the sixty-second day of his fifty-seventh year. Mr. Lincoln had the perfect male body. There was not a single flaw in any part.[89] Dr. Leale said he could have been the model for Michelangelo's Moses, possessing the same massive grandeur.[90] The medical men made no secret that they would be unable to save the president. They were simply waiting for the slow exhaustion of his vital energy.[91] From time to time, a member of the cabinet would try to talk to the president. He could not respond.

Hugh McCullough, secretary of the treasury, pushed his way into the house and made his way to the bedroom where the president was breathing heavily. Scanning the faces of the other cabinet members, the astute politician instantly read that there was no hope. Every face was bathed in tears. McCullough must have been reeling. When he'd seen Mr. Lincoln earlier in the day, he'd noted that the worn look that had long been on his president's face even when he was telling a funny story had finally vanished, along with the war. McCullough thought that he had never seen the president as happy and cheerful as on the morning of April 14. And now this.[92]

Secretary of the Navy Gideon Welles stood at the foot of the bed, his frame shaking.[93] Senator Charles Sumner was sobbing profusely, his head bowed so close to the comatose president that they were almost sharing a pillow.[94] Mary Lincoln's rueful moans were plainly audible, even when the parlor doors were closed. Even in the Petersens' separate kitchen building, there was no escaping them.[95]

The Petersen children were spared no details of the president's suffering. Pauline gave the doctors a pair of scissors to snip hair away from the bullet hole.[96] Her stomach turned whenever she passed the bloody bedding, discarded bandages, and dripping mustard plasters piled up by the door, but the waste was cleared only when the first lady headed down the hall.[97] Whenever she came, doctors would drape Anna Petersen's clean cloth napkins over the blood-soiled pillowcases, using more than a dozen for her nearly hourly visits to the bedside.[98]

William Petersen, before he left, had instructed his daughter to fetch the good tea set and prepare tea for Mrs. Lincoln, but by the time Pauline finished ripping sheets for bandages, it was late.[99] Mrs. Lincoln's friend Elizabeth Dixon, the attractive wife of a Connecticut senator, arrived around midnight with her sister Mary Kinney, a millionaire hotelier's wife, and Mrs. Kinney's daughter Constance.[100] They were comforting the first lady in the front parlor when Pauline headed there with her family's nicest tea tray.

As Pauline passed Miss Harris in the front hallway, she overheard that John Wilkes Booth was the assassin. It could not be the same John Wilkes Booth she knew, Pauline thought. Then she realized her family might be suspect if anyone learned that one week earlier Booth had spent the night in the same bed where the president now lay dying. Frightened but aware of her task, Pauline walked into the parlor with the tea tray. She never forgot the look in the first lady's eyes that night—sad but darting from side to side as if watching for another attack.[101]

People were coming and going all evening, but all had to get past the guards posted at every door and window and even atop the wet slate roof.[102] As they passed the front parlor, visitors could hear Mrs. Lincoln's shrieks through the closed doors.[103]

The death room was in stark contrast. A solemn silence pervaded it. The only sound was the president's labored breathing. People came and went with soft footfalls. Nary a word was spoken, except by Stanton, who brought his deep barrister's voice down to a whisper to direct the men chasing the assassins.[104] On normal days, he sometimes worked eighteen hours; he was not about to slow down now.[105]

Outside, blacks and whites stood vigil together in the dismal rain. Tenth Street was teeming with people from F Street down to the avenue, despite temperatures dipping into the high forties.[106] The street in front of Petersen's was so jammed that to move at all it was necessary to push a path through to wherever you wanted to go. The men who had carried the president across the street stood among the crowd, put out of Petersen's as soon as their part was finished.[107] Father Jacob Walter, the thin, bespectacled pastor of St. Patrick's Roman Catholic Church, around the corner, stood praying in the cold rain most of the night. Exactly twelve weeks later, he would stand on the gallows with convicted coconspirator Mary Surratt until the trap door was sprung.[108]

Around town, couples who had been reveling hours earlier walked home with compressed lips. Men threw their arms around one another's necks and cried like babies.[109] They sobbed so much that their tears blinded them.[110] Beyond the sadness, people were wild with fright. It was, as Chief Justice Salmon Chase told his diary, "a night of horrors."[111] L. P. Brockett wrote that Washingtonians that night were like men awakened at midnight by an earthquake and bewildered to find everything they trusted wavering and falling.[112]

Wives and children headed home to lie awake in locked rooms, lest the invading rebels find them. Helen Moss, who had been advised to leave Grover's promptly, was one of thousands of women who huddled around windows in the dark, fearful any light would attract attackers. She said women leaned out into the rainy night just far enough to catch the news but ducked back beneath their windowsills whenever horses' hooves echoed in the darkness. They had no rest, she said, until their men came home and told them it was all over.[113]

Every route out of the city was picketed. Every street was patrolled. Steamboats about to depart down the Potomac were stopped and searched. Messengers galloped in every direction. Prominent officials heard the heavy "tramp-tramp" of military boots beneath their windows all night.[114]

For soldiers like Lieutenant John Toffey, it meant working all night, keeping order and searching houses. Because no one knew the whereabouts of the assassins, police turned the neighborhood around the theater upside-down. Newspapers said authorities were confident there was no way for the attackers to escape the city, but hunting for them in the nation's capital was like looking for a needle in a haystack. The city had 230 miles of streets and 77 miles of alleys.[115]

Everywhere, men swore vengeance on the rebels. A mob of about two thousand went to Old Capitol Prison, intending to set fire to the Confederates jailed there, but police and soldiers put a stop to it. Senator William Stewart of Nevada said there was just one phrase that seemed to calm a drink-fueled crowd. Lawmen would jump on a box or climb a flight of stairs and shout, "What would Mr. Lincoln say?"[116] As Edwin Bates and his friend Sawyer headed back to their hotel through knots of hotheads, they were plumb certain the man they had seen on Ford's stage would be discovered to be some sort of insane person.[117] Even a rebel of the worst type, they reasoned, would not commit such a horrible deed in so bold a manner before thousands of people. There was just too little chance of escape.

Everywhere, citizens were stunned. Why, just nine months earlier, Secretary Seward himself had said, "Assassination is not an American practice or habit, and one so vicious and so desperate cannot be engrafted into our political system." Now his throat was cut.[118]

14

Enough Evidence to Hang Booth

When the legless war vet who had calmed the audience at Grover's returned to his Tenth Street boardinghouse, he found armed guards blocking the porch. Soldiers were checking identities because the house shared its south wall with Petersen's boardinghouse, where the president lay dying. Once James Tanner was cleared to return to his front room, the dark-haired clerk surveyed the undulating masses from his balcony just one floor above the street.[1] The crowd calmed as the night progressed. Still, Tanner knew that any man whispering one word in justification of Booth's deed would have been torn to pieces. As Mose Sanford wrote to his friend John Beatty in Jersey City, New Jersey, two days later, "It don't do for a man to open his mouth unless he talks the right way."[2]

The balcony outside Tanner's room was brimming with boarders, so when a general came out of Petersen's and asked if anyone could write phonography, a precursor to shorthand, someone shouted Tanner's name. As quickly as he could get there, the clean-shaven phonographer was sitting next to bushy-bearded Secretary Stanton, taking testimony from witnesses at a round wooden table in the Francises' vacated first-floor bedroom. He was so excited that he didn't think his scribbles looked like standard phonography, but he could read them well enough. They took testimony from midnight until four a.m., but within fifteen minutes they had enough to hang Booth. The nation's first presidential assassination would be an open-and-shut case.[3]

Early on, Stanton interrupted the questioning to check the president's condition. When he walked back into the parlor, Tanner looked at him expectantly. The secretary slowly forced the answer from his mouth: "There is no hope."[4]

The small parlor was teeming with the most eminent men in the capital, some dictating dispatches, others conversing in hushed tones. As Tanner wrote to a friend two days later, "Never in my life was I surrounded by half so many impressive circumstances."[5]

Ironically, the room where they all worked that night had once been rented to a member of Jefferson Davis's cabinet. John C. Breckinridge, Davis's secretary of war, had boarded at Petersen's in the early 1850s, when he was a Kentucky congressman, before he was elected vice president under President James Buchanan and long before he joined the secessionists.[6]

On assassination night, Tanner noticed that Stanton positioned himself facing the hallway so he could see anyone who approached the president's bed.[7] The secretary of war was the busiest man in the house during those sleepless hours. He pumped witnesses. He directed the manhunt. He dictated news bulletins. He ran the country. He grieved for his president and put up with the piercing cries of the first lady, whom he heartily disliked. As Stanton worked in the back parlor, he no doubt could hear Mary Lincoln's hysterics in the front parlor, although she was seated on a couch on the opposite side of the room, and the heavy folding doors were shut tight.[8]

Stanton had enough experience with the Lincoln family to know there were some things even someone with his pluck could not change. Leonard Grover, the theater owner, told a story about Stanton once interrupting Mr. Lincoln while he was watching a play. Stanton whispered questions at the president, and Lincoln answered them, but his eyes kept straying to the stage. Finally, Stanton yanked his boss's suit lapel and pulled him around so that they were face to face. The president just smiled the way you would with a mischievous child, but he returned his gaze to the stage. Stanton gave up and left.[9]

Now it fell to Stanton to tell the world the president was insensible. He filed an official news bulletin at one thirty a.m. Stanton's missive was as direct and informative as any of the reporters': "This evening at about 9:30 o'clock at Ford's Theatre, the President, while sitting in his private box with Mrs. Lincoln, Miss Harris and Major Rathbone, was shot by an assassin who suddenly entered the box and approached behind the president. The assassin then leaped upon the stage, brandishing a large knife, and made his escape in the rear of the theatre. The pistol ball entered the back of the President's head, and penetrated nearly through the head. The wound is mortal. The President has been insensible ever since it was inflicted, and is now dying"[10]

15

Waiting for History

Mary Lincoln and her friends walked back to the death room several times during the night, perhaps squeezing their full skirts to make it through the thirty-seven-inch hallway. One time, Mary sank by the bed and cried, "Kill me. Kill me. Kill me. Shoot me too!"[1] She alternated between begging her husband to live and loudly imploring him to take her with him. He never responded. There is no way of knowing whether he was thinking about her or whether, perhaps, his life was passing before him. Maybe he was thinking of May 18, 1860, when he won the Republican nomination in Chicago inside a hastily built pine-board convention hall called the Wigwam. In a little less than five years, the Wigwam would slip into history too, burning to ashes on November 12, 1869.[2] With each rise and fall of Mr. Lincoln's chest, there issued a dismal moan.[3] As the night wore on, the dark patch around his right eye spread.

Dr. Robert Stone arrived on the scene and approved Dr. Leale's treatment.[4] Stone was the Lincolns' family physician. He had treated the president for chills, headaches, ringworm, and a mild form of smallpox. He was the one who had cared for Willie when he was dying. Stone had never agreed with the president's politics, but he described him as "the purest-hearted man with whom I ever came in contact."

He examined the wound with his finger and a silver probe, repeating what Dr. Leale had done instinctively with his pinky at Ford's. He was unable to alter the calculus. As Dr. Leale had discovered early on, whenever the president's wound was blocked, his breaths became loud and labored. When doctors released the pressure, breathing improved.

About two a.m., Surgeon General Barnes introduced a long porcelain-tipped probe into the wound and came to the same conclusion Dr. Leale had in the theater. The bullet was lodged behind the president's right eye. While Barnes was probing, Major J. R. O'Beirne was feeling nervous as a cat. Stanton had assigned him to fetch Andrew Johnson from his room at the Kirkwood House and escort him the three and a half blocks to Peter-

Vice President Andrew Johnson, shown here in a formal portrait, wore a high silk hat as he was escorted through the swarm of angry men on Tenth Street on assassination night. Credit: National Archives

sen's. Neither of O'Beirne's two law degrees had prepared him to push his way up Tenth Street with the vice president on his left arm. The muscular Irishman's head kept swiveling. He wanted to be certain no would-be assassin was following them. O'Beirne left his overcoat open so onlookers would see his military brass, and just to be sure, he kept his right hand on his revolver. Even his tenure as a member of the hard-fighting Thirty-seventh New York Regiment, nicknamed the Irish Rifles, had not prepared him for this. Although the vice president had a clear and resonant voice, O'Beirne did all the talking on Tenth Street. As they moved slowly uphill through the crowd, he stated that he was the provost marshal and had to make his way into the house. Any assassin could have picked the powerfully built vice president out of the crowd. He was taller than average, and his thinning hair was combed into one distinctive dark brown curl at the back of his neck. As if that weren't sufficient to make him an easy target, that night he wore a high silk hat. The moment the vice president was safe behind Petersen's windowless front door, O'Beirne walked into the front parlor and picked up a family Bible. It wasn't necessary though. The president looked like he might rally, so the swearing-in was put off.[5]

Johnson stayed only another two minutes. Unbeknownst to anyone in the room, his life had been spared only because Booth's accomplice George Atzerodt hadn't followed orders.

Nine blocks south at the National Hotel, night clerk Walter Burton was at his desk when investigators came to search Room 228. They told him John Wilkes Booth had killed the president. Burton laughed at the absurdity of such a thing—along with all the others within earshot. Booth was a hotel regular. Why, he'd often sit behind the night desk with Burton, drinking and smoking twelve-cent cigars while they waited for the newspapermen who lived there to arrive with the morning news.[6]

It seemed even more absurd when the investigators said they'd discovered a gag, a set of handcuffs, a military dress coat, and a letter from a woman who pleaded for Booth to forget his plot. They had also found a monogrammed pair of black cashmere pantaloons that might have come in handy right then if their owner had packed them.[7]

Over at Petersen House, the night seemed long, so long that John Usher, the portly secretary of the interior, climbed into the Francises' unmade bed and took a nap.[8] The Reverend Dr. Phineas Gurley, Mr. Lincoln's pastor, arrived around three a.m. and prayed at the president's bedside. Bob Lincoln later told his cousin Kate Helm he thought the hours of hopeless watching would never end.[9] The twenty-one-year-old perfectly composed himself whenever his mother entered the death room. He would remind her to put her faith in God. The moment she left, his calmness invariably gave way. His breakdowns brought tears to the eyes of everyone in the room.[10]

Fred Petersen was sitting on a trunk at the foot of the deathbed when he began to nod off. Secretary Gideon Welles touched him and said, "My boy, you are tired out, and you had better go out and get some sleep, and we will call you if we need you." The fifteen-year-old nestled into a rocking chair in the next room and was soon asleep, at least until a rough hand caught his shoulder. He heard Stanton's deep voice saying, "My boy, this is no time to sleep. You had better go in and watch." Fred returned to the bedroom briefly. Then, unable to keep his eyes open, he found a private nook at the back of the house and fell off to sleep again.[11]

Some artists asked the doctors to pose as they tried to recreate the deathbed scene in the small, crowded bedroom. Credit: Library of Congress

Around four a.m. Mrs. Lincoln returned to the death room and became so hysterical Pauline could hear her screams downstairs in the kitchen.[12] The first lady was a strong, strikingly physical woman. She suddenly began tearing her own hair out of her head by the handful. Major O'Beirne was horrified, but like the others in the room, the Medal of Honor winner did nothing. They were all relieved when Bob Lincoln persuaded his mother to stop.[13]

When Pauline heard Mrs. Lincoln's footfalls returning to the front parlor, she made more tea. When she entered the parlor, the girl gently placed her hand on the first lady's shoulder and handed her a china cup. Mrs. Lincoln, whose face was red and blotchy from sobbing, thanked her. Then she broke into another cry. Pauline sat down next to her, stroked her arm, and let her cry. The look in Mary Lincoln's eyes reminded her of the look in her own mother's eyes when she lost a baby, but it was ten times more terrible. The first lady told Pauline she was the only one who had not told her to stop crying. At first light, around five thirty a.m., Mary Lincoln unpinned a small brooch with a big diamond from her dress and placed it in Pauline's palm. Although the thirteen-year-old protested, Mrs. Lincoln told her to take it in appreciation of all her kindnesses on the worst night of her life.[14]

Oddly, during the deathwatch, the occasional artist would crowd into the room and set to capturing the somber scene. Artists kept coming and going all night. Some dignitaries were eager to be included in the historic paintings. Dr. Leale himself posed for three.[15]

16

That's the Last of Him

Fred, who was sleeping in a back bedroom, awoke with the gray dawn. He heard President Lincoln in the next room. His breathing was so heavy you could have heard him in any part of the house. When Fred entered the sick room, he noticed the president's jaw had fallen down upon his chest, baring his teeth and gums.[1] As a Raleigh reporter described it later, "His features were fixed to that calm, stony solemnity which only the hand of death can mold."[2]

Mr. Lincoln's skin was waxen.[3] His breaths had become shorter, and occasionally, they would cease entirely for a few seconds.[4] The smell in the room was nauseating, but few people left.[5] From a spindle-backed rocking chair, Secretary Welles watched his friend's blood drain from his face. Bob Lincoln clung to the side of the bed with his head buried in the blanket.[6] When Stanton wasn't reading dispatches or writing them, he sat motionless in a chair near the window, his large head bent slightly to the right, resting on his hand.[7] Perhaps he was thinking of the day earlier that week when he had resigned from the cabinet. He had handed Mr. Lincoln his written resignation, saying the secretary of war's job should be over when the war ends. The president had torn the resignation into pieces and thrown his arms around Stanton.[8] General Grant later wrote that the secretary and the president were opposites in almost every particular, except that both possessed great ability. The president often compromised because he didn't like to disappoint others, Grant wrote, but Stanton cared nothing for the feelings of others. In fact, Grant wrote, Stanton seemed to get more pleasure out of disappointing others than gratifying them. No matter, Stanton was plainly bereft that evening.[9]

Outside, on Tenth Street, Sergeant Smith Stimmel had been riding his steed up and down the block for almost seven hours, since the previous evening, when he had been jolted out of a sound sleep to go on patrol. He'd almost convinced himself he was just having a nightmare that the president was dying a few yards away.[10]

Dr. Leale could attest it was no dream. His agile mind was moving ahead to what the president would feel as he exited this life. The doctor's knowledge of physiology told him that the president was totally blind as a result of the pressure on his brain. He didn't know if Mr. Lincoln could hear or feel, but he decided to act as if he could. He held the president's right hand firmly to let him know, in his blindness, that he was still in touch with humanity and still had a friend.[11]

Dr. Leale hoped that the president could hear his wife's voice when she visited him for the last time just as the day was struggling with the dim candles in the room.[12] She certainly must have noticed a change the moment she saw him, because she fell into a faint. The one who caught her in her arms and brought her to the window for air was her friend Elizabeth Dixon. Mrs. Dixon might have fallen over herself, because she had been up for most of the last twenty-four hours. She had gone to bed about nine thirty p.m. but had been abruptly awakened by Bob Lincoln's messenger.[13] When Mrs. Lincoln recovered from her swoon, she seated herself in a cane-bottomed chair by the president, tears flooding her face. She kissed him and purred every endearing name. "Love, live but for one moment to speak to me once—to speak to our children," she begged.[14] Doctors holding both of the president's hands were counting every pulsation. They felt them growing weaker, moment by moment, until they dropped to barely a third of the normal rate. The president's breathing grew unnaturally loud, more like a snore or a bray. It panicked his wife, who let out a yowl. With that, Stanton had had enough.

The secretary's relationship with Mary Lincoln had always been frosty, and his patience had given out. He snapped. He barreled in from the adjoining parlor with his arms raised and shouted, "Take that woman out, and do not let her in again."[15] Secretary Usher said the scene that occurred then beggared description.[16] As she left her husband's side, Mary wailed, "Oh, my God, I have given my husband to die." James Tanner said he had never heard so much agony in so few words. He called it the sound of her heart breaking.[17]

Even after the first lady was banished, the room was thick with at least twenty-one visitors, including Major A. F. Rockwell, who stood behind the headboard, his eyes continually darting from person to person without exception.[18]

They were all huddled into a space eighteen feet by ten feet.[19] It seemed a humble setting for the death of a president of the United States, but Abraham Lincoln had entered the world in a log cabin the same length and only six feet wider.[20]

Everyone knew the president was sinking. The surgeon general sat on the edge of the bed, holding the president's left hand, his finger on Mr. Lincoln's pulse. Occasionally, he bent over, placed his ear next to the heart, and listened. When it became plain the body was shutting down, doctors' eyes moved like pendulums from their pocket watches to his pale face and back.[21]

The president looked perfectly natural, except for the deep black stain around his eyes.[22] His breaths were shorter and less labored, and the dismal moan that had issued from his throat all night was replaced with a gurgle. The battle veterans in the room recognized the sound. They called it a death rattle, the deep, guttural noise that signaled the last convulsions of the heart.[23] Stanton's facial muscles began to twitch when he heard it.[24] His large glasses focused on his president's face.

Whenever Mr. Lincoln fell quiet, the doctors would fix their eyes to their watches, but when another fluttering breath came, they'd sigh with relief and shift their eyes back to his face. In the last seconds, some of them held their breaths, lest they drown out the president's last feeble inhalation.[25] Dr. Taft made a mental note that the greatest men in the nation were standing around the bed like statues.[26] The next week he wrote this in the *Medical and Surgical Reporter:* "The death-like stillness and suspense were thrilling."[27]

When they heard nothing but unbroken quiet, the doctors' eyes returned to their watches—five seconds short of 7:22 a.m. One of the physicians whispered, "This pulse has ceased beating."[28] All eyes went to the president's face, which looked normal, except for his jaw, which had fallen toward his chest so his teeth and gums were bared. His arms were lifeless. The surgeon general crossed them atop the president's chest. For more than four minutes, no one moved.[29]

Then Stanton made a queer gesture. Not everyone saw it because he was toward the back of the room, but he picked up his hat in his right hand and slowly extended his arm until the hat was high in the air. Tears falling down his face, he placed it on his balding head for an instant. Then he removed it with the same flourish.[30]

Dr. Leale, a devout Episcopalian, had hoped the last sound his patient would hear would be his pastor's prayers committing his soul to God. Mr. Lincoln had lost his hold on this world, though, and his pastor hadn't opened his mouth. Rev. Dr. Phineas Gurley just stood near the president's head.[31]

Stanton asked Gurley if he would say something.

Booth escaped over the Navy Yard Bridge into Maryland. Credit: National Archives

Gurley said, "I will speak to God."

Stanton replied, "Do it just now."[32]

Gurley dropped to his knees and began, but he was quickly interrupted by the deep sobs of Stanton, who had buried his face in the bedclothes. Gurley went on, but his voice was nearly inaudible among the sobs of more than twenty-one people packed into the room. Tanner pulled his pencil from his pocket to copy the prayer for posterity, but its point caught in his coat and broke.[33] Bob Lincoln stood at the headboard leaning over his father, then sobbing on the shoulder of Senator Sumner.[34]

Stanton, tears still streaming down his cheeks, looked longingly at the president's face and said, "Now he belongs to the ages."[35]

Major O'Beirne remembered him saying, "That's the last of him."[36]

Sweet peace came to Abraham Lincoln.

As quickly as he could, the army major who had been eyeballing every person in the death room bustled back to his office to draw a diagram showing the exact positions of the witnesses to the president's demise.[37]

At this moment, while the newspapers had him all but nabbed, John Wilkes Booth was resting in a much larger bedroom thirty miles away, in the gracious home of Dr. Samuel Mudd in rural Waldorf, Maryland.[38]

In Boston, Edwin Booth had already received a note from his theater manager saying his popular play would be closed until further notice.[39]

And stunned June Booth was making plans to quietly leave Cincinnati, where he had just wrapped up a two-week engagement at Pike's Opera House. He turned himself in to a federal marshal upon his arrival in Philadelphia.[40]

No one immediately ventured to tell Mrs. Lincoln her husband was no more. Several surgeons were packing to leave by the time Bob Lincoln and Dr. Gurley walked into the front parlor to deliver the news. Passersby could hear her moans through the half-opened door.[41]

The throng outside learned the bleak news at about the same time, because Fred Petersen and Henry Ulke both left the house. Word spread lip to lip from Pennsylvania Avenue to F Street: "President Lincoln is dead." As soon as Fred walked onto the porch, he saw it was a nasty day to walk to his father's shop—cloudy, dark, and drizzling. Henry Ulke was surprised that the crowd had grown even larger and most of the faces were black. "How is he now?" several black mourners asked simultaneously. "Your best friend is dead," Ulke answered gravely.[42] He called what came next the saddest sight of his life: liberated slaves, hundreds of them, men and women, crying out loud in the streets.

Maunsell Field had just left Petersen's for Willard's when he met the chief justice turning onto Tenth Street, hurrying in the opposite direction. Field noticed Salmon P. Chase's eyes were bloodshot and his face was as distorted as he had ever seen it. "Is he dead?" Chase asked.[43] Field told him he was. Chase was soon climbing two flights of stairs to reach Vice President Andrew Johnson's suite at Kirkwood House, where the swearing-in would take place.[44]

Elsewhere around town, soldiers standing atop the five-story Winder Building on Seventeenth Street, the tallest building in Washington, raised flags, sending sad signals to the troops across the river in Virginia.[45]

17

Caught in the American Nightmare

Fred Petersen found his father sound asleep in his tailor shop.[1] Soon they were heading home on the wet clay streets, a cold mist enveloping them as they walked.[2] By the time they returned, Stanton had thrown open the death room windows to let in some fresh air.[3] The president's face was cold as stone, and the blackness had spread beyond the eyes to the forehead. That wasn't what threw William Petersen off, though.

When Petersen's eyes fell on the stinking piles of bloody bandages and leaking mustard plasters, he became unglued.[4] The heaps of medical refuse loomed large in the narrow hallway. The boardinghouse owner stormed into the death room and rudely grabbed the stained top pillow out from under the dead president's head, terrifying the Ulke brothers.[5] Raising the thick window blinds, he tossed the pillow, possibly still wet with Mr. Lincoln's blood, out onto the fieldstone courtyard two stories below.[6] As soon as he came to his senses, Petersen loudly explained that his house was a mess, full of blood and mud and unwashed basins.[7] Before the president was buried, Petersen would try to bill the federal government for every single thing he had provided for the president's makeshift hospital. Even, falsely, for his own time.[8]

Dr. Leale gently smoothed the president's contracted facial muscles. He moved the fallen jaw upward and knotted the handkerchief to hold it in place. He said he took two silver dollars from his pocket to cover the eyelids, although other men have also claimed they were the ones who placed the 1854 and 1861 coins on President Lincoln's face.[9] When the coins were in place, Leale drew a white sheet up over the martyr's face. The doctor had not been seated once since he sprang from his cane-bottomed chair at Ford's. He was tired and sad, and his shirt was stained with the president's blood. He left Petersen's house in a contemplative mood, but he was shocked back to reality by the cold rain dropping on his bare head. He realized he had left his hat inside the theater.[10]

His quick thinking had prolonged President Lincoln's life for nine hours—long enough to keep the fragile union from falling apart. Not bad for a twenty-three-year-old just forty-five days out of medical school. As he walked back to his office in the drizzle, Dr. Leale could hear the hammers of homeowners and shopkeepers putting up mourning crepe to honor the president. The bells of Washington City's thirty-seven churches broadcast the president's demise with a rapid tintinnabulation that began about seven thirty when the news first got out. The two sounds Leale heard gradually spread around the city and, eventually, around the country.[11]

At Petersen's, Stanton locked the door to the death room and stationed a sentry in front of it. Reverend Gurley was still praying in the front room, where Mrs. Lincoln was lying on a stiff horsehair sofa. Her son Bob was standing at her head.[12]

When Billy Ferguson returned to Petersen's at nine a.m., Fred came down to the kitchen to meet him. While the widow was still praying in the parlor, Fred placed a piece of the president's shirt and a strip of blood-stained linen in Ferguson's hands.[13]

Most Washingtonians learned who had been assassinated and who had been spared at the breakfast table. The morning papers reported all the details. Papers across the country carried the news the same day, thanks to the new transcontinental telegraph lines, barely four years old. The *New York Herald* headline blared: "Important!"[14] The *Dayton Extra Journal* headline was "National Calamity: President Lincoln Assassinated."[15] The *Chicago Tribune* reported that people who walked into Petersen House could hear shrieks and cries from the room where Mrs. Lincoln and her son were.[16] It was the first time such sad tidings were instantly sent coast to coast. Ironically, the first president to embrace the new technology of the telegraph was also the subject of the worst news that telegraph operators had ever tapped out. Exactly forty-seven years later, the telegraph would figure in another catastrophe when the HMS *Titanic* tried in vain to rouse a sleeping telegraph operator on the SS *Californian* on the weekend of April 14–15, 1912.

The city's weather seemed to match its mood. The beautiful spring day previous had turned dark and cool.[17] Sable clouds hung overhead.[18] As private secretary Al Daggett wrote to his mother that day from his room next door to Petersen's, "Even the sky is weeping great tears."[19] In New York City, Gustave Dieterich's eyes fell upon the morning paper when he was walking to breakfast. It was framed in an unusual deep black border. When he read that President Lincoln had been assassinated at Ford's and carried to a private house directly across the street, he instantly recalled Anna Petersen's unlucky feeling.[20]

In Washington, perhaps another wife remembered Friday was her unlucky day. As Mrs. Lincoln left Petersen's and headed home without her husband, she paused on the iron-railed front porch. Looking over at Ford's, she blurted out, "Oh, that dreadful house! That dreadful house!" Her life was about to fork.[21]

The widow Lincoln descended the brownstone steps to her carriage, wearing her blood-splattered checkered dress and one of Huldah Francis's bonnets. She couldn't find her own. Boarders found it later. They cut it up for souvenirs.[22] By the time she arrived home, a thoughtful servant had preserved the purplish-red coffee cup the president had left on the windowsill for his post-theater supper.[23] Mary's doctor instructed her to go to bed immediately. Her friend Elizabeth Dixon steered her into one room after another, but each time, she shrank back, crying, "Not there! Oh, not there!" Finally, they settled on a room where the president liked to write.[24]

Back at Petersen's, Secretary Stanton was still waiting for the custom-built pine box to arrive from the undertaker's workshop. He was unwilling to leave Petersen's until his president's body was in safe hands, but Stanton had work to do. Protocol was never his strong suit, so he called a cabinet meeting at Petersen's while the corpse still lay across the bed. He had to divine the assassin's end game.[25]

In the meantime, an extra-long pine box arrived. The nude corpse was wrapped in an American flag and placed inside the box before it left the boardinghouse at about nine thirty a.m.[26] The flag that cloaked it had thirty-five stars only because Mr. Lincoln had refused to remove the stars for the states that seceded. The citizens standing vigil in front of Petersen's in the rain parted into clumps as the narrow hearse wheels struggled through the wet sand.[27] Dark clouds hid the morning sun as six soldiers carried the pine box down the same steps the living president had been carried up the previous night.[28]

Some citizens followed the hearse as it rounded F Street. Many others watched from their doors and windows, their faces stamped with grief. The crowd was, for the most part, subdued, but one man ventured a shout for Jeff Davis. He was set upon and nearly torn to pieces by onlookers.[29]

As the day unfolded, onlookers rushed a street preacher foolhardy enough to say that, if Andy Johnson kept the same policies as the late president, he would be assassinated within two weeks.[30] And later, when a man dared to say he was glad President Lincoln was dead, the words had hardly

Jefferson Davis, president of the Confederate States of America, was described as being as cold as a snake and ambitious as Lucifer. Credit: National Archives.

left his mouth when a bullet from a Union soldier's pistol went crashing through his brain. Even Booth's theatrical agent, Matthew Canning Jr., accustomed to writing glowing press releases about his client, began telling people, "Booth has oil in the brain."[31]

The route back to the Executive Mansion took the coffin near the Church of the Epiphany. Although it had been retrofitted as a hospital in 1862, ironically, it had also once served as the parish of both Jefferson Davis and Edwin Stanton. The Confederate president and his wife, Varina, had stopped attending services when the war began. The Stanton family took over their pew.[32]

After the cabinet members left Petersen's, a boarder secretly photographed the death room. Maybe as soon as the coffin was carried out, one

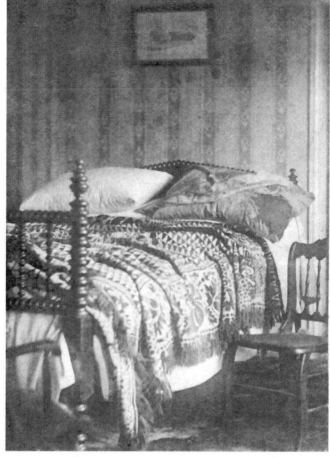

This deathbed photo was taken by one of the Ulke brothers after President Lincoln's body was removed to the Executive Mansion. The Ulke family kept it under wraps until 1961. Credit: Houmes Collection

of the Ulke brothers pointed a large wet-collodion camera at the deathbed. He must have thought he was preordained to take the historic photograph. After all, what were the chances a president would die in a room beneath his own? After convincing Willie Clark not to move a thing, the photographer prepared his plates for the historic photo. He may not have realized that one crucial relic had been moved. There was a bloodstained pillow on the bed, but the small pillow that had propped the president's head was probably still lying in the courtyard, where William Petersen threw it after he ripped it from under the corpse's head. Perhaps one of the Ulkes ran to the courtyard and retrieved it, but even if they weren't trying to evade Stanton's guard, they would have had to move quickly. Collodion, the flammable, syrupy solution used to coat their glass negatives, dries in ten minutes.

The complicated wet process required several difficult steps, but it produced finely detailed brownish photos with a lush, glossy surface. Its main advantage was a negative that could produce unlimited prints. Julius Ulke, who sold small photo portraits to tourists, would have grasped the whopping market for a photograph of Mr. Lincoln's deathbed.[33]

Tourists were just discovering Petersen's house that Saturday morning, but the government officials were through with it. Or at least they thought they were until May 3.

18

Grief and Greed

The official focus shifted back to the Executive Mansion, where the hearse rattled up the pavement around eleven a.m. on Saturday, April 15.[1] Inside, Elizabeth Dixon was just leaving Mary Lincoln in an upstairs room, a full twelve hours after Bob Lincoln's messenger had arrived at her door. As she started down the stairs, Dixon met the men carrying the president's remains to the undertaker's cold board. Suddenly, it crystallized for her. She realized she was leaving her friend a lonely widow. She thought how everything had changed for Mary Lincoln since she and her husband rode down the driveway on their merry way just fifteen hours earlier. Mary had lost her anchor.[2]

The hastily built pine box would be replaced with an elegant fifteen-hundred-dollar coffin lined in lead, fitted with satin, and accented with silver. The silver plate over the breast would be inscribed: "Abraham Lincoln, 16th president of the United States, Born February 12, 1809. Died April 15, 1865." Even the six-foot, six-inch custom-made coffin was a close fit for the six-foot, four-inch president.[3]

Over at Petersen's boardinghouse, the odor of sweat and blood lingered on mustard plasters and bed linens. Mud and horse droppings had been tracked throughout the first floor. The wallpaper, window curtains, and furniture were perfectly intact though.

Willie Clark, home from his night out, quickly grasped that the ordinary items in his rented room had been conferred relic status. A candle stub had been transformed into the light surgeons used to examine President Lincoln's fatal wound. A bloody napkin had morphed into a keepsake. Clark kept a close eye on every individual who entered his room for fear they would boost something. As he wrote to his sister a few days later, "Everybody has a great desire to obtain some memento from my room, so that whoever comes in has to be closely watched for fear they will steal something."[4] Naturally, Clark squirreled away a few things for himself. He collected a piece of linen with a portion of the president's brain and a lock

Soldiers guarded Ford's Theatre, draped in black mourning bunting after the assassination. Credit: Library of Congress

of coarse black hair. He framed the hair. He fully intended to keep other items, but his landlord caught on to their commercial value.[5]

That morning, an officer instructed Clark to hang the first piece of mourning crepe for the murdered president on the light green trim that framed Petersen's front door.[6] His action would be repeated so many times that dry-goods stores would run out of every black fabric, from inexpensive black muslin to pricey silk crepe. Hammers clinked in every direction as Washingtonians replaced their red, white, and blue bunting with black crepe that drooped in the rain. Ministers everywhere draped their pulpits in black. Reverend Gurley's was covered in fashionable black alpaca.[7] Nearly every building was draped, no matter whether its occupants were pinched or prosperous. Even secesh families hung crepe. Sometimes, the more secesh, the more crepe. It was the same way across the country, as Sarah Morgan, a young Baton Rouge belle, wrote in her diary. "The more violently secesh and the more thankful they are for Lincoln's death, the more profusely the houses are decorated with emblems of woe," she wrote. "Men who have hated Lincoln with all their souls, under terror of confiscation and imprisonment, which they know is the alternative, tie black crepe from every practicable knob and point."[8]

The bleak news spread all over Baltimore that day, but John Barron never heard it. The naval officer, in town just briefly, knew only one man in the city, and he had neglected to buy a newspaper that morning. Barron had no idea his old acting chum was the most wanted man in America until he walked aboard the steamer *Highland Light* to visit his friend Ferdinand Benner. Benner greeted him with, "What do you think of the awful news?" When Barron asked what awful news, Benner said, "For God's sake, John, don't you know that your friend John Wilkes Booth has assassinated President Lincoln?"[9]

An avalanche of dismal thoughts swept through Barron's head. He thought back to that day on Broadway the month before when Booth must have used every ounce of his acting ability to suppress his emotions. Immediately, Barron thought that if he had not shown his uniform that day, then the president might be alive. He doubtless would have hastened to the Navy Yard and reported Booth's words. He could have saved the president and also saved John Booth from himself.[10]

All weekend, Barron's thoughts kept returning to the assassination. He found it hard to imagine Booth's delicate, tapered fingers pulling the trigger that killed the president. They were as dainty as a girl's.[11]

Washington was tightly wrapped in a cloak of gloom. Flags that had floated proudly on Friday now drooped to half mast. Stores, theaters, and barrooms closed. Black mourning bands were buckled over standard hatbands. Those who couldn't buy a mourning badge made their own, retrofitting 1864 campaign buttons with black ribbon. At Grover's National Theatre, the ambiguous transparencies of the previous night quickly came down, replaced by large letters spelling out a clear sentiment: "The National mourns a martyred father."

The moment the military guard was removed from Petersen's boardinghouse, curiosity seekers rushed to the door. William Petersen, who had been about to go downstairs to his bed, heard their knock. He did not wish to welcome more strangers into his home, but manners dictated he should allow the president's admirers to see the room where he had succumbed.[12] Instead of respectfully filing past the bed, some strangers busied the family members with questions while others made off with bloody bandages and used mustard plasters. They took everything they could lay their hands on. They pulled paper from the bedroom walls and snipped pieces of the Brussels carpet. They even whittled away at the furniture. Some stole spoons. One asked to purchase the pillows.[13]

The Petersens slowly caught on that their house had become a national shrine overnight. When Fred, a natural go-getter, watched men whipping out paper to blot up dripped blood from the oilcloth in the hallway, he saw a golden opportunity. The fifteen-year-old went into the relic business. He ran to the writing desk in the front parlor and grabbed some plain white paper. He cut it into squares and signed and dated each one. Then he dipped them in the blood from the front hall, probably Major Rathbone's. The people knotted outside clamored to buy Fred's grim souvenirs. He made $1.12 in fewer than ten minutes.[14]

Thousands walked up and down Tenth Street, moving as slowly as pallbearers as they eyeballed the theater and the boardinghouse. Some were on a pilgrimage, others a treasure hunt. Souvenir hunters blotted blood from steps and chipped away at the brick buildings to retrieve slivers. Strangers tiptoed up to the Petersens' windows and peeked in. Artists drew the house from the street. Relic seekers knocked day and night. At some point, the newspapers reported, someone in the Petersen House started charging admission.[15]

The fervor for relics was intense in the uncertain days leading up to the funeral, and it brought out the worst in ordinary people. Even some officials entrusted with cherished items took whatever they could. Mose Sanford, who worked in the hardware department at Frank Sands's government undertaking office, was one of them. Within minutes after the pine box that transported the president was left in his care, Sanford unscrewed its lid and went fishing for relics. As soon as the coast was clear, Sanford not only swiped Mr. Lincoln's necktie and a portion of his shirt but also removed every screw in the box and put other screws in their places. He mailed a piece of the shirt to a friend in New Jersey with a not-so-subtle note that he could have sold every inch of it for five dollars, but he preferred dividing it among his friends because he knew they would appreciate it and "also remember the donor" and "recollect that he never forgets his old and true friends."[16]

After Anna Petersen's carriage inched through the sea of gawkers Saturday evening, she took one look at her home's rifled interior and went to bed for weeks.[17] It couldn't have helped if she read the words a New York newspaper used to describe her gracious home with its marble mantelpieces and Brussels carpets: "There is nothing about the building to make it attractive." Or if she saw the erroneous report of a Washington City paper:

"The frail Petersen house, built rather on a tenement style, will not long stand as a memento of the great man who died in it."[18]

The swell of visitors didn't stop even on Black Easter. Washingtonians had brushed off Good Friday to celebrate the surrender, so naturally, many cut short their Easter celebrations to visit the saddest room in America—and possibly glean some grim souvenirs. Mrs. Petersen was spared the anguish of watching relic hunters parade through her house. She remained in bed. Her sister-in-law Louisa Kloman filled in for her, at least until sixteen-year-old Louisa Petersen packed her belongings at Moravian Seminary for Girls and headed home.[19]

Just as Mary Lincoln never again entered the bedroom where her son Willie died, Anna Petersen never again sat on the horsehair sofa the first lady had occupied all night. She couldn't bear to look at the round table where Mary Lincoln had left her things, so she had it moved to the basement.[20]

While Anna Petersen and Mary Lincoln brooded in their beds, Stanton moved ahead like a steam engine. He was busy planning the most extraordinary funeral in American history and capturing the first presidential assassin. At the moment, he was having more luck with the first task. The assassin's comfortable stay at Dr. Mudd's immaculate home had been short-lived, but he was well hidden in a Maryland pine barren, awaiting his chance to escape across the Potomac to Virginia. Booth and Davy Herold were waiting for a backwoods guide to signal them with a peculiar whistle. He would bring them food and let them know when the coast was clear.[21]

Booth was cold, sniffling, and in pain. The fine frock coat and thin dress pants he had chosen for his final stage performance would have worked better if he were spending Easter Sunday at a holiday table rather than a makeshift camp. His clothes provided little protection against the elements, and they were beginning to wrinkle and smell.[22] That must have been vexing for Booth, an unusually smart dresser who depended on his looks to charm people. He was lucky he had Davy Herold at his side. It was as if a playwright had cast the perfect companion for a man on the run in a rural setting. A well-spoken college man with a warm personality that opened doors for Booth, twenty-two-year-old Herold was also an avid hunter, so he knew Maryland's back roads and even many of the residents who lived on them.[23]

Booth really would have chafed if he'd known how people across the country were reacting as the news of the assassination spread. Broadway was hung with black. Old men wept in the streets in Council Bluffs, Iowa. Gun salutes were fired every sixty seconds outside the state capitol building in Nashville, Tennessee. In Baltimore, an indignant mob rushed a photography studio rumored to have a single picture of Booth. Fifteen thousand San Franciscans attended a memorial, the largest spectacle ever seen on the West Coast. Even the Canadian flag on Nova Scotia's government house drooped to half mast.[24]

John Ford, on business in Richmond, heard nary a word about the assassination until Sunday afternoon, and then he just heard that Edwin Booth had killed the president somewhere in Washington. He laughed at that. Ford knew Edwin Booth had been in Boston Friday night. He thought it was an impossible rumor. "It never occurred to me at all that John Wilkes Booth had been in Washington," Ford later testified. "I treated the matter with not the slightest credence. It was only on Monday morning, before the boat was leaving the wharf, that I got a newspaper and learned the actual fact."[25]

Booth's feat was the biggest news story in all thirty-five states. The *Newburyport Herald Extra* jumped the gun and told Massachusetts readers that "the assassinator" had already been nabbed.[26] Philadelphians who paid two cents for an *Inquirer* must have been stopped in their tracks when they saw twenty-one assassination headlines on the front page. The headlines were not what Booth was banking on though. Surely his beautiful face would have winced if he'd seen the banner head on the *Dubuque Daily Times*' Easter Sunday edition: "Horrible News: Culmination of Southern Fanaticism and Barbarism—Latest and Most Hellish Exhibition of Pro-Slavery Spirit."[27]

The greatest sting, if Booth had any way of knowing about it, would have been the condolence telegram Edwin Stanton received from the governor of Virginia.

F. H. Pierpont, a Lincoln supporter who headed the "restored" Virginia government, wrote this on April 15: "Loyal Virginia sends her tribute of mourning for the fall of the nation's president by the hands of a dastardly agent of treason, who dared to repeat the motto of our state at the moment of the perpetration of his accursed crime."[28]

19

The Most Elaborate Funeral in US History

When the Executive Mansion's doors opened at ten a.m. on Tuesday, April 18, its 170-foot façade was festooned with crepe.[1] The casket, nestled on a platform and topped with a regal domed canopy, reached so high that one of the East Room's three ornate gasoliers had to be removed to fit it.[2] Benjamin French, the commissioner of public buildings, had spared no expense. The canopy was fashioned from black alpaca with an underside of fluted white satin. Yards of black velvet flowed down its sides. It was draped with black crepe and dotted with sixteen oversized black satin rosettes. French, a Thirty-third Degree Mason, had designed the catafalque and its trappings to resemble the elaborate Lodges of Sorrow used in Masonic rites.[3]

The body was dressed in the same plain black suit the president had worn to his second inaugural just forty-five days earlier. This time it was dotted with strategically placed white flower petals and green leaves. Mourners noted the blackness around Mr. Lincoln's eyes. Stanton had instructed the mortician to leave the effects of the bullet as part of history.[4]

Mary Lincoln stayed in bed as twenty-five thousand men, women, and children climbed the steps to the platform and filed past her husband's corpse in the funereal darkness just one floor below. Even armless and legless soldiers made the climb with their canes and crutches and wooden limbs.[5]

People were able to view the body on the third day after death for one reason: Abraham Lincoln was embalmed.[6] Americans considered the practice a throwback to the ancient Egyptians until the Civil War, when embalming gained popularity as a way to preserve soldiers' bodies long enough so that they could be shipped home. As 1.5 million Americans stood in line to view President Lincoln's body, the embalming industry got a bounce. The bar was high because Mr. Lincoln had been the most photographed man in America.[7] Mourners arrived with an image of their lean, craggy-faced president in their minds, and the embalmers delivered. Dr. Charles Brown, who had preserved the president's body and his son Willie's, became a national celebrity. He was famous enough to visit Edwin Booth backstage on Broadway.[8] The president's body was actually embalmed repeatedly during his eighteen days of funeral services across seven states, so much that mourners in the last cities noted his skin had turned goldish. When the coffin was opened in 1901, Lincoln's face was still intact, although it was an unnatural grayish chestnut color.[9]

It is not known whether any of the Petersens joined their fellow Washingtonians in the thick line of mourners. It is certain the mood at the boardinghouse was funereal. Louisa described it in her diary on Black Easter: "Our hearts are filled with terrible grief over the sad death of the President, who was shot in Ford's Theatre Good Friday evening and brought into our house. . . . Papa is distraught and Mamma has taken to her bed so upset."[10]

While thousands were paying homage to President Lincoln in Washington on April 18, his assassin's dreams of glory had dead-ended in a Maryland pine thicket. On Tuesday, Booth's backwoods guide Thomas Jones finally delivered the newspapers the actor had been pining for. Booth was hiding among the pines like a hunted animal, but the actor in him still itched to read his reviews. He was horrified to read that it was Lincoln, and not he, who was hailed as a hero. The fame and honor he expected would never come his way. The headlines must have percolated in Booth's mind because that Friday he wrote this in the slim red 1864 pocket calendar he had started using as a diary: "After being hunted like a dog through swamps, woods and last night being chased by gun boats till I was forced to return wet and cold and starving, with every man's hand against me, I am here in despair. And why? For doing what Brutus was honored for, what made Tell a hero. And yet I, for striking down a greater tyrant than they ever knew, am looked upon as a common cutthroat."[11]

Booth was so convinced of his appeal that the news stories sparked an irrational desire in him to turn around and return to Washington. He told his diary later in the week that he would try to escape to Virginia, but he admitted, "I have a greater desire to return to Washington and, in a measure, clear my name, which I feel I can do."[12]

His life as a stage star must have seemed far off that Tuesday night, although four of the five carte de visite photographs Booth was carrying on his person were of actresses—Fannie Brown, Effie Germon, Alice Grey, and Helen Western. The fifth photo was of his true love, Lucy Lambert Hale. The government appropriated one of Booth's own publicity poses for wanted posters advertising the fifty-thousand-dollar price on his head.[13]

Major Henry Rathbone probably would have been pleased to read of Booth's predicament. That very day he sat up in bed for the first time since Booth nearly sliced his arm off.[14] Four days after the assassination, Rathbone just couldn't shake the feeling that he should have saved the president or at least kept hold of his assassin. He never would.[15]

Washington woke up to fire bells and church bells on April 19, the day of President Lincoln's Washington funeral. Cannons boomed with the first rays of sunlight, but the widow remained in bed.[16]

Every window and housetop was filled with people as the whopping procession crept almost two miles, from the East Room to the Capitol rotunda, where the president would lie in state.[17] Official condolences poured in from Austria, Argentina, Brazil, Belgium, Costa Rica.[18] In Berlin, altars were draped in black.[19] Queen Victoria of Britain, who had lost the father of her nine children just four years earlier, sent a personal note of condolence to Mary Lincoln.

The soldiers who led the way down the avenue were African Americans. The fifteen-foot-high, glass-sided hearse that followed them captured so much attention that few noticed the hero riding in the carriage directly in front of it. Dr. Leale, in his dress uniform with his ceremonial sword draped in black crepe, rode along with two other favored physicians.

As Leale's coach inched toward the Capitol, a high-ranking officer put his head inside and congratulated him. "Dr. Leale," he said, "I would rather have done what you did to prolong the life of the president than to have accomplished my duties during the entire war." The twenty-three-year-old shrank back in his seat as the importance of his role registered with him for the first time. As soon as he returned to his private office after the ceremony, he pulled down the window shade and locked the door. Then he knelt prostrate on the bare wood floor and asked God for advice. The answer came to him as distinctly as if another person had been in the room: "Forget it all."[20] "It was, for a youngster as I was, a terrible experience," Dr. Leale wrote decades later. "After it was all over, the reaction from the enormous responsibility that had been thrust up at me by fate was depressive." Rather than seeing himself as a hero, Dr. Leale thought he had come up short. "I couldn't help wondering if I had done my best," he wrote. "I couldn't sleep."[21] Although the villain saw himself as a hero, the hero did not. He saved his bloodstained shirt cuffs for the rest of his life, and he never took the ceremonial crepe off his sword, but Dr. Leale kept mum about his role in President Lincoln's assassination for at least the next forty-four years.[22]

On Thursday, April 20, the doors of the Capitol swung open at six a.m., and thirty thousand people filed by Mr. Lincoln, the second person ever to lie in state in the rotunda. The first had been the other presidential candidate in Mary Lincoln's life—Kentucky senator Henry Clay.[23]

At eight a.m. the next morning, the president began his journey back to Springfield, Illinois, following roughly the same route he had taken to Washington as president-elect. Once again, Willie Lincoln would be riding with him. The family had the eleven-year-old's body disinterred for reburial in Springfield. It was waiting in the funeral car when his loving father's remains arrived.[24]

When Congressman Lincoln took the round trip to Washington, he got there on his own power, put in for mileage, and was reimbursed $1,300.80.[25] This time, workers moved passenger platforms and erected three-story arches to welcome his funeral car. Special timetables were printed to inform citizens of the route, and farmers forgot their fields for a brief glimpse of the moving train.[26] A separate engine moved down the track ten minutes before the funeral train to alert citizens of its approach. It was hard to miss. It was festooned with flags and flowers, and a framed photograph of the president was perched over the cowcatcher. The trip that started this Friday would last thirteen days. The country had never seen anything like it.[27]

Meanwhile, Friday morning, April 21, found Booth and Herold on the wrong side of the Potomac. After paddling hard through the night, daybreak revealed they had put in to a Maryland creek. Either they had been thrown off course while trying to avoid a Yankee ship anchored nearby, or Booth didn't know beans about using a compass.[28]

When they left Washington on April 14, Booth and Herold had a head start. They could have outrun the news of the assassination. But the longer they went without crossing the Potomac, the more ordinary citizens got wind of the largest manhunt in US history.

Even with the news spreading, crafty Herold found someone willing to help them. For a seventh night, though, they would have to sleep on the ground in the wetlands near Nanjemoy Creek. Booth might have been less downcast if he had only known that hucksters at the presidential funeral were selling carte de visite photos of him, along with mourning pins and

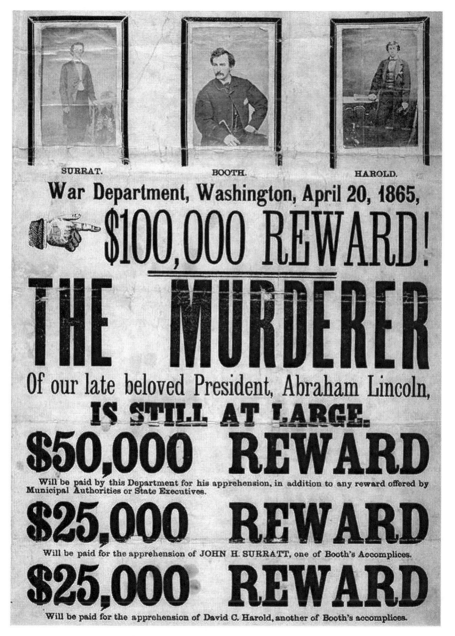

The manhunters used Booth's theatrical publicity photo on this wanted poster. Credit: Library of Congress

Lincoln mementos. Of course, the actor's immaculate appearance on the cartes de visite was a far cry from his current look. His perfectly oval face was pinched with pain.[29] It was blanketed with a week's growth of coal-black whiskers. His trademark mustache was growing back straggly, despite his compulsive efforts to groom it with his fingers. His black suit was spotted with dirt and brambles and rumpled from sleeping in cold, miry fields. His blackened left leg was swollen up.[30] His diary entry reflected his mental state: "For my country I have given up all that makes life sweet and holy, brought misery on my family, and am sure there is no pardon in Heaven for me since man condemns me so."[31]

Booth's ambitious plan was fast unraveling. Nine days after his stunning escape from Ford's, he was still in Union territory, and the cavalry was on a crooked path to nab him. On Sunday, April 23, he and Herold crossed the Potomac into Virginia, wet, cold, and disheveled.

At dusk that evening, they traveled down the long lane that led to the gracious T-shaped frame farmhouse of Confederate sympathizer Dr. Richard Stuart. Booth was confident this relative of Robert E. Lee would attend to his leg and take them in for the night. Stuart, who already had news of the assassination, wouldn't hear of it.

At the very moment Booth and Herold were cast out in Virginia, the remainder of half a million mourners were still lined up outside Philadelphia's Independence Hall to view the president's casket.[32] Red, white, and blue calcium lights shone on the building where the Declaration of Independence had been signed eighty-eight years earlier. The air inside was perfumed by twenty-five vases of rare blooms positioned around the casket, plus more exotic blooms on an oversized floral wreath. The room was lit by eighteen blazing candelabra and more than one hundred burning tapers. The ornate casket was positioned so that Mr. Lincoln's head rested next to the Liberty Bell.[33]

On the same day in Washington, Rev. Abraham Dunn Gillette, a Baptist pastor, spoke from the pulpit about the small back bedroom where the president's soul had taken flight. "Though the wound was mortal, he did not die, thank Heaven, amid the unhallowed surroundings where he received it. Kind arms bore him to a Christian home," Gillette said. "His breath and spirit went out of its clay tabernacle into the presence of his God and Judge from the house of a worthy family, belonging to the Lutheran Church . . . in a room sacred to them, as from it, a few months since, went two cherub children to the bosom of the good Shepherd above. . . . He died in a religious home, his friends and pastor around him—the most sacred place this side of Heaven."[34]

Meanwhile, Booth and Herold finally had some success on Monday, April 24. With the help of three Confederate soldiers, one of whom would later betray them, Booth and Herold made it across the Rappahannock River to Port Royal. They were in the South, but they were far from home free.

Back in Washington, Booth's escape was becoming a bitter pill for the nation to swallow, and official Washington was scrambling for a quick fix. Photographer Matthew Brady wrote to Stanton, offering life-size photos of Jeff Davis and "other criminals." S. J. Bowen, the Washington City postmaster, had no qualms about searching citizens' mail to find the culprit.[35]

As the funeral train wound its way north and then west to Springfield, Booth's pursuers tracked him to the east and the south. It was beginning to look like a wild goose chase.

On the evening of Monday, April 24, the president's corpse was rolled off a ferry in Lower Manhattan and carefully transported to New York's City Hall, where almost every surface was draped with black crepe. Eighty mourners filed by every sixty seconds in the pitch black. At midnight, one thousand German American voices chanted dirges.[36]

The same midnight brought to an end a restorative day for Booth. He had enjoyed the hospitality of Richard Garrett, a kindly Caroline County, Virginia, farmer who lived on a ridge near Port Royal with his second wife, Fanny, her sister, and far more children than bedrooms. The actor was passing himself off as John Boyd, a wounded Confederate soldier heading home. Garrett, whose own sons had fought for the Confederacy, offered him a warm supper. While Herold went off to town with some others, Booth relaxed on the front porch with John Garrett, a real Confederate veteran. The assassin bummed some pipe tobacco. Young Garrett had no inkling he was whiling away the afternoon with America's most wanted fugitive. And Booth had no idea that Willie Jett, the Confederate soldier he had confided in, was about to point the manhunters his way.[37]

Their houseguest had a fifty-thousand-dollar price on his head, but the Garretts would actually lose money hosting him. Twelve people lived in the Garrett's four-room house. John Wilkes Booth made an unlucky thirteen.[38]

That very day in Washington, Booth was the subject of an exchange between Secretary Stanton and a pushy detective. Allan Pinkerton, the former Union Intelligence Service chief, had wired Stanton. The enterprising sleuth didn't want to be left out of the largest manhunt in America's history.

Famous detective Allan Pinkerton tried to butter up Edwin Stanton so he'd hire him to nab Booth, but Stanton didn't bite. He didn't even spell Pinkerton's name correctly in his rejection letter. Credit: James O. Hall, from the Collection of Edward Steers Jr.

In his telegram, Pinkerton boasted that he might have been able to prevent the assassination if he were still on the job. He urged the secretary to take great personal caution and added a fawning, "The nation cannot spare you." Pinkerton offered Stanton the services of his entire detective agency.[39]

Stanton didn't bite.

On April 24, he sent Pinkerton a lukewarm letter suggesting he might earn the reward money if he scoured an area where few others were hunting. "Booth may have made his way West with a view of getting to Texas or Mexico," Stanton wrote. "You will please take measures to watch the Western rivers, and you may get him." Not only did Stanton fail to bite, but he misspelled Pinkerton's first name.[40]

The next day was a grim one for the assassin but a glorious one for the president's memory. While Booth wore out his welcome at the Garretts' Virginia farm, hundreds of thousands of New Yorkers filled the streets for President Lincoln. Most wore mourning badges on their left arms and grim looks on their faces. Sixteen gray horses pulled the grandiose fourteen-foot-long canopied black bier around Manhattan for almost four hours. Mourners lined both sides of every street, like dense human hedges.[41] A future president was among the spectators. Six-year-old Teddy Roosevelt was watching from an upper-story window at his grandfather's Broadway mansion.[42]

The funeral train left Manhattan at four fifteen, headed for Garrison's Landing, a spot near the US Military Academy at West Point. The entire cadet corps was lined up to pay its respects.[43]

Mrs. Lincoln missed all of it. Still muffled in grief at the crepe-draped Executive Mansion, she sat up in bed that day for the first time.[44]

20

The Manhunt Closes In

In Virginia, Booth's soldiering fiction began to unravel when he abruptly ordered one of Garrett's children to run for his pistols when a man walked onto the property. Up until that day, Booth had played his role perfectly, but he suddenly began slipping in and out of character. First Booth abruptly shouted for his sidearm, and then he and Herold scrambled for cover when a visitor mentioned the cavalry was nearby. The Garrett men never dreamed their houseguest was a presidential assassin, but they were growing suspicious. They agreed the "Boyd cousins" should get on their way.

While the funeral train was rolling toward Albany, New York, on April 25, Garrett's son John gathered the courage to ask Booth and Herold to leave his family's farm. The likelihood of another night on the cold ground galled Booth. Herold suggested they sleep under the porch, but Garrett humiliated them by saying his dogs had that spot. Herold then announced, in a no-ifs-ands-or-buts way, that they would sleep in the tobacco barn. The barn, a good distance downhill from the house, was a low-lying affair with boards placed inches apart to allow air to cure the tobacco. John Garrett allowed it. Booth limped down to the barn, still wrapped in the shawl he had been using to cover the initials tattooed on his left hand.

Unlike the well-appointed room Booth had enjoyed at Dr. Mudd's house just ten days earlier, this time the actor would be sharing his space with Herold, all manner of farm equipment, and the bedsteads and chairs and dining room tables the Garretts' neighbors were hiding from Union raiders.[1] As soon as the two men settled inside, the Garrett brothers, thinking the "Boyds" just might be horse thieves, quietly closed the lock. Then they returned to the house for evening prayers.[2] Locking the door was a misstep that later cost the family its barn and everything inside it.

The irony is that the Garrett sons knew the War Department had offered a fifty-thousand-dollar reward for the president's assassin and a smaller bounty for his accomplice. They simply had not pegged Booth and Herold as assassins. If they had, they might have turned them in and col-

Dr. Samuel Mudd treated John Booth's injury. He was convicted of conspiring to murder the president. Credit: Author's collection (public domain)

lected the reward. William Garrett had said as much to "Boyd" at the lunch table that day. Again, Booth's acting skill saved his neck.

As Albany, New York, residents were herded past the casket at the rate of seventy per minute in the pre-dawn hours of April 26, the cavalry was closing in on Booth in Virginia.[3] The soldiers tracking Booth were certain he had passed toward the Garretts'. They found sets of footprints with a queer little hole left by the tip of Booth's wooden crutch.[4] If she had known, that might have been some comfort to Albany native Clara Harris, whose mind kept returning to being barred in with Booth in the box at Ford's. Most nights since the assassination, she just tossed in her bed. She told a friend her only thought was that the fiend was still at large.[5]

Actually, Booth would soon be cornered. The Sixteenth New York Cavalry had him and Herold surrounded in Garrett's tobacco barn. He was cold and filthy, and his luck was about to run out. As the soldiers neared, they could hear the fugitives arguing inside the barn. Herold, who instantly deduced they were no match for the cavalry, wanted to surrender. Booth did not want to be taken alive. Perhaps he was thinking back to that crisp December day when he watched John Brown's body dangle at the end of a noose. He had almost fainted then, and he was ten yards from the gallows.[6]

When Herold insisted on leaving, Booth walked to the door and announced in a mocking voice, "Oh, Captain! There is a man here who wants to surrender awful bad." Outnumbered fifty to one, Booth seemed not to comprehend that his odds had fundamentally changed. He still taunted the cavalry: "Captain, I could have picked off three or four of your men already if I wished to do so."[7] He was grossly outmanned, but the openings between the barn slats were wide enough for Booth to put his carbine through, even wide enough to squeeze his muscular arm through. He had the advantage for the moment because, even with just a sliver of a crescent moon, it was easier for him to spot the soldiers than it was for them to peer into the barn's blackness. Booth likely knew daybreak would change that.[8]

He had no reason to imagine how he'd be silhouetted if the barn were set afire, at least not until the cavalry gave him a surprising ultimatum: he could surrender, or they'd light a match to the place. The nonchalant assassin parried with, "No, I have not made up my mind, but draw your men up fifty paces off and give me a chance for my life." Booth acted as if he were engaged in a backyard game instead of a life-or-death struggle.

He did stop grandstanding long enough to help Herold though. Perhaps realizing Herold had passed on several opportunities to abandon him that week, Booth told him, "Go out and save yourself, my boy, if you can."[9] Herold walked out, his empty hands first. The soldiers demanded his weapons, until Booth shouted, "I own all the arms, and may have to use them on you gentlemen."[10] As soon as Herold was collared, Booth shouted to the officers, "I declare, before my Maker, that this man here is innocent of any crime whatsoever."[11]

Suddenly, a handful of burning pine brush was tossed inside the tobacco barn, and the advantage instantly switched to the cavalry men. Booth's every movement was silhouetted in the flames. The gypsy's prophesy was coming true: "You'll die young. You'll make a bad end."[12]

Preparing to stand his ground, Booth raised his carbine and leveled it. Little did he know that the reasonable cavalry officer out front was not the only one he had to worry about. It is unlikely any Booth had ever come in contact with a man as crazy as the man who, just then, was training his revolver on John Wilkes's back. Consider that Junius Booth Sr. once dug up his dead child's body, thinking he could breathe life back into it, and that

John Wilkes himself had shot the president of the United States. Still, the man who stood less than twelve feet behind him may have been, quite literally, a mad hatter.[13]

Trigger-happy Sergeant Boston Corbett was a small, sober-looking man who parted his dark hair down the middle so severely that a swath of his white scalp was always visible. He wore a brush mustache and scraggly beard that strayed aimlessly down his neck. A New York City hat maker until his wife died in childbirth, Corbett moved to Boston after the burial. There, he drank heavily until a street preacher brought him to God. Corbett became a Methodist, grew his hair long like Jesus, and renamed himself in honor of the city where he found religion. But that wasn't the end of it.[14]

What happened next might be explained by the medical effects of the mercury used in hat making—delusions, mood swings, and aggressiveness. When Corbett was approached by two prostitutes who inspired lust in his heart, he went home and read Matthew 19:12, a Bible passage that mentions eunuchs. Taking the passage literally, Corbett cut open his own scrotum, pulled out his testicles, and cut them off. That night, he attended a prayer meeting, ate an ample meal, and took a walk. He sought medical help only after his scrotum turned black and swollen.[15]

Corbett joined the Union army when war broke out, but he often landed in the doghouse when he scolded other soldiers for cursing, even his commanding officer. Each time Corbett shot his weapon at a rebel, it was his habit to say, "God have mercy on your soul." It is not known whether he said that at three fifteen a.m. on April 26 when he shot Booth in the back of the neck. If he did, Booth likely heard his words, because Corbett was standing less than twelve feet behind him, aiming his Colt revolver through one of the barn slats.[16]

At least one soldier thought he heard Booth cry out as he crumpled to the ground, paralyzed. When the manhunters sped in to pull Booth out of the fire, he was armed with a Spencer carbine, a seven-shooter, a pocket pistol, a revolver, and the knife he had used on Major Rathbone. He had left his prized souvenir, the silver-clad derringer he used to assassinate the president, on the floor of the presidential box.[17] Along with Booth's hopes, the fire also destroyed the Garretts' farm equipment and their neighbors' stored furniture. As the fire flared, some soldiers lifted the limp rebel and carried him several yards up a slight incline through the trees and past the white-picket gate to the Garretts' narrow porch.[18]

Just two days earlier, Booth had sat on the same porch, filled his pipe with the Garretts' pungent tobacco, and entertained them with his tales. Now, the star-crossed actor lay helpless on a small straw mattress the Garrett women had placed on the porch floor. His speech was fading. He was unable to command his own arms and legs.[19] When Corbett's bullet penetrated his neck just about an inch from the spot where his own bullet had struck the president, it triggered a paralysis that would soon make it impossible for him to breathe. He was left like he had left President Lincoln twelve days earlier—unable to move and gasping for breath.

Lucinda Holloway, Mrs. Garrett's unmarried sister, who boarded at the farm, had been charmed by Booth's stories the night before. Now that he was having difficulty speaking, the prim-looking schoolteacher knelt at his side, moistening his lips with a wet handkerchief. She later described his skin as luminous. It is not known whether Miss Holloway was aflutter over Booth, as Washington, DC, waitresses, actresses, and maids had been, but when it was all over, she wrapped one of his coal-black curls around her finger and stealthily motioned to the doctor to snip a lock of hair for her.[20]

While still stage-star handsome, Booth looked nothing like the publicity photo on his wanted poster. His hair was somewhat shorter and dirty and disarranged. His mustache had been cut off but had grown back straggly. The lips of the corpse were tightly compressed. His face was freckled and weathered from exposure to the elements. Dark blood pooled around the chin and neck.[21]

Soldiers disagreed about whether John Wilkes Booth ever said another word. Some said he whispered, "Tell Mother I died for my country." Some said he asked to have his hands held up before him and said, "Useless. Useless." Others said they never heard a sound from him in the almost three hours after they pulled him from the burning barn, save the same gurgling noise the president had made minutes before he died.[22]

Like the president, his assassin died shortly after seven a.m., just after the sun's rays had overtaken the darkness. While the president's body was making its way west in a fifteen-hundred-dollar casket lined in white satin, Booth's was enveloped in scratchy wool.[23] An army officer borrowed a darning needle from Mrs. Garrett so he could sew the assassin's body into his used army blanket. He didn't bother to sew one end, so Booth's motionless feet hung out the bottom. The corpse was heaved into a rickety wagon, a far cry from the flower-bedecked luxury train car that bore the president's remains. John Wilkes Booth met a bad end, just as the palm reader had predicted.[24]

His fame far outlasted his father's and his brother Edwin's, though. The first full-length book about him, *J. Wilkes Booth, the Assassinator of President Lincoln,* by Dion Haco, was available twenty-eight days after his death. By June 1, *Confession de John Wilkes Booth, Assassin du President Abraham Lincoln* was also available in French.[25]

The day after Booth was shot, an autopsy was performed aboard the USS *Montauk,* the ship the Lincolns had visited on their April 14 carriage ride. Afterward, Booth's body was secretly buried. His victim's burial was anything but secret. Although President Lincoln's funeral train only moved through seven states, 1.5 million Americans viewed his remains, and 7 million greeted his train or one of his hearses in white dresses, mourning clothes, and military uniforms. There were plumed hearses, processions, three-story floral arches, one-thousand-voice choirs, and so many mourners that many lines moved forward only one foot per hour. Bands played dirges. Guns fired salutes. Train stations were draped in black. In some towns, the entire population turned out with torches to watch the train speed by in the night. Writer Lloyd Lewis called it "half-circus, half-heartbreak."[26]

21

Unrivaled Honors and an Unexpected Invoice

Exactly twenty-four hours after Booth's death, former president Millard Fillmore was up early to escort President Lincoln's body to St. James Hall in Buffalo, New York, where thousands viewed it, including many Canadians who crossed the border for the occasion.[1]

The train didn't stop at the little village of Westfield, New York, where, the last time Mr. Lincoln visited, he left his train car and walked through the crowd to kiss Grace Bedell, an eleven-year-old girl who had written him a letter suggesting that he grow a beard.

While the train was still moving toward Lincoln's grave, the first advertisements for pictorial items inspired by the assassination popped up in publications. The April 29 issue of *Harper's Weekly* featured ads for Alonzo Chappel's fictional painting *The Death of Lincoln*. Bob Lincoln and U. S. Grant both ordered the one-hundred-dollar version with forty-seven figures.[2]

As the funeral car moved into Indiana on Sunday, April 30, it passed under a specially constructed thirty-foot-wide arch decorated with Mr. Lincoln's words: "With malice for none, with charity for all." A triple arch greeted the casket at Chicago, where more than 150,000 citizens turned out. This one was inscribed: "We honor him dead who honored us while living. Rest in peace, noble soul, patriot heart, faithful to right, a martyr to justice."[3] That same day, but almost four thousand miles away, Americans living in London mourned together in the balcony at St. James Hall, which was draped in black cloth bordered in white lace and decorated with three American flags for the occasion.[4] On Wednesday, May 3, the entire population of Dwight, Illinois, turned out to see the funeral train pass at two a.m. Despite the hour, guns and bells signaled the train's arrival through the dark night. It may have been too dark for passengers on the train to make out the four words on the memorial arch at Bloomington, Illinois, when

This elaborate plumed hearse carried the president's body around Springfield, Illinois Credit: The Collection of Edward Steers Jr.

they passed by at five a.m. that morning: "Go to thy rest." When the train rolled through the president's namesake town of Lincoln, Illinois, at seven a.m., another overhead arch quoted the president: "With malice to none, with charity for all." The casket arrived home in Springfield, Illinois, at nine a.m. that day, remarkably just one hour behind schedule.[5]

As the train rolled into Springfield, spectators crowded the tracks for several miles, and every roof was covered with them. The president's body would ride to its final resting place in the ornate hearse used for the funeral of Senator Thomas Hart Benton. Except for its black color, it looked like a fairy-tale carriage, decorated with silver, gold, and crystal and crowned with eight tall black plumes.

As more than seventy-five thousand people viewed the body in the lobby of the state capitol, each passed a cornice painted with this rewritten version of the prophetic words President Lincoln had spoken at Independence Hall in 1861: "Sooner than surrender these principles, I would be assassinated on the spot."[6]

The next day, as solemn strains of music played, the plumed hearse

Mary Surratt was the first woman hanged by the US government. Credit: James O. Hall Collection

Edman Spangler (shown here) and Dr. Samuel Mudd became close friends in prison. Credit: Library of Congress

Michael O'Laughlen caught yellow fever while he was imprisoned at Fort Jefferson. Dr. Samuel Mudd tried unsuccessfully to save him. Credit: Library of Congress

Sam Arnold was involved in the plot to kidnap the president, not to kill him, but he was convicted and jailed. Credit: Library of Congress

crawled through a surging black sea of mourners to the rural cemetery where President Lincoln was put to rest.

Less than a week later, the trial of the conspirators began. Of the scores of people locked up after the assassination, only nine were ever charged. They were an odd lot—immigrant carriage painter George Atzerodt, who botched his assignment to kill the vice president; Mary Surratt, whose boardinghouse President Andrew Johnson called "the nest that hatched the egg"; young Davy Herold, who accompanied Booth into the country-side; carpenter Edman Spangler; Dr. Samuel Mudd, who examined Booth's leg; Lewis Powell, who attacked the Sewards; Booth's boyhood chums Samuel Arnold and Michael O'Laughlen, early conspirators who left the group when Booth's original plan to kidnap the president took a murderous turn; and John H. Surratt Jr. All except John Surratt were convicted by a military tribunal. Herold, Atzerodt, Powell, and Mary Surratt were sentenced to be hanged. The others were imprisoned at a massive hexagonal fortress on a remote isle off the coast of Florida in the Gulf of Mexico. John Surratt was tried later in a civilian court. His jury deadlocked, and he was released.

William Petersen didn't wait for the first trial or even for the president to be laid to rest before he submitted a bill for the use of his house to the federal government.[7]

Mary Surratt, Lewis Powell, Davy Herold, and George Atzerodt wait on the scaffold. Credit: Library of Congress

General John Hartranft reads the death warrant from the scaffold while the convicted prisoners wait in the hot sun. Credit: Library of Congress

The condemneds' ropes are adjusted. Credit: Library of Congress

The four hooded bodies dangle under the scaffold. Credit: Library of Congress

22

Paltry Meanness

Someone at the War Department must have been stunned when he opened the mail on May 3 and discovered that $550 rent was due on the modest bedroom where the president had spent his last eleven hours. A bill from William Petersen sought compensation for the use of his home, his furniture, his linens, his servants' time, and his own time—although he had left the house at least seven hours before the president succumbed.[1]

When the War Department sent the bill to the quartermaster general's office for payment, a snappish note was scrawled on it: "Pay Mr. Petersen a reasonable sum for the property consumed and for the use of his house, and inform him that the War Department has no authority to pay anything further." The reasonable sum was $293.50 for a nine-hour stay. That might have been the end of it, but the newspapers got wind of the story.[2]

The *Louisiana Democrat*'s response was representative. The paper blasted William Petersen as "rather cool" for billing the government $550 for the few hours "distinguished officials" used his home "on such an unfortunate occasion."[3] After all, even the president of the United States earned only $480 a week in 1865. The *Philadelphia Inquirer* headlined its editorial "Paltry Meanness": "There is certainly no limit to the gapping avarice of some men," the editor wrote. "They have actually put in a claim, in the office of the auditor of the treasury, for losses incurred by the damaging of sheets, pillowcases and carpets caused by the ebbing out of the lifeblood of the great American martyr. Can greater meanness be imagined? Hundreds would gladly have sacrificed half their worldly possessions to have had the honor of soothing the last moments of the great statesman, who was sacrificed that his country might live united and free." The paper particularly blasted Petersen for charging for the bloodstained linens: "Thousands would deem the possession of blood-stained relics as priceless mementoes." Newspapers also reported that, during the weeks when mourners flooded into Washington, the Petersens charged fifty cents for admission to the death room: "These Washington house owners have had their premises exhibited for weeks at high rates of admission, and have gleaned a golden harvest out of the nation's calamity," the *Inquirer* reported on June 26. "They have the audacity to claim compensation. Out on such paltry meanness!"[4]

On June 28, William Petersen wrote a letter to the editor of the *National Intelligencer* lambasting the reports. "I never presented such a bill," Petersen wrote. "The day after the late president's remains were removed from my house, [a] general called and offered to pay me the amount of damages incident in connection with the calamity. I respectfully declined to accept the offer."[5] Petersen also wrote a sheepish denial that his house was open to sightseers at fifty cents a head during the mourning period. He said he gave orders that no one should be admitted to the death room, but it didn't work out that way. "During the grand reviews, there were many persons desirous of visiting the room where the president died," Petersen wrote. "I gave orders to admit no one, but, during my absences on those occasions, my servant opened the house and accepted, as I afterwards understood, small donations from several visitors."[6] He said the visitors stole silver spoons, knives, forks, tumblers, and other articles that were used the night President Lincoln died.[7]

Fred Petersen told relatives he blotted up the blood in the hallway with a piece of paper and sold small squares of it to eager relic hunters, but his younger brother told a much different version years later. In 1878, Charles Petersen told a reporter he had been offered ten dollars for a small piece of towel dotted with the president's blood, but his father had become indignant at the mere thought of selling relics. "He was annoyed at the publicity which that event gave his residence and assiduously sought to avoid doing anything in that connection which might result in pecuniary benefit to himself," Charles said, referring to his father. Reacting to rumors that the Petersen children were currently asking the government to take the house off their hands for several times its real value, Charles Petersen also attempted to mitigate old stories that his father had charged admission and rent after the assassination. "It is very unkind and unjust, to say the least, to pull a dead man out of his shroud and smirch him with the filth of falsehood," young Petersen said. By then, William Petersen wasn't around to speak for himself. Charles Petersen said his father's dying request was that the house should be sold without mentioning it was where Lincoln had died. Actually, it is unlikely William Petersen had time to relate his last wishes to his children.[8]

With the war ended and the American economy entering a slump, Petersen's lucrative uniform business dried up. He slipped from proprietor of his own shop to cutter in other tailors' shops.[9] Around the same time, his rental income shrank as the theater closed and the long-term boarders began to move out. The housewares business was so slow that the Francises gave up their rooms on June 1 to go on an extended holiday in upstate New York and New England.[10] Others left too. By 1870, a twenty-year-old photographer named Victor Schanang was the sole boarder.[11] William Petersen took to going on drinking sprees once or twice a week. He liked to finish them off with laudanum, a legal mixture of opium and alcohol. On Saturday night, June 17, 1871, he bought some laudanum from S. E. Bishop's druggist shop and sat down on a bench on the grounds of the red Smithsonian Castle, probably with a spree in mind.[12]

By the time Sergeant Clayton of the Fifth Precinct found him, Petersen was in a stupefied condition with an empty vial labeled "laudanum" by his side. The sergeant was able to rouse him long enough for him to say it was his habit to take about twenty-five cents' worth of laudanum to finish off his sprees. He was taken to a central guardhouse, where Dr. Hartigan and Dr. Muncaster both tried to revive him. They tried emetics to induce vomiting. They pumped his stomach. Still, they lost him sometime after midnight. Coroner Potter summoned a jury of inquest and heard testimony from the druggist and the officers. The verdict was that Mr. Petersen had died of an "overdose of laudanum taken through mistake." His body was taken to 453 Tenth Street, where it lay in repose. His obituary appeared in the *New York Times,* where he was identified as the owner of the house where President Lincoln died. The *Times* labeled it a suicide.[13]

Following his funeral at four thirty Tuesday afternoon, Mr. Petersen was buried in a gently terraced section of Prospect Hill Cemetery. The cemetery, on the crest of a hill at the city limits, had opened twelve years earlier as a burial ground for Washington City's German Americans. The first two German immigrants killed in the Civil War were interred there.[14] Petersen's double plot, situated amid small willows and cedars, cost the family sixteen dollars, twice the fee for Prospect Hill's least expensive plots.[15] Mr. Petersen's body, and soon his wife Anna's too, were surrounded by the remains of bakers, brewers, engineers, shoemakers, cabinet makers, saloonkeepers, bookbinders, and other tailors. Many of them were Civil War veterans from the Eighth Battalion, a volunteer company from Washington, DC, whose members spoke German and elected their own German American officers.[16]

Exactly four months after William Petersen died, his wife, Anna, was also dead. She was buried on the same Wednesday she died. Her family never disclosed the circumstances of her death, and death certificates from that period were not preserved. The obelisk that marks their grave rivals the tallest in the cemetery. It is embellished with the flowers that were the style in the 1870s and with the words, "Lo, where this silent marble weeps, find Father Mother peaceful sleep."[17]

Eventually, the bodies of many other individuals connected with the Lincoln assassination would surround them. Among them were Louis Kettler, a merchant tailor like Petersen who was at Ford's on assassination night, and Louis Schade, the newspaperman who bought the Petersens' house. George Parkhurst, who played the bailiff in *Our American Cousin*, was also interred at Prospect Hill. So was W. Henry Walther, who was on guard duty in Georgetown the night the president was assassinated. Walther was one of the artists who painted the flowers on the Capitol dome, but as a new immigrant, he was so eager to work that he accepted a job as a bartender in Alexandria, Virginia, and commuted by swimming the Potomac daily.[18]

Within three weeks of Anna Petersen's death, her furniture and personal belongings were auctioned off, right down to her spittoons, picture frames, and four flatirons. A sofa went for $3.75; one bureau sold for $6.25; a bookcase garnered $4.00. William Boyd, publisher of the Washington and Georgetown directory, bought the deathbed, the mattresses, and a certificate of authenticity signed by Fred Petersen for $80.00 when similar beds were selling for $6.00.[19]

When Pauline Petersen wed a Baltimore businessman in 1873, the twenty-one-year-old bride took two bloodstained pillowcases with her to Baltimore and deposited them in a bank vault along with the diamond brooch Mary Lincoln had given her on assassination night.[20]

23

History Forgot Tenth Street

History almost forgot Tenth Street for three decades.

John Ford was never permitted to reopen Ford's Theatre. Federal officials paid him one hundred thousand dollars for it, and a contractor converted it to a three-story government office building. Abraham Lincoln would not be the last man to die inside.[1]

As for Petersen's boardinghouse, Louis Schade, a German American newspaper publisher who already lived on Tenth Street, bought it for forty-five hundred dollars in 1878. He used its upper floors as a private home for his growing family, and in its English basement, he published the pro-immigration *Washington Sentinel*. Because the death room was the sunniest one in the house, Louis and Anna Schade turned it into a playroom for their five fair-haired children. Like the Petersens, though, the Schades found their lives continually interrupted as tourists knocked at their door, displaying all sorts of bad manners and acting as if they were inspecting a public museum. Anna Schade was so annoyed by visitors who scolded her for allowing her children to play in the death room that the family moved away in 1893.[2]

The Schades then leased the house to a historical association that allowed Osborn H. Oldroyd to live there rent-free. A newsman once called Oldroyd "probably the most remarkable instance of American hero worship on record." Oldroyd had read one of Mr. Lincoln's speeches when he was eighteen years old. From then on, he was hooked. He spent the next sixty years collecting any Lincolniana he could get his hands on—the original wanted poster for John Wilkes Booth, a real Lincoln log split by the president, the letter Grace Bedell wrote advising candidate Lincoln to grow a beard. One of his prize possessions was the family Bible with "Abraham Lincoln" scrawled in a nine-year-old's handwriting.

Oldroyd and his wife, Lida, had the distinction of living in two homes where the Lincolns had also lived. They had moved to Washington City from the Lincolns' former residence in Springfield, Illinois, bringing Mary Lincoln's cookstove along with them.

Louis Schade, an attorney and newspaper editor, bought Petersen's boardinghouse and published his *Washington Sentinel* from the English basement. Credit: McCoy Family Collection

Anna Schade, wearing the gown she chose for President U. S. Grant's inaugural ball. She became irritated with pushy visitors who criticized her for turning the death room into a playroom for her children. Credit: McCoy Family Collection

Oldroyd had more than three thousand relics. To get the last note the president ever wrote, he had to outlive a man and his wife. After their deaths, the wife's sister finally gave it up for $125. He walked eighty miles to get another relic. Retracing Booth's eighty-mile escape route mostly on foot, Oldroyd visited the late Dr. Samuel Mudd's farmhouse near Bryantown, Maryland, while it was still occupied by the doctor's wife, Frankie. She told Oldroyd a man who lived nearby had the spur her husband cut off Booth's boot when he examined him. After some dickering, the man sold it to Oldroyd for fifty dollars.[3]

Oldroyd had a rose taken from the president's bosom before his casket was closed. He owned the chair Mr. Lincoln used when he practiced law in Springfield and the desk where the Emancipation Proclamation was written. His collection included one thousand Lincoln biographies, a wheel from the Lincolns' surrey, and the furniture the couple sold to neighbors when they moved to Washington. After Willie Clark's death, his widow mailed Oldroyd the candle and carving knife surgeons had used to probe the president's wound. His ownership of one item was short-lived: Mrs. Lincoln's cookstove eventually was returned to Illinois because Oldroyd had removed it from the Springfield house without Robert Lincoln's permission.[4]

The Civil War veteran, who called himself "captain" although he never achieved that rank, opened a museum in Petersen's old boardinghouse with the death room as one of the exhibits. Henry Ford offered Oldroyd fifty thousand dollars for his collection, but the captain, albeit in his eighties, held off. He firmly believed the artifacts should be owned by the American people, and he was hoping Congress would appropriate the money to purchase his collection.

The federal government bought Petersen House from the Schades in 1896. The thirty-thousand-dollar price tag was almost six times what the Schades had paid for it in a down market eighteen years earlier. Oldroyd continued to operate his popular Lincoln museum in the boardinghouse rent free.[5] A movie-studio researcher once spent three days there. One clergyman wanted to know exactly how Mr. Lincoln had stood when delivering an address so that he could adopt the same posture.[6] They each paid Oldroyd twenty-five cents admission, half of what William Petersen had reportedly charged three decades earlier.[7]

Across the street, the old Ford's Theatre building still looked as it had on April 14, 1865, because the government contractor had renovated the inside only. Then, in 1893, calamity returned to Tenth Street.

24

Lincoln Would Not Be the Last to Die at Ford's

Without warning, at nine thirty a.m. on Friday, June 9, 1893, a basement support in the Ford's Theatre building gave way. All three floors fell like a house of cards. Employees and their desks slid into the breach, killing twenty-two and injuring sixty-eight. Every window was blown out. A cloud of dust rose to the roof.[1] It happened at the precise moment when hundreds of mourners were solemnly watching Edwin Booth's heavy oak coffin being loaded into a waiting hearse outside the Church of the Transfiguration in New York City.[2]

That morning, Louis Rosafy, exhausted after running five and a half blocks from Judiciary Square so he wouldn't be late for work, was sitting at his desk on the third floor of the building when he noticed dust coming up through the tile floor. When the floor started sinking underneath him, Rosafy scrambled to get to a section that was still horizontal, but the next thing he knew, he was lying at the bottom of a pit, his skin slashed open and his right arm fractured. When Samuel Cottrell saw bricks falling from the ceiling, he dashed for a doorway with his pen still in his hand. On the way, he stepped into the arms of an overturned chair and stumbled to the floor. Stampeding workers walked over him until he extricated himself.[3]

One of the first responders on the scene was Father Jacob Walter, the priest who had prayed outside Petersen House on assassination night and walked Mary Surratt to the gallows.[4] Firemen hoisted ladders to catch people hanging out of windows. The crowd cheered as survivors emerged. The dead were carried out with newspapers and clothing veiling their faces. Investigators found the cause: astonishingly, the iron girders supporting all three floors were neither fixed nor bolted, just haphazardly propped across a bearing beam.[5]

After the collapse, one man saved Petersen House and Ford's Theatre for posterity. He was a US congressman reared in Germany by par-

All three floors of Ford's Theatre collapsed without warning at nine thirty a.m. on June 9, 1893. It happened at the precise moment when Edwin Booth's heavy oak coffin was being loaded into a waiting hearse outside a New York City church. Credit: Courtesy of Ford's Theatre National Historic Site, National Park Service

ents who were close enough to smell the gun smoke when John Wilkes Booth shot Abraham Lincoln. Henry Riggs Rathbone, the son of Clara and Henry Rathbone, was born on Lincoln's birthday in 1870 and elected to Congress from Illinois in 1922. He was raised by an aunt after his father, still tormented about letting Booth loose, shot and stabbed his mother at Christmastime 1883. In 1910 Congressman Rathbone had burned the bloodstained white dress his mother wore on assassination night, convinced it had been nothing but a curse on his family, but he pushed for the purchase of the Oldroyd Collection and the preservation of Ford's Theatre.[6] In 1926, Congress paid Captain Oldroyd fifty thousand dollars for a collection one newspaper said was easily worth one hundred thousand dollars.[7]

25

A Place to Make Him Comfortable

When you stand in the museum in the basement of Ford's Theatre, you are inches away from John Wilkes Booth's silver-plated derringer and his desperate, scribbled notes in his slim red pocket diary.

You can gaze upon Mary Lincoln's opera glasses or the coffee cup that her husband left on the windowsill, awaiting the late supper that never was served.

When you visit the Center for Education and Leadership next to Petersen House, you can almost touch the fat ring of keys John Wilkes Booth used for the last time on April 14. You can stare at the tiny metal handcuffs and heavy foot shackles Dr. Samuel Mudd wore en route to his Florida jail cell. You can almost picture Lewis Powell hightailing it out of Lafayette Square when you examine his bulky brown leather saddle with its ornate white stitching and rough wooden stirrups.

What you cannot see are the ghosts of Petersen House—the Ulkes rushing an iconic photo, Mary Lincoln pulling her hair out by the roots, and William Petersen seething because his Friday-night plans were upended. You cannot see the timid girl holding the first lady's hand, the frantic comedian burning the assassin's letter, or the young surgeon placing silver dollars on the eyes of the dead president.

Petersen House once held the high hopes and dashed dreams of a family and its boarders, but now few remember that President Lincoln wasn't the first person to breathe his last in its small back bedroom. Four-year-old Anna Augusta Petersen succumbed there on January 13, 1863, and her one-year-old sister Caroline Augusta died the next day.[1] All that was forgotten in an instant when Abraham Lincoln was carried through the creaky front door, just as his work on earth was finished.

The president was larger than life. The shot that killed him was aimed at our country, as Rev. Henry Fowler told his flock of Presbyterians on April 23. America's grief was personal, large, national, and enduring.[2]

To this day, every visitor to the dark, slant-ceiling room where Abraham Lincoln succumbed can feel the specter of that grief there.

To history, Petersen House will always be a place to make him comfortable.

Epilogue

What's Past Is Prologue

The Lincoln assassination, for better or worse, changed the lives of ordinary and extraordinary Washingtonians. The event was so jarring to nineteenth-century America that the slightest connection to it usually merited a mention in an otherwise ordinary obituary, even into the mid-1950s.

The event brought nightmarish endings to the lives of all five people who were barred inside the presidential box—Abraham Lincoln, Clara Harris, and John Wilkes Booth were killed by madmen. Colonel Henry Rathbone and Mary Lincoln were committed to insane asylums.

Mary Lincoln

Mary Lincoln spent months staring out the window at the diamond-embossed bars after her son Robert had her committed to a posh insane asylum in Batavia, Illinois, in 1875. Her confinement lasted only four months, ending when a Chicago newspaper took up her cause.

The first lady could never get over the fact that she was not accorded special recognition as the widow of Abraham Lincoln. After all, lesser widows were accorded places of honor. Sallie Pickett spent fifty years writing and lecturing about Confederate general George Pickett, rarely mentioning her husband's infamous and futile charge at Gettysburg. Elizabeth Custer wrote a children's book that used her husband, General George Custer, as a model for manliness. Varina Davis, widow of Jefferson Davis, became a columnist for the *New York World* and, ironically, a good friend of Julia Grant.[1]

Mary, meanwhile, was roundly criticized, even by her own pastor, but the most vulgar wag was Oregon senator James Nesmith. After enjoying the Lincolns' hospitality at an 1862 party, Senator Nesmith sent his wife a letter with this coarse description of his hostess: "The weak-minded Mrs. Lincoln had her bosom on exhibition. . . . As I looked at her I could not help regretting that she had degenerated from the industrious and unpretentious woman that she was in the days when she used to cook old Abe's

Mary Lincoln was roundly criticized after her husband's death. A senator said she had her bosom on exhibition. Her own pastor called her queer. Credit: Collection of Edward Steers Jr.

dinner and milk the cows with her own hands. Now her only ambition seems to be to exhibit her own milking apparatus to the public gaze."[2]

Even Reverend Gurley, who had said the prayer at her husband's death-bed, wrote a catty letter about her less than two months later: "Everybody in Springfield loves Mr. Lincoln, but, as for Mrs. L., I cannot say as much." He continued: "Hard things are said of her by all classes of people. . . . She is queer, but it may be that her failings have been somewhat exaggerated. She has always been very kind to Emma and myself, and I cannot but feel very sorry for her. The ladies of Springfield say Mr. Lincoln's death hurt her ambitions more than her affections."[3]

The Rathbones

Just like the Lincolns, one of the Rathbones was killed by a madman, and the other was committed to an insane asylum. In the Rathbones' case, the husband was the madman.

The couple was living in Germany with their three young children when Henry Rathbone shot and stabbed his forty-nine-year-old wife just before Christmas 1883. Fully dressed before daylight, Rathbone wandered to the room where the children and their nurse were sleeping. He asked to see the children. Clara Harris Rathbone awakened and bravely distracted her husband, although he was armed with a new dagger and a new six-shooter. Tricking him into leaving the children's room, she told the nurse to lock the door behind them. As soon as they were alone, he stabbed her in the heart, fired bullets into her breasts, and then wounded himself. German police found his six-shooter and a knife covered with gore. Rathbone told police his children had been abducted and he had been wounded in a fight with their kidnapper.[4] His lawyer said the major's mind was still clouded with scenes from Ford's Theatre. It was like a seam that was never properly closed.

The shooting was an absorbing topic of conversation in Albany, New York, social circles that holiday season because the Harrises and the Rathbones were among the city's leading families. The major was committed to the Hindesheim Asylum for the Criminal Insane in Hanover, Germany, coincidentally the city where William Petersen had been born. He lived in luxury there for another twenty-eight years, with servants attending him. Because of his wealth, he occupied the largest suite of rooms, including a choice library and a private dining room. He was permitted to ride his own carriage around the countryside, despite telling doctors he was surrounded by enemies who made him drink liquids through the walls.[5]

John Wilkes Booth

Of the five people barricaded in the presidential box on assassination night, John Wilkes Booth was the only one ever to return to Baptist Alley. When his body was exhumed for return to his mother in the winter of 1869, the corpse was briefly stored in a Washington undertaker's garage. Ironically, the garage was on the former site of Booth's stable in Baptist Alley behind Ford's Theatre.[6]

Dr. Charles Leale

Dr. Charles Leale, who did his best to undo what Booth had done, lived until 1932. He spent a long, happy life using his skills to help others, just as he had on assassination night.

He mustered out of the army as a captain, married socialite Rebecca Medwin Copcutt at her parents' elegant three-story stone home in Yonkers, New York, and fathered four children. They lived in a mansion on Manhattan's posh Madison Avenue, but his work always focused on public health and infectious disease.

President Lincoln wasn't the last presidential assassination victim Dr. Leale would treat. When Charles Guiteau shot President James Garfield in a Washington train station on July 2, 1881, Dr. Leale was called in to consult. President Garfield died eleven weeks later.

Dr. Leale kept mum about his heroic effort to prolong President Lincoln's life for forty-four years, until he was invited to tell his story to a veterans' group on the one-hundredth anniversary of President Lincoln's birth.[7]

Lucy Lambert Hale Chandler

Lucy Hale, the smitten senator's daughter who gave John Wilkes Booth tickets to Lincoln's second inauguration, remained single until she was almost forty. Her parents had spirited her away to Europe immediately after the assassination. She returned to their New Hampshire home four years later but did not marry for another decade. The lucky man was William Chandler, an old flame and recent widower who went on to serve as secretary of the navy under President Chester A. Arthur. They had one son in 1885, when Lucy was forty-four. In 1882, the *Los Angeles Times* reported that protocol then called for the wife of the secretary of the navy to be escorted by the secretary of war on state occasions. The report pointed out that this would call for Robert Lincoln, secretary of war under President Arthur, to escort the woman whose one-time fiancé had shot his father.[8]

Elizabeth Dixon

Elizabeth Dixon, the friend who caught the swooning Mary Lincoln in the death room, was so publicity shy that she offered to pay newspaper reporters to keep her name out of the papers. Ironically, her daughter Clementine married James Welling, a former managing editor of the *National Intelligencer.*[9]

Willie Clark

Willie Clark, who crawled into the bed where President Lincoln died and fell asleep, became a Boston real estate agent. He was purchasing a pair of gloves at a men's store in 1888 when he fell back into a chair and died of a heart attack.[10]

Father Jacob Walter

Crucifix in hand, Father Walter comforted Mary Surratt atop the gallows. The gawkers who watched them didn't know that he was, at that very moment, in the doghouse with his archbishop. After Father Walter told newspapermen there wasn't enough evidence against Mary Surratt to hang a cat, the Most Reverend Martin Spalding warned Walter to do nothing further to draw attention to himself. The archbishop already had his hands full. A Charleston bishop had been accused of disloyalty, and anti-Catholic Know-Nothings were squawking that several conspirators were Catholic. Father Walter, who joked that he took his superior's warning as a suggestion rather than an order, went to the Executive Mansion anyway and attempted to meet with President Andrew Johnson, with Mrs. Surratt's twenty-two-year-old daughter in tow.[11] Walter told reporters that no one could make him think that a Catholic woman would take Holy Communion on Holy Thursday and commit murder on Good Friday.[12] Despite what Father Walter believed, Mary Surratt became the first woman ever executed by the US government. Father Walter, who stood atop the gallows with Mrs. Surratt, was the only person besides the conspirators who could be certain whether she was innocent. As she waited outside her cell for her walk to the scaffold, he heard her last confession. She declared her innocence.[13]

Boston Corbett

Sergeant Boston Corbett, the man who shot Booth, received $1,653.85 in reward money. Owing to his celebrity as Booth's killer, he was offered a job as assistant doorkeeper of the Kansas House of Representatives in Topeka. That lasted until the fanatically religious Corbett brandished a revolver at a person who mocked the legislature's opening prayer. Corbett was arrested and sent to the Topeka Asylum for the Insane. A year later, while taking a walk on the grounds, he escaped. His final whereabouts are unknown.[14]

Annie Sardo Sheehy

Annie Sardo Sheehy, the six-year-old who never forgot the thundering noise of Tenth Street on assassination night, lived into her nineties. When she led her grandchildren on a twentieth-century road trip tracing John Wilkes Booth's escape route, she told them everyone on Tenth Street had supported Mrs. Surratt. Her grandson Dr. J. Rush Shanahan got the impression the family was sesech, just as neighbor Henry Safford suspected in 1865.[15]

William J. Ferguson

Billy Ferguson, the handsome fifteen-year-old who helped Fred Peterson remove a shutter and climb into his home on assassination night, enjoyed a successful career as a comic and a movie actor. In 1915, he played Abraham Lincoln in the silent film *Battle Cry for Peace*.[16]

Ned Emerson

Ned Emerson, the actor often mistaken for John Wilkes Booth, stashed his memories in an attic trunk. Six decades after the assassination, Emerson's son Charles opened the trunk and found a photo of Booth, an April 14 theater program bearing a single dot of blood, and his father's own vivid account of assassination night. Ned Emerson's description of his friend Booth was generous: "He was a kind-hearted, genial person, and no cleverer gentleman ever lived. Everybody loved him on the stage, though he was a little excitable and eccentric."[17]

Asia Booth Clarke

John Wilkes Booth believed one of his pregnant sister's twins would be named for him. He was not. Instead, Asia Booth Clarke and her husband, John Sleeper Clarke, almost divorced over her brother's act.

She named her newborn Creston, not John, but he became an actor.[18]

Joseph Hazelton

The little program boy whose hair John Wilkes Booth tousled on the day of the assassination grew up to be a Hollywood actor. Joseph Hazelton performed with stars like Lon Chaney, Norma Shearer, and Jackie Coogan.[19]

Samuel Seymour

Samuel Seymour, who was five years old when he saw John Wilkes Booth fall to the stage, appeared on TV's *I've Got a Secret* in 1956, when he was ninety-six. His secret: "I Saw John Wilkes Booth Shoot Abraham Lincoln."[20]

Peter Taltavul

When his business was shuttered after the assassination, Taltavul worked as a casket maker.

His descendants ran a funeral home business in Washington, DC.[21]

Henry Ulke

When Henry Ulke heard German actress Veronica Neuberg Schultze was booked to appear in New York City, he felt he just had to meet her. He left his room at Petersen House and went to Manhattan. Before the end of 1865, the two were married. They set up housekeeping at their own home in Washington City and reared six children.[22]

Ulke painted more than one hundred portraits of the famous. His work still hangs in the White House and the National Portrait Gallery.[23] He introduced painted backgrounds into photography, an innovation that would influence portrait photography for the next one hundred years.[24]

The beetle collection he was working on in his room at Petersen's boardinghouse eventually included one hundred thousand meticulously preserved specimens. Now housed at Carnegie-Mellon University, it is still considered one of the finest of its kind.

Julius Ulke

In his own time, Julius Ulke was well known as a hotel investor and a nature photographer who traveled to Africa to photograph the transit of Venus. Now he is remembered as the cameraman who took the haunting secret photograph of the Lincoln deathbed. Although the Ulke brothers shared a photo studio, and Henry's stamp is on the back of some copies of the deathbed photo, Julius is most often credited with the deathbed photo, possibly because one of his descendants first revealed it almost a century after it was taken. Probably fearing confiscation, the family kept the photo under wraps until a ninety-three-year-old descendant agreed to sell it to author Dorothy Kunhardt to raise thirty-seven hundred dollars for her British church in 1961.[25]

Just like Edwin and John Booth, Henry Ulke's work was much better known in his lifetime, but Julius's photo is more immediately recognizable now than any of his brother's stunning oil portraits.

James Tanner

The injured war veteran who calmed the crowd at Grover's National Theatre became an attorney, a public official, and, as the powerful US commissioner of pensions, a well-known advocate for the country's two million veterans.[26] He was riding on a night train to Indianapolis after the turn of the century when a gentleman mentioned he was the son of Major Rathbone and Miss Harris, who were in the presidential box on assassination night. After the other passengers dispersed, James Tanner spoke up. He told Henry Riggs Rathbone that he had watched his mother, as a young woman, helping Mrs. Lincoln down the narrow hallway that night.[27]

John Mathews

John Mathews, the childhood chum who burned Booth's confession while the president lay dying one floor below, lived his last twenty-one years in a single room near Manhattan's theater district. Friends said he was alone, except for his blind Irish setter.

His innocence had long been established, but Mathews never fully recovered from accusations that he conspired with Booth. Friends said any reference to the assassination made him so wildly excited that he earned the reputation of being erratic, although he was anything but.

Mathews quit acting in 1891 and became an investigating agent for the Actor's Fund. His job was to dole out money to sick and needy actors. Some weeks, he included most of his own fifteen-dollar salary. When he died in his sleep in 1905, one actor called him "an angel of mercy." Others described him as a warmhearted, conscientious man who always knew how to do just the right thing. His funeral drew a packed house. After his death at age sixty-nine, friends learned Mathews hadn't been so lonely. His seventy-one-year-old landlady, Mary Kimball, had also been his sweetheart.[28]

The Lincoln Carriage

The head-turning green carriage the Lincolns rode in to Ford's Theatre was a gift from several New York merchants. After the assassination, Robert Lincoln sold the carriage to a New York doctor, who sold it to carriage maker Clement Studebaker for his carriage museum. A twenty-first-century restoration proved surprising. For almost 150 years, historians had called the carriage black, but it was actually a soot-covered green. Conservators uncovered green body paint, elaborate presidential monograms, and gold, white, and maroon detailing. The partially restored carriage is part of the Studebaker National Museum collection in South Bend, Indiana, but its original detailing was never restored.[29]

Helen Coleman Wynkoop
(Stage Name: Helen Truman)

Helen Truman, who took such note of Mrs. Lincoln's gray-checked silk dress on assassination night, followed the acting jobs to Hollywood in the early twentieth century, like many of Ford's players. Interviewed before her death in 1924, she said that assassination night stood out in her memory as the hell of hells. She pointed out that, ironically, President Lincoln's death in the theater proved to be one of the great dramas of American history.[30]

The Petersens

The gawkers who stood on their tiptoes to peek inside Petersen's boardinghouse on assassination weekend should have been thanking their lucky stars that the president wasn't brought to their homes. History shone a harsh light on the Petersen family's private business, and the children attempted to change the direction and intensity of that light.

After William Petersen overdosed on a bench in front of the red Smithsonian Castle and his wife, Anna, died four months to the day later of an undisclosed cause, their grown children, consciously or unconsciously, set about distancing themselves from the newspaper stories about their family. As Washington segued from an overcrowded rough-edged capital to a more genteel Victorian-era one, the Petersens attempted to burnish their family's reputation as well.

Charles Petersen was nine years old when he saw John Wilkes Booth drop to the stage. He worked as a clerk at the War Department and died of heart disease at fifty.[31]

Fred Petersen and his partner Albert Childs opened a carpet showroom on Pennsylvania Avenue, taking advantage of innovations in carpet making that had begun in 1839 with Erastus Bigelow's invention of the steam-driven loom, which multiplied the number of yards that could be produced in an hour. Petersen & Childs's 1884 ad in the *National Republican* boasted: "We keep only the best grades of Bigelow, Wiltons, and Body Brussels, Smith's Moquettes, Roxbury and Smith's Tapestry Brussels."[32]

By 1910, Fred was retired and living in Baltimore with his daughter Anna, his son-in-law Harry Thomas, and their three children. Their eldest was named after him. The census taker recorded him as widowed, but Fred's divorce was well documented in the local papers. The first story appeared under the headline "More Happy Apart" on July 28, 1891, when he was forty-two. His wife, Emily Tew Petersen, thirty-four, had won a divorce, alleging "the well-known dealer in carpets" had beaten her until she was black and blue, pulled out great bunches of her hair, and once dragged her down the stairs by the hair. He told the court he had only slapped her with his open hand when she exasperated him beyond endurance and locked her in a room when she was intoxicated and that she once threw a hammer at his head. Fred said all the unhappiness that came to them during their married life was caused by his wife's intoxication, her ungovernable temper, and her utter disregard for the wishes or comfort of anyone but herself. Although he listed an income of eight thousand dollars a year and a net worth of forty thousand dollars, he suggested that she apply for assistance to her male friends—a handsome, blond, mustachioed police officer in the Second Precinct and one of the highest officials in the Census Office. The court ordered Fred to pay her two hundred dollars a month in support for herself and their ten-year-old daughter.[33]

Two years later, the *Washington Post* reported on a row at the Howard House in Baltimore after Fred Petersen found his former wife in a bedroom there with a streetcar conductor. Later that week Fred petitioned the court to cancel his alimony and give him custody of his twelve-year-old daughter. He alleged her mother was teaching her to drink and smoke cigarettes.[34]

Until his death in 1915, Fred routinely answered newspaper reports critical of his family with the same fervor that he answered his wife's charges of cruel and abusive treatment. In 1913, he wrote a letter to the editor in which he said his father never received any thanks from anyone for what he did. The letter his father wrote to the editor of the *National Intelligencer* in 1865 contradicted that: William Petersen wrote that a general called the day after the president's body was removed and offered to pay him for any inconvenience, but he declined the offer.[35]

Pauline Petersen Wenzing and her husband, Otto, owned a large four-story industrial building on one of Baltimore's main streets. Oddly, it adjoined Ford's Theatre—John Ford's Baltimore venue.[36] When her husband died in 1905, Pauline ran his dyeing business briefly before leasing the prime commercial building to another company. The headline in the *Baltimore Sun* was "Big Price for Realty."[37]

When Pauline died in 1932, her grandsons went to court to probate her will. They lost to her son.

They said he had "undue influence" upon her because he lived with her.[38]

William Felix Petersen

William Felix Petersen, the oldest surviving Petersen son, moved to Galveston, Texas, and eventually Los Angeles with his wife, Jennie. He worked as a druggist.[39]

Louisa Petersen

Louisa Petersen, who had to leave boarding school and return home after the assassination, met her future husband in Washington City. Charles Rector, who had served as a drummer boy with the New York infantry, was working as a clerk in the War Department when they met. They married on his twenty-fifth birthday, in May 1869. She was twenty-one. Soon he was managing the country's first coast-to-coast railroad dining car, following in the footsteps of his father, a restaurateur in upstate New York. The couple moved to Chicago, where Rector opened the eatery that introduced Chicagoans to oysters on the half shell. It featured the first cash register with a bell west of the Appalachians. When the Columbian Exposition opened in Chicago in 1893, Rector wrangled the only license to sell food inside the fairgrounds. His Café Marine made history. It claimed the first female patron to smoke a cigarette in public. Princess Eulalie of Spain lit up first, but Chicago party girls immediately followed suit. Encouraged by famous World's Fair customers who raved about his food, Rector moved his family to New York City and opened a lobster palace just four months before the century turned. Rector's boasted Broadway's first revolving door, and people would come just to push it. The place was dubbed "the cathedral of froth" for its Louis XIV–style interior of gold and crystal. Floor-to-ceiling mirrors made it easy to see which stars were coming and going through the revolving doors. Actress Lillian Russell, Commodore Cornelius Vanderbilt, Diamond Jim Brady, ill-fated architect Stanford White, and leggy songstress Anna Held were all regulars. Rector bragged that, while New Yorkers paid to see Broadway stars, the stars paid to see Rector's.[40]

O. Henry, the writer, Thomas Lipton, the tea magnate, and George M. Cohan, the lyricist, also ate at Rector's, where sixty waiters buzzed from table to table. A waiter there could make nearly one thousand dollars a month in tips, and the coatroom alone brought in ten thousand dollars a year, according to George Rector, Louisa's son. Rector's was so popular that the Ziegfeld Follies sang about it in 1913. Maybe too popular. When a Broadway musical called *The Girl from Rector's* gave the impression that the restaurant served fast women, its reputation nosedived. That, and the impending passage of Prohibition, led to Rector's demise on New Year's Day 1919. Louisa, Charles, and George went on to build a hotel on the site. George Rector wrote six books, including *Dine at Home with Rector—A Book on What Men Like, Why They Like It, and How to Cook It*. In one of his books, he wrote, "Rector's may not have been the center of population in the late 90s and early 1900s, but it was the center of all the population worth knowing."[41]

When Louisa died in 1889, her short obituary referred to her only as "an hotelier's wife." It devoted more inches to reporting that President Lincoln had breathed his last in her bed and that she owned a pillow stained with his blood. Several years after Louisa's death, the second Mrs. Charles Rector donated that pillow to the Chicago History Museum.[42]

In 1921, William Petersen's famous grandson sugarcoated the family history in a *New York Times* interview. George Rector said he had heard his uncle Fred Petersen, an eyewitness to Lincoln's demise, repeat every detail of that night many times, and he had never mentioned any boarders.

"It was not a boardinghouse at all," Rector told the *Times*. "I know that my grandfather did not conduct a rooming house."[43]

Acknowledgments

The seed for this book has been growing since I visited Petersen House as a child and glimpsed a small blue-and-white pillow stained with President Lincoln's blood. In those days, the original artifacts were still on display in the death room.

That seed might never have grown into a manuscript if Gloria Swift had not been curator of Ford's Theatre in 2009. Because Ford's has no formal archive, Ms. Swift kindly shared her office day in and day out while I searched through files. I cannot imagine a better person to run a national shrine.

The manuscript surely would have gone nowhere if not for Ed Steers Jr., esteemed author of *Blood on the Moon*. Dr. Steers shepherded it to publication. Without his quick mind and extraordinary kindness, it would never have made it into print. Not only did he spend weeks patiently reading and correcting footnotes for someone who was then a complete stranger, but he gave me sage advice, made invaluable introductions, even freely offered rare prints from his own collection as illustrations. Aside from being the greatest Lincoln expert alive, he is also a marvelous person. Dr. Steers applies the same exacting focus to Lincoln research that he employed as a Fulbright Scholar, biomedical researcher, and deputy director at the National Institutes of Health before he retired to write his groundbreaking book on the Lincoln assassination. An editor told me that many authors who write the definitive book on their subjects swat away new authors, but Dr. Steers is quite the opposite and quite like Mr. Lincoln in his treatment of others.

He is not alone in that. I found a nationwide community of pay-it-forward Lincoln experts and enthusiasts who share their knowledge as authors, speakers, docents, and guides. Add to that the archivists, librarians, and museum professionals thrilled by the discovery of a single new fact.

I'm especially indebted to the National Parks Service staff of Ford's Theatre, where my five years of research began. I found an extraordinary welcome there from Ms. Swift but also from Laura Anderson, Allison Dixon, William Cheek, Kym Elder, Rae Emerson, Jim Garrett, Sylvia Jarvi, Eric Martin, and Roger Powell.

I'm grateful for the nineteenth-century occupants of Ford's too. The theater's small archives are filled with their statements, many verging on poetry. One of my favorites is Major Henry Rathbone's vivid description of his failed attempt to get his arms around the athletic, muscle-bound assassin: "I might as well have tried to hold a machine of iron." Washington City residents were skilled wordsmiths. Their phrases paint pictures for readers even 150 years later.

I owe a debt to the members of the Surratt Society in Clinton, Maryland, where I first went as a stranger in 2011 and now feel very much at home. Laurie Verge, the director who does so much more than direct, is prime among them. Ms. Verge has been correctly referred to as a matchmaker who matches people and information. I'd also like to thank Lindsey Horne, Louise Oertly, Susan Proctor, Richard Smyth, Dave Taylor, Sandra Walia, and, especially, historian Joan Chaconas.

Surratt Society members treat each other like extended family. I'd like to thank the generous Dr. Blaine Houmes for offering a rare photo for this book within ten minutes of our meeting. Most of all, I'm grateful to Betty J. Ownsbey, author of Alias Paine, for her willingness to share her knowledge of everything from Photoshop to nineteenth-century horseback-riding styles.

At the Lincoln Discussion Symposium, I am thankful for Eva Lennartz, Roger Norton, Robert G. Wick, and other members of this knowledgable online community.

I'm grateful for the important work being completed by the research associates of the Papers of Abraham Lincoln and especially indebted to Helena Iles Papaioannou and David Gerleman, without whom I, no doubt, would not have found key documents at the National Archives.

I owe a special debt to the descendants who shared information and photographs of their ancestors present at the assassination—Bob Cecil, Colleen Gibson, Thomas Gourlay, Myron and Malon Richardson, Ken Schade, Dr. J. Rush Shanahan, John J. Toffey IV, Caroline Welling Van Deusen, and Carey and Olga R. Weiss.

At the Kiplinger Research Library of the Historical Society of Washington, DC, I am grateful to Laura Barry, Karen Harris, Ann Kesler, Jennifer Krafchik, Adam Lewis, Elizabeth Ratigan, and Anne Rollins.

At the Library of Congress, I thank Arlene Balkansky, Matthew Braun, Jeff Bridgers, Loretta Deaver, Eric Frazier, Bruce Kirby, Amber Paranick, and, especially, John R. Sellers.

At St. Elizabeth's Hospital, thank you to Dr. Patrick Canavan, Cassandra Jackson, and Dr. Surya Kanhouwa.

I am grateful to Rodney Orme of the Cornell University Registrar's Office.

At the US Senate Historical Office, I thank Heather Moore.

At the Lincoln Heritage Museum of Lincoln College, I thank Ron Keller.

At the Office of Public Records Management for Washington, DC, thanks go to Bill Branch, Clarence Davis, and William Walker.

Many archivists and museum professionals went above and beyond to add to this manuscript. They include Ted Bennicoff of the Smithsonian Institution; Raymond Wemmlinger of The Players; Scott S. Taylor of Georgetown University's Special Collections Research Center; John Richter III at the Center for Civil War Photography; SaVern Fripp of the Office of the Chief Medical Examiner for Washington, DC; Bryant Johnson at the US District Court for Washington, DC; Stephanie Lucas of the Benson Ford Research Center; and, at the National Archives, Juliette Aria, John P. Deeben, Robert Ellis, Cynthia Fox, Trevor Plante, Katherine Vollen, and Karen Needles, who makes research easier for everyone fortunate enough to come in contact with her.

I'm also grateful for the assistance of Dr. Eric Boyle at the National Museum of Health and Medicine; Matthew Goldman at Meserve-Kunhardt Foundation; Lincoln funeral train experts May Cay and Wayne Wesolowski; Maria Downs at the White House Historical Association; Michelle Ganz of Harrogate Library; Pauly Iheanacho at Morris Library of the University of Delaware; Susan Haake of the Lincoln Home National Historic Site; Rev. George E. Stuart, archivist for the Catholic Archdiocese of Washington, DC; Melissa Naulin of the Curator's Office at the White House Museum; Judy Gemmell at the Moravian Academy Archives; David Schappert and Cathy Welsko at Moravian College; Dr. Paul Peucker at Moravian Church Archives; and Laetitia Combrinck of the United Church in Washington, DC.

I owe much to the helpful researchers at the Chicago History Museum, who even pulled a piece out of storage to answer a question; to the obliging staff at the New York Historical Society; to James Mundy at the Union League of Philadelphia; o Scott Daniels at the Oregon Historical Society; and to Gwen Thompson, executive director of the Mary Todd Lincoln House in Lexington, Kentucky, who brought a tape measure from home to answer my questions with precision.

Several fellow journalists lent their talents or encouragement. I thank Mike Renshaw for reading the book with a first-rate editor's eye, Erik Larson for reviewing it, Geoffrey Johnson for allowing me use of his Chicago magazine articles, and John Sweeney for sharing his deep knowledge of American history. I also thank Denise Foley, Dick Hughes, Ron Ivey, Ken Lockerby, Anita Manning, Gary Rawlins, Ellie Reader, John Taylor, Sam Waltz, Patricia Rooney Wandling, Katherine Ward, and Karen Wilson for their encouragement.

Many historians laid the groundwork for my research, including James O. Hall, whose decades of research became the bedrock for many writers. I am also grateful for the work of Karen Getzinger, Timothy S. Good, James Edward Kelly, Clara E. Laughlin, Roger Norton, George J. Olszewski, W. Emerson Reck, Edward Steers Jr., James L. Swanson, and Nora Titone.

Many of the people instrumental in bringing this research to light are neither historians nor authors, but their work made mine possible. Chief among them is Richard Brodie, the programmer who created the search function of Microsoft Word. Without fingertip search, this book would have taken years longer. The importance of that technology crystallized for me when I turned the onion-skin pages of the David Rankin Barbee papers at Georgetown University. Mr. Barbee, who researched Abraham Lincoln from 1928 to 1958, copied newspaper articles in longhand because there were no copy machines available to him and certainly no stick drives like the ones I used to copy the same articles in seconds.

At the University Press of Kentucky, I am grateful for the help of Anne Dean Dotson, Bailey Johnson, Iris Law, Cameron Ludwick, Patrick O'Dowd, Carol Sickman-Garner, and Blair Thomas.

Thanks to friends and family members who cheered and commiserated along the way—the Reverend Michael Angeloni, Karen Beavers, Ruth Ann Bunnell, Valerie Butler, Dr. Patrick Canavan, Virginia Canavan, Virginia Delavan, Anne Dubuisson, Suzanne Duffy, Rana Fayez, Judy Fetters, Deborah Flaherty, Lisa Fleetwood, Linda George, Brother Ronald Giannone, Bobby Green, Dr. Judy Green, Barbara Hearne, Carl La Va, Susan Mahler, Lois Mayhorn, Frank McIntosh, Dan McNeil, Ziggy Mielnikiewicz, Mike Mika, Peggy Mika, Christi Milligan, Kay Moyer, Mary Murphy, Mark Nardone, Laurie Orsic, Drew Ostroski, Brother Robert Perez, Brother Rudolph Pieretti, Anthea Piscarik, Faith Pizor, Brother Miguel Ramirez, Jeanne Renshaw, Carl Schnee, Ellen Schonbach, Ray Siegfried, Avie Silver, Rachel Simon, Anne Slaton, Lucy Stone, Greg Sweeney, Matt Sweeney, and Donna Urban, who never left a flea market without scanning the stands for Lincoln photos.

Notes

In the course of research, I consulted many manuscript and records sources, chiefly including the Kiplinger Research Library at the Historical Association of Washington; the National Park Service (N.P.S.) files at Ford's Theatre; the James O. Hall Research Center in Clinton, MD; the Rare Book Room, the Manuscript Division, and the Newspapers and Periodicals Collection at the Library of Congress; and the Special Collections Research Center at Georgetown University Library. I also consulted the Chicago History Museum Research Center; the California Digital Newspaper Collection; the Smithsonian Institution Archives; the White House Museum; the Moravian Archives in Bethlehem, PA; the Free Library of Philadelphia; the New York Historical Society; the Union League of Philadelphia; the Delaware Public Archives; and the District of Columbia Archives.

1. The Secret about Booth

1. News clipping, Lincoln Assassination folder, National Park Service files, Ford's Theatre, Washington, DC (N.P.S. files hereafter).

2. Testimony of Joseph M. Dye, in *Trial of John H. Surratt*, 2 vols. (Washington, DC: French and Richardson, 1867), 1: 139.

3. J. C. Hemphill, "Deathbed Relics Here Tell of Lincoln Tragedy," *New York Times Sunday Magazine,* Feb. 9, 1913, 5.

4. Petersen Family folder, N.P.S. files; *Philadelphia Press,* Dec. 4, 1881; Louis J. Weichmann, *A True History of the Assassination of Abraham Lincoln and of the Conspiracy of 1865* (New York: Knopf, 1975), 158.

5. Hemphill, "Deathbed Relics," 5.

6. "Lincoln's Murder as I Saw It from the Stage," *San Francisco Chronicle,* Feb. 12, 1905.

7. Roeliff Brinkerhoff, *Recollections of a Lifetime* (Cincinnati: Robert Clarke, 1904), 166.

8. M. Helen Palmes Moss, "Lincoln and Wilkes Booth as Seen on the Day of the Assassination," *Century Magazine,* Apr. 1909, 952-53, Unz.org, http://www.unz.org/Pub/Century-1909apr-00950; playbill, reproduced in Moss, "Lincoln and Wilkes Booth."

9. Moss, "Lincoln and Wilkes Booth," 951–53.

10. James Tanner to Hadley F. Walch, Apr. 17, 1865 (copy), James Tanner folder, N.P.S. files.

11. Moss, "Lincoln and Wilkes Booth," 951–53.

12. Ibid., 951.

13. *Washington Post,* Apr. 16, 1905.

14. Moss, "Lincoln and Wilkes Booth," 951–53.

15. Ibid.

16. Ibid.

17. Hemphill, "Deathbed Relics."

18. *William A. Petersen House: The House Where Lincoln Died,* Historic Structure Report (Washington, DC: National Park Service, 2001), 16.

19. W. J. Ferguson, "Lincoln's Death," *Saturday Evening Post,* Feb. 12. 1927, 39; "Lincoln's Death," *Los Angeles Times,* Apr. 12, 1896.

20. W. J. Ferguson, "Lincoln's Death," 49.

21. *William A. Petersen House,* part 1A, 2, part 1B, 20.

22. *Boyd's Washington and Georgetown Directory 1865* (Washington, DC: Boyd's Directory, 1865), 412, Kiplinger Research Library, Historical Society of Washington, DC; Judy Gemmel, Moravian Academy, to author (email), n.d.; William C. Reichel and William H. Bigler, *A History of the Moravian Seminary for Young Ladies* (Bethlehem: Moravian Seminary, 1901); Petersen Family folder, N.P.S. files.

23. Clara E. Laughlin, *The Death of Lincoln* (New York: Doubleday, Page, 1909), 100; Robert T. Bain, *Lincoln's Last Battleground* (Bloomington: Author House, 2005), 16.

24. Bain, *Lincoln's Last Battleground,* 16.

25. Ibid., 14; "Paper Scrap," Lincoln Relics Registry, Chicago Historical Society, http://www.chicagohistory.org/wetwithblood/private/partners/relictable.htm (accessed 2010); Matthew R. Virta, *Archeology at the Petersen House* (Washington, DC: National Park Service, 1991), 12; Laughlin, *Death of Lincoln,* 100; "Memories of Lincoln: Furniture That Suddenly Becomes Valuable," *New York Times,* Feb. 16, 1887, http://query.nytimes.com/mem/archive-free/pdf?res=F00D10FD3C5E1A73 8DDDAF0994DA405B8784F0D3; "Corn Husk Mattress," Lincoln Relics Registry.

26. "Horrible News," *Dubuque Daily Times,* Apr. 16, 1865, Stern Collection of Lincolniana, Library of Congress, http://www.loc.gov/collection/alfred-whital-stern-lincolniana/about-this-collection/; "Northern News: An Account of Mr. Lincoln's Death by an Eye Witness," *Raleigh Daily Progress,* Apr. 27, 1865. (I frequently used the Library of Congress's extensive collection to access newspaper accounts; hereafter the Library of Congress is not specifically cited for individual newspaper articles, although I have retained the Library of Congress's URL when available.)

27. W. J. Ferguson, "The Story of the Assassination," *Independent,* Apr. 4, 1895, reprinted in *Abraham Lincoln: Tributes from His Associates, Reminiscences of Soldiers, Statesmen and Citizens* (New York: Crowell, 1895), 15–16, Internet Archive, https://archive.org/details/abrahamlincoln2415ward; "Lincoln's Death."

28. "Eyewitness Recalls Scene of Lincoln's Assassination," *Kansas City Star,* Feb. 8, 1925.

29. W. J. Ferguson, "Lincoln's Death," 37.

30. Hemphill, "Deathbed Relics," 5.

31. Petersen Family folder, N.P.S. files.

32. Harry Clay Ford, statement to investigators, Primary Source Microfilm, M599, roll 5, National Archives and Records Administration (NARA hereafter).

33. Hemphill, "Deathbed Relics," 5; Bain, *Lincoln's Last Battleground*, 16.

34. Bain, *Lincoln's Last Battleground*, 17; tour of Petersen House kitchen, May 14, 2010; Laughlin, *Death of Lincoln*, 100.

2. Washington City Then

1. *Boyd's Washington and Georgetown Directory 1865*, 404–5; John B. Ellis, *The Sights and Secrets of the National Capital* (New York: U.S. Publishing, 1869), 445; vertical files, Washingtoniana Division, Martin Luther King Jr. Memorial Library, Washington, DC.

2. Ellis, *Sights and Secrets of the National Capital*, 445.

3. Ibid., 445.

4. Gloria Swift, National Parks Service curator, Ford's Theatre, interview with the author, n.d.

5. Civil War Washington folder, N.P.S. files; "Civil War Washington Collaborative Research Grant Narrative," CivilWarDC.org, http://civilwardc .org/introductions/other/collaborative.php (accessed Dec. 1, 2013).

6. Petersen House folder, N.P.S. files.

7. "Sites of Interest in President Lincoln's Washington 1861 to 1865," Civil War Washington folder, N.P.S. files.

8. Stephen M. Forman, *Guide to Civil War Washington* (Washington, DC: Elliott & Clark, 1995), 13, 21; George S. Bryan, *The Great American Myth: The True Story of Lincoln's Murder* (New York: Carrick & Evans, 1940), 4, Internet Archive, https://archive.org/stream/greatamericanmyt00brya#page/n9/mode/2up.

9. Forman, *Guide to Civil War Washington*, 13, 21; Bryan, *Great American Myth*, 4; Diane Shields, US Department of Agriculture geologist, telephone interview with the author, n.d.

10. Bryan, *Great American Myth*, 6.

11. Stanley Kimmel, *Mr. Lincoln's Washington* (New York: Bramhall House, 1957); Jeanne Fogle, Kiplinger Research Library, guided tour of Washington, DC, Apr. 18, 2009.

12. Fogle, Kiplinger Research Library, guided tour; Edward G. Longacre, *Lincoln's Cavalrymen* (Mechanicsburg: Stackpole, 2000).

13. "Lincoln Children for Lincoln Boyhood Memorial," and "Lincoln Notebook," N.P.S. files.

14. Thomas P. Lowry, *The Civil War Bawdy Houses of Washington, D.C.* (Fredericksburg: Sgt. Kirkland's Museum and History Society, 1997), 18–20.

15. Noah Brooks, *Washington in Lincoln's Time* (Washington, DC: Century, 1895), 38.

16. Margaret Leech, *Reveille in Washington, 1860–1865* (New York: Harper & Bros., 1941), photo plates, 132–33.

17. Margaret Leech, "Wartime Washington," *Life*, Sept. 29, 1941, 92.

18. Leech, *Reveille in Washington*, 67, 68.

19. *Boyd's Washington and Georgetown Directory 1865*; "Armory Square Was a Military Hospital," n.d., History Engine, University of Richmond, http://history-engine.richmond.edu/episodes/view/5393 (accessed Apr. 1, 2014); Billy J. Harbin, "Laura Keene at the Lincoln Assassination," *Educational Theatre Journal* 18, no. 1 (Mar. 1966): 48, Jstor.org, http://www.jstor.org/discover/10.2307/3205119?uid=2&uid=4&sid=21103814871917.

20. Harbin, "Laura Keene at the Lincoln Assassination," 47.

21. Fogle, Kiplinger Research Library, tour; Garnett Laidlaw Eskew, *Willard's of Washington* (New York: Coward-McCann, 1954), 50.

22. "Sites of Interest in President Lincoln's Washington 1861 to 1865."

23. Kimmel, *Mr. Lincoln's Washington,* 19; Leech, *Reveille in Washington,* 393.

24. "Ford's Theatre History," National Park Service, http://www.fords.org/home/explore-lincoln/learn-story/fords-theatre-history (accessed Apr. 1, 2011).

25. *Boyd's Washington and Georgetown Directory 1865,* 433.

26. Kimmel, *Mr. Lincoln's Washington.*

27. G. H. Stuart, *The Life of George H. Stuart* (Philadelphia: J. M. Stoddart, 1890).

28. *Boyd's Washington and Georgetown Directory 1865,* 123.

29. Ulke folder, N.P.S. files; "Baird as Assistant Secretary and the Growth of a Dream," Smithsonian Institution, http://siarchives.si.edu/history/exhibits/baird/bairdc.htm (accessed July 10, 2012).

30. Ulke file, General Correspondence 1892–1964, R.U. 311, Box 018, Smithsonian Institution Archives; "Megatherium Club," Smithsonian Institution, http://www.150.si.edu/chap3club.htm (accessed June 10, 2012); "Family Affair," Smithsonian Institution, http://siarchives.si.edu/blog/family-affair (accessed Apr. 7, 2014).

31. Cornelius W. Heine, "Abraham Lincoln in Washington," Lincoln anniversary program, Lincoln Museum, Feb. 10, 1963, N.P.S. files.

32. Dorothy M. Kunhardt and Philip B. Kunhardt, *Twenty Days* (Secaucus: Castle, 1965), 72.

33. Heine, "Abraham Lincoln in Washington."

34. Clayton R. Newell, Charles R. Shrader, and Edward M. Coffman, *Of Duty Well and Faithfully Done: A History of the Regular Army in the Civil War* (Lincoln: University of Nebraska Press, 2011), 37.

3. The Great Illumination

1. *Meteorological Journal 1865,* Washington City Observatory, Sunday, Apr. 9, 1865–Saturday, Apr. 15, 1865.

2. Daniel Mark Epstein, *The Lincolns: Portrait of a Marriage* (New York: Ballantine, 2008), 49.

3. Tanner to Walch, Apr. 17, 1865.

4. "Mourning: Further Details of the Terrible Tragedy at Washington," *New York Herald,* Apr. 18, 1865, ProQuest Historical Newspapers. (I frequently used

ProQuest Historical Newspapers to access newspaper accounts; hereafter ProQuest is not specifically cited for individual newspaper articles.)

5. Nan Wyatt Withers, *The Acting Style and Career of John Wilkes Booth* (Madison: University of Wisconsin Press, 2009), 129.

6. Megan Gambino, "Ask an Expert: What Did Abraham Lincoln's Voice Sound Like?" Smithsonian.com, June 6, 2011, http://www.smithsonianmag.com/history/ask-an-expert-what-did-abraham-lincolns-voice-sound-like-13446201/?no-ist.

7. Testimony of Eaton G. Horner, in Benn Pitman, *The Assassination of President Lincoln and the Trial of the Conspirators* (Cincinnati: Moore, Wilstach & Baldwin, 1865), 235.

8. Charles A. Leale, US passport, issued June 4, 1877, Passport Applications 1795–1905, Record Group 59, M1372, Roll 0217, NARA; Charles A. Leale, *Lincoln's Last Hours,* Address Delivered before the Commandery of the New York State Military Order of the Loyal Legion of the United States (New York: privately printed, 1909), 2; "Armory Square Was a Military Hospital."

9. Leale, *Lincoln's Last Hours,* 2.

10. James L. Haley, *Sam Houston* (Norman: University of Oklahoma Press, 2004), 411.

11. Guy Gugliotta, "New Estimate Raises Civil War Death Toll," *New York Times,* Apr. 2, 2010, http://www.nytimes.com/2012/04/03/science/civil-war-toll-up-by-20-percent-in-new-estimate.html?_r=0; census estimate, University of Illinois, https://mste.illinois.edu/malcz/ExpFit/data.html (accessed Mar. 26, 2014).

12. *The Terrible Tragedy at Washington: Assassination of President Lincoln* (Philadelphia: Barclay, 1865), 44.

13. W. Emerson Reck, *A. Lincoln: His Last 24 Hours* (Jefferson: McFarland, 1987), 81.

14. Series 2: Lincoln Death Series, David Rankin Barbee Papers, Georgetown University Library Special Collections Research Center; Epstein, *Lincolns,* 496.

15. Ellis, *Sights and Secrets of the National Capital,* 77.

16. "The Calcium Light," *New York Times,* June 1, 1861, http://www.nytimes.com/1861/06/01/news/the-calcium-light.html.

17. Samuel J. Seymour, in Timothy S. Good, *We Saw Lincoln Shot* (Jackson: University Press of Mississippi, 1995), 55.

18. *Washington Star,* Apr. 14, 1865.

19. *Philadelphia Daily Evening Bulletin,* Apr. 4, 1865.

4. The Making of an Assassin

1. *Washington Evening Star,* Apr. 14–15, 1865.

2. Testimony of Charles H. M. Wood, in *Trial of John H. Surratt,* 1: 495–98.

3. Asia Booth Clarke, *The Unlocked Book* (New York: G. P. Putnam's Sons, 1938), 56–57.

4. Nora Titone, *My Thoughts Be Bloody* (New York: Free Press, 2010), 29–31.

5. Ibid., 32.

6. Ibid., 55–63; Withers, *Acting Style and Career of John Wilkes Booth,* 54.

7. W. J. Ferguson, "Lincoln's Death," 35–37.

8. Stanley Kimmel, *The Mad Booths of Maryland* (Indianapolis: Bobbs-Merrill, 1940), 209.

9. Ibid., 71–72; Titone, *My Thoughts Be Bloody,* 76–84.

10. Titone, *My Thoughts Be Bloody,* 80–82.

11. Ibid., 91–93.

12. Ibid., 91–93, 134–35; Clarke, *Unlocked Book,* 59.

13. Titone, *My Thoughts Be Bloody,* 134–35; *Washington Evening Star,* Dec. 7, 1881.

14. Titone, *My Thoughts Be Bloody,* 123.

15. Withers, *Acting Style and Career of John Wilkes Booth,* 62–66.

16. Titone, *My Thoughts Be Bloody,* 154.

17. *Account of the Terrific and Fatal Riot at the New-York Astor Place Opera House* (New York: Ranney, 1849), 16.

18. Titone, *My Thoughts Be Bloody,* 163.

19. "Edwin Booth and Lincoln, with an Unpublished Letter by Edwin Booth," *Century Illustrated Monthly Magazine* 77 (Nov. 1908): 119.

20. Withers, *Acting Style and Career of John Wilkes Booth,* 75.

21. John Ford, testimony, in "Investigation and Trial Papers Relating to the Assassination of President Lincoln," Record Group 153, M599, Roll 4, NARA; Withers, *Acting Style and Career of John Wilkes Booth,* 67; Titone, *My Thoughts Be Bloody,* 178.

22. Titone, *My Thoughts Be Bloody,* 179–83; Withers, *Acting Style and Career of John Wilkes Booth,* 9.

23. Withers, *Acting Style and Career of John Wilkes Booth,* 66.

24. "The Life of Philip Whitlock, Written by Himself," Jewish-American History Foundation, http://www.jewish-history.com/civilwar/philip_whitlock.html (accessed Apr. 3, 2011).

25. Ibid.

26. *Washington Evening Star,* Dec. 7, 1881.

27. W. J. Ferguson, "Lincoln's Death," 35–37.

28. Clara Morris, *My Life on the Stage* (New York: McClure, Phillips, 1901), 103.

29. Withers, *Acting Style and Career of John Wilkes Booth,* 127–28.

30. W. J. Ferguson, " Lincoln's Death," 37.

31. Ibid.

32. *Terrible Tragedy at Washington.*

33. Morris, *My Life on the Stage,* 98–100.

34. Ibid.

35. Alexander Hunter, writing in the *Portsmouth (VA) Occasional,* quoted in "Booth and Bob Lincoln," *Chicago Inter Ocean,* June 18, 1878.

36. Reck, *A. Lincoln: His Last 24 Hours,* 65.

37. Hunter, quoted in "Booth and Bob Lincoln."

38. Withers, *Acting Style and Career of John Wilkes Booth,* 66.

39. Ibid., 157.

40. Ibid., 108.

41. Ibid., 72, 137, 147, 179.

42. Ibid., 72.

43. Ibid., 179.

44. Ibid., 137.

45. John M. Barron, "With John Wilkes Booth in His Days as an Actor," *Baltimore Sun,* Mar. 17, 1907.

46. Box 30, John T. Ford Papers, Library of Congress.

47. Titone, *My Thoughts Be Bloody,* 331–32.

48. Ray Wemmlinger, curator, Player's Club, telephone interview with the author, n.d.

49. Ernest C. Miller, *John Wilkes Booth, Oilman* (New York: Exposition Press, 1923), 27, Internet Archive, https://archive.org/details/johnwilkesbootho00mill.

50. *Boston Globe,* June 17, 1878.

51. Edward Steers Jr. and William C. Edwards, eds., *The Lincoln Assassination: The Evidence* (Urbana: University of Illinois Press, 2009), 1156.

52. Harry Hawk to his father, Apr. 1865 (copy), N.P.S. files.

53. Moss, "Lincoln and Wilkes Booth."

54. *New York Day Book Caucasian,* Apr. 22, 1865, http://www.loc.gov/resource/lprbscsm.scsm1215/?st=gallery.

5. Plans and Dreams

1. *Washington Evening Star,* Dec. 7, 1881.

2. John Mathews, testimony, War Department Records (copies), Box 4, Folder 212, Barbee Papers.

3. "The Assassin Booth," *Chicago Tribune,* June 30, 1878.

4. George J. Olszewski, *Historic Structures Report: Restoration of Ford's Theatre* (Washington, DC: National Park Service, 1965), 107–22.

5. "Mourning: Further Details of the Terrible Tragedy at Washington"; *Meteorological Journal 1865,* Washington City Observatory, Sunday, Apr. 9, 1865–Saturday, Apr. 15, 1865.

6. *Washington Evening Star,* Dec. 7, 1881.

7. Good, *We Saw Lincoln Shot,* 31.

8. Thomas Proctor folder, N.P.S. files.

9. "Find Actor's Story of Lincoln's Death," *New York Times,* Feb. 14, 1926.

10. H. W. Brands, *Andrew Jackson: His Life and Times* (New York: Doubleday, 2005), 503–4; Jon Meacham, *American Lion* (New York: Random House, 2008), 298–99.

11. Object Report 29.1451.1, Collections of Henry Ford, Henry Ford Museum, Dearborn, MI; Stephanie Lucas, research specialist, Henry Ford Museum, interview with the author, n.d.; Pitman, *Assassination of President Lincoln*, 75.

12. "Ford's Theatre," National Park Service, http://www.nps.gov/foth/faqs.htm (accessed Dec. 12, 2012); tour of Ford's Theatre, 1991.

13. Gustave Dieterich to *New York Sun*, from the scrapbook of Dieterich's sister K. Gotthielde Barthel, Petersen Family folder, N.P.S. files.

14. "The Metropolis of Today," *Illustrated New York* (1888): 254, available in collection edited by International Publishing, New York, Internet Archive, http://archive.org/stream/illustratednewy00unkngoog/illustratednewy00unkngoog_djvu.txt; Dieterich to *New York Sun*.

15. James C. Ferguson, testimony, and James Tanner, notes (copies), both courtesy of Union League of Philadelphia.

16. Joseph H. Hazelton, "The Assassination of President Lincoln," *Good Housekeeping*, Feb. 1927, N.P.S. files.

17. "Interview with W. J. Ferguson," *Independent*, Apr. 4, 1895.

18. Hemphill, "Deathbed Relics."

19. "Where Lincoln Walked," *Washington Post*, Feb. 10, 1989.

20. Hemphill, "Deathbed Relics."

21. John Mathews, testimony, in *Trial of John H. Surratt*, 2: 821–22; Pitman, *Assassination of President Lincoln*, 44.

22. John Mathews file, James O. Hall Collection, James O. Hall Research Center, Surratt House Museum, Clinton, MD; John Mathews, testimony, in *Trial of John H. Surratt*, 2: 821–22.

23. "An Actor's Reminiscences of the Crazy Assassin of Lincoln," *Boonville Weekly Advertiser*, May 20, 1881, John Mathews folder, N.P.S. files.

24. John Mathews, testimony, in *Trial of John H. Surratt*, 2: 821–22; Pitman, *Assassination of President Lincoln*, 44.

25. John Mathews, testimony, in *Trial of John H. Surratt*, 2: 821–22.

26. Dieterich to *New York Sun*.

27. Associated Press, "1846 Carriage to Return to Public Display," *USAToday.com*, Feb. 7, 2008, http://usatoday30.usatoday.com/travel/news/2008-02-07-lincoln-carriage_N.htm; Drew van De Wielle, interview with the author, n.d. (The carriage was never restored to its original colors.)

28. *Meteorological Journal 1865*, Washington City Observatory, Sunday, Apr. 9, 1865–Saturday, Apr. 15, 1865.

29. Emily Todd Helm, "Mary Todd Lincoln," *McClure's*, Sept. 1898.

30. Bessie L. Putnam, "Lincoln Exercises," *Journal of Education* 71, no. 2 (Jan. 13, 1910): 40; Leslie W. Dunlap, "Lincoln's Autobiography," *Quarterly Journal of Current Acquisition* 4, no. 3 (May 1947): 57; John G. Nicolay, "Lincoln's Personal Appearance," *Century Magazine* (Oct. 1891); F. B. Carpenter, *Six Months at the White House* (New York: Hurd and Houghton, 1866), 333; T. D. Stewart, *An Anthropologist Looks at Lincoln* (Washington, DC: Government

Printing Office, 1952), 432–35; Charles Snyder, "Abe's Eyes," *Arch Ophthalmology* 75 (Feb. 1966).

31. Gambino, "Ask an Expert."

32. Carl Sandburg, *Mary Lincoln: Wife and Widow* (New York: Harcourt, Brace, 1932), 38.

33. Kunhardt and Kunhardt, *Twenty Days,* 67.

34. Douglas L. Wilson, "William H. Herndon and Mary Todd Lincoln," *Journal of the Abraham Lincoln Association* 22, no. 2 (Summer 2001).

35. Harry E. Pratt, *The Personal Finances of Abraham Lincoln* (Springfield: Abraham Lincoln Association, 1943), 3.

36. Claude S. Fischer, *Made in America: A Social History of American Culture and Character* (Chicago: University of Chicago Press, 2010), 66; David Herbert Donald, *Lincoln* (New York: Simon and Schuster, 1995), 38–60.

37. John G. Nicolay and John Hay, *Abraham Lincoln, A History* (New York: Century, 1905), 1: 43.

38. Stephen Dickey, "Shakespeare's Influence on Abraham Lincoln," Folger Shakespeare Library, http://www.folger.edu/template.cfm?cid=3137 (accessed July 9, 2011).

39. Katharine Helm, *Mary, Wife of Lincoln* (New York: Harper & Bros., 1918), 44–58.

40. Gwen Thompson, director of Mary Todd Lincoln House, Lexington, KY, telephone interview with the author, n.d.

41. "History," Mary Todd Lincoln House, http://www.mtlhouse.org/history.html (accessed June 5, 2013).

42. Ronald D. Reitveld, "The Lincoln White House Community," *Journal of the Abraham Lincoln Association* 7, no. 2 (Summer 1999): http://quod.lib.umich.edu/j/jala/2629860.0020.204/—lincoln-white-house-community?rgn|=main;view=fulltext.

43. Jason Emerson, "Mary Todd Lincoln," *Times Topics,* http://topics.nytimes.com/top/reference/timestopics/people/1/mary_todd_lincoln/ (accessed June 2, 2013); Dan Guillory, "Courtship and Politics: Lincoln and Douglas as Suitors," *Illinois Heritage* (Jan.–Feb. 2004), Illinois Periodicals Online, http://www.lib.niu.edu/2004/ih011004.html.

44. Ward Hill Lamon, *Recollections of Abraham Lincoln, 1847–1865* (Chicago: A. C. McClurg, 1895), 231.

45. K. Helm, *Mary, Wife of Lincoln,* 100.

46. Abraham Lincoln, "Buoying Vessels over Shoals," US Patent No. 6469, issued May 22, 1849.

47. Forman, *Guide to Civil War Washington,* 104.

48. Catherine Clinton, *Mrs. Lincoln: A Life* (New York: Harper Collins, 2009), 184–87.

49. K. Helm, *Mary, Wife of Lincoln,* 101.

50. Leonard Grover, "Lincoln's Interest in the Theater," *Century Magazine* 77 (Nov. 1908–Apr. 1909): 942.

51. Reitveld, "Lincoln White House Community."

52. Smith Stimmel, *Personal Reminiscences of Abraham Lincoln* (Minneapolis: William H. M. Adams, 1928), 39–40; Forman, *Guide to Civil War Washington,* 90–91.

53. K. Helm, *Mary, Wife of Lincoln,* 101.

54. Kunhardt and Kunhardt, *Twenty Days,* 72.

55. Carpenter, *Six Months at the White House,* 293.

56. K. Helm, *Mary, Wife of Lincoln,* 225.

57. Elizabeth Keckley, *Behind the Scenes* (New York: G. W. Carleton, 1868), 101.

58. Julia Gates Green, *Abraham Lincoln on the Niagara Frontier* (n.p., n.d.), 3–4, Library of Congress, http://lccn.loc.gov/32009746.

59. "The California Bear Flag," Virtual Museum of the City of San Francisco, http://www.sfmuseum.org/hist6/toddflag.html (accessed June 6, 2013).

60. Pratt, *Personal Finances of Abraham Lincoln,* 13.

61. Ibid., 40.

62. Sculptor James E. Kelly's interviews with Civil War generals, in William B. Styple, ed., *Generals in Bronze: Interviewing the Commanders of the Civil War* (Kearny: Belle Grove, 2005), 180.

6. Nothing Exactly According to Plan

1. The Church of Jesus Christ of Latter-Day Saints, "Vital Records Index: Individual Record: Washington, D.C. birth records," Microfilm 1994617; Ninth Census of the United States, 1870, Washington, DC, Ancestry.com (accessed at Delaware State Archives, June 2011); Karen Getzinger, "Anna Petersen: Her Life in Washington, D.C. and the Petersen Boarding House," N.P.S. files.

2. William Petersen obituary, *New York Times,* June 19, 1871.

3. Jesse W. Weik, "A New Story of the Lincoln Assassination," *Century Magazine* (Feb. 1913): 561, http://books.google.com/books?id=iL5AAQAAMAAJ&pg=PA483&lpg=PA483&dq=century+magazine+february+1913&source=bl&ots=vnpsEpMovx&sig=3A1YeTkCwy5aBPxE8snLsFlzEM8&hl=en&sa=X&ei=L_XrU7HiDMGMyASrqYDIDQ&ved=0CDoQ6AEwCA#v=onepage&q=sic%20semper%20tyrannis&f=false.

4. *Trial of John H. Surratt,* 1: 176–78.

5. Ibid.

7. Shuffling History

1. *New York Day Book Caucasian,* Apr. 22, 1865.

2. *Louisville Daily Union Press,* Apr. 17, 1865, http://www.loc.gov/item/scsm001223/.

3. "Mourning: Further Details of the Terrible Tragedy at Washington."

4. *Trial of John H. Surratt,* 1: 329.

5. Col. G. V. Rutherford, statement, and Report of James Tanner before Chief Justice Carter, both Lincoln Assassination Eyewitness Accounts, N.P.S. files.

6. John Wilkes Booth's key ring, displayed at the Ford's Theatre Collection, Center for Education and Leadership, Washington, DC.

7. "Edwin Booth and Lincoln," 919.

8. Bain, *Lincoln's Last Battleground,* 1.

9. Ibid., 11.

10. *Boyd's Washington and Georgetown Directory 1865,* 3, 199.

11. William C. Davis to James O. Hall, 1996, James O. Hall Research Center.

12. Kunhardt and Kunhardt, *Twenty Days,* 47; Henry Safford to Osborn Oldroyd, June 25, 1903, N.P.S. files.

13. Unidentifiable 1909 news clipping, Henry Safford folder, N.P.S. files.

14. Clarke, *Unlocked Book,* 168–69.

15. Ulke folder, N.P.S. files; Joe Nickell, *A Handbook for Photographic Investigation* (Lexington: University Press of Kentucky, 2005), 121.

16. Unidentified newspaper clipping, William Clark folder, N.P.S. files.

17. Dr. Charles Sabin Taft to Osborne Oldroyd, N.P.S. files; Col. George Rutherford, statement, N.P.S. files; Charles S. Taft, *Abraham Lincoln's Last Hours* (Chicago: privately printed, 1934), 11; Kunhardt and Kunhardt, *Twenty Days,* 47.

18. David Rankin Barbee, "Lincoln and Booth" (unfinished manuscript), 778, Box 15, Barbee Papers; tour of Petersen House, May 14, 2010; Hemphill, "Deathbed Relics."

19. Stanley McClure, *The Lincoln Museum and the House Where Lincoln Died* (Washington, DC: National Park Service, 1949), 38.

8. The Turning of the Tide

1. "Lincoln's Murder as I Saw It from the Stage."

2. Ibid.

3. Ibid.

4. Harbin, "Laura Keene at the Lincoln Assassination," 47–54.

5. Notes of sculptor James E. Kelly's May 4, 1887, interview with William J. Ferguson (copy), courtesy of New York Historical Society.

6. Edward Steers Jr., *The Lincoln Assassination Encyclopedia* (New York: Harper Perennial, 2010), 430–31; *Boyd's Washington and Georgetown Directory 1865,* 5.

7. Olszewski, *Restoration of Ford's Theatre,* 56.

8. "John Wilkes Booth's Other Victim," *Broadway Magazine,* May 1904, N.P.S. files; "An Unsung Song Prevented Panic When Lincoln Was Shot," *San Jose Evening News,* Feb. 12, 1912, America's Historical Newspapers.

9. Titone, *My Thoughts Be Bloody,* 150–51, 350.

10. Booth's horn-handled dagger and its sheath can be found in the museum collection at the Ford's Theatre National Historic Site in Washington, DC.

9. Looking Forward to a Memorable Evening

1. Leale, *Lincoln's Last Hours*, 2.

2. Ibid., 3.

3. Ibid., 2–3.

4. Irving A. Watson, *Physicians and Surgeons of America* (Concord: Republican Press Association, 1896), 36.

5. Collection, Ford's Theatre Museum; "White House Coffee Cup," Smithsonian Institution, http://collections.si.edu/search/record/nmah_515538 (accessed Jan. 4, 2011).

6. George R. Brown, *Reminiscences of Senator William M. Stewart of Nevada* (New York: Neale, 1908), 190, 224.

7. Edward Steers Jr., *Blood on the Moon: The Assassination of Abraham Lincoln* (Lexington: University Press of Kentucky, 2001), 98.

8. U. S. Grant, *Personal Memoirs of U. S. Grant* (Cleveland: World, 1952), 565.

9. *Danville (IL) Commercial News*, Dec. 9, 1921, Robert Lincoln folder, N.P.S. files.

10. Robert T. Lincoln to Dr. J. G. Holland, June 6, 1865, in Rufus Rockwell Wilson, *Intimate Memories of Lincoln* (Elmira: Primavera, Elmira, 1945), 499, Internet Archive, https://archive.org/stream/intimatememories00wils#page/498/mode/2up/search/holland.

11. *Danville Commercial News*, Dec. 9, 1921.

12. Thomas Keneally, *American Scoundrel: The Life of the Notorious Civil War General Dan Sickles* (New York: Doubleday, 2002), 300–301.

13. *Meteorological Journal 1865*, Washington City Observatory, Sunday, Apr. 9, 1865–Saturday, Apr. 15, 1865.

14. Affidavit of Maj. Henry R. Rathbone, Apr. 17, 1865, in Steers and Edwards, *Lincoln Assassination*, 1080.

15. Van De Wielle, interview.

16. Clara Harris, letter, Apr. 25, 1865 (copy), courtesy of New York Historical Society.

17. Michael Burlingame, *Abraham Lincoln: A Life, Vol. 2* (Baltimore: Johns Hopkins University Press, 2008), 802.

18. Clara Harris, letter, Apr. 29, 1865 (copy), Clara Harris Rathbone folder, N.P.S files.

19. John H. Ketcham, *The Life of Abraham Lincoln* (1884; rpt., London: Forgotten Books, 2008), 428–30.

20. Reck, *A. Lincoln: His Last 24 Hours*, 81.

21. Olszewski, *Restoration of Ford's Theatre*, 7.

22. Ibid., 5.

23. Ibid., 9.

24. Leech, *Reveille in Washington*, 438.

25. Olszewski, *Restoration of Ford's Theatre*, 11.

26. Ibid., 19.

27. Ibid., 33.

28. Ibid., 45.

29. George Francis to Josephine (his niece), May 5, 1865, copy courtesy of Chicago Historical Society.

30. Olszewski, *Restoration of Ford's Theatre*, 26; Thomas A. Bogar, *Backstage at the Lincoln Assassination* (Washington, DC: Regnery History, 2013), 23.

31. Olszewski, *Restoration of Ford's Theatre*, 53; Steers, *Blood on the Moon*, 98, 107.

32. Benjamin Poore, ed., *The Conspiracy Trial for the Murder of the President*, 3 vols. (Boston: J. E. Tilton, 1865) 2: 91.

10. Booth's End Game

1. Untitled newspaper clipping, Henry Safford folder, N.P.S. files; Dr. J. Rush Shanahan (grandson of Annie Sardo), interview with the author, n.d.

2. Carpenter, *Six Months at the White House*, 325.

3. Stern Collection of Lincolniana.

4. Snyder, "Abe's Eyes."

5. Michael E. Ruane, "Tracing Lincoln's Footprints," *Washington Post*, May 14, 2009.

6. J. B. Wright, scrapbook, N.P.S. files; "Lincoln's Murder as I Saw It from the Stage."

7. Captain Joseph R. Findley, eyewitness account, Lincoln Assassination Eyewitness Accounts, N.P.S. files.

8. J. B. Wright, scrapbook, N.P.S. files; "Lincoln's Murder as I Saw It from the Stage."

9. Captain Oliver Gatch, eyewitness account, in "Accounts of the Assassination of Abraham Lincoln," Lincoln Financial Foundation Collection, 183, Internet Archive, https://archive.org/stream/accountsofassassefhlinc#page/n5/mode/2up (accessed Aug. 8, 2014).

10. "Lincoln's Murder as I Saw It from the Stage"; J. B. Wright, scrapbook, N.P.S. files.

11. Julia Shepherd, letter, Apr. 16, 1865, *Century Magazine* (Apr. 1909), Unz .org, http://www.unz.org/Pub/Century-1909apr-00917.

12. *Trial of John H. Surratt*, 1: 571.

11. 'Tis the Wink of an Eye

1. J. B. Wright, scrapbook, N.P.S. files; "Lincoln's Murder as I Saw It from the Stage."

2. Ruane, "Tracing Lincoln's Footprints."

3. J. E. Buckingham Sr., *Reminiscences and Souvenirs of the Assassination of Abraham Lincoln* (Washington, DC: Darby, 1894), 13.

4. A. S. Crawford, testimony, Tanner notes, copy courtesy of Union League of Philadelphia.

5. Helen Truman Wynkoop, letter to the editor, *Los Angeles Times,* Feb. 16, 1916; "Eyewitness Recalls Scene of Lincoln's Assassination"; Keckley, *Behind the Scenes,* 30. (Keckley described the dress slightly differently, as a black-and-white-striped silk.)

6. Nicolay and Hay, *Abraham Lincoln,* 10: 295.

7. Ibid., 295.

8. Olszewski, *Restoration of Ford's Theatre,* 45.

9. Artifacts in the museum collection, Ford's Theatre National Historic Site, Washington, DC.

10. Nicolay and Hay, *Abraham Lincoln,* 10: 299; Dr. J. J. Woodward, autopsy report, National Institutes of Health, http://www.nlm.nih.gov/visibleproofs /galleries/cases/lincoln.html (accessed Aug. 8, 2014).

11. Affidavit of Maj. Henry R. Rathbone, Apr. 17, 1865, in Steers and Edwards, *Lincoln Assassination,* 1080.

12. Ibid.

13. L. P. Brockett, *The Life and Times of Abraham Lincoln* (Philadelphia: Bradley, 1865), 620.

14. James Ferguson, statement to investigators, Conspiracy Trial Testimony, M599, Roll 7, NARA.

15. Miss Clara Harris, affidavit, Apr. 17, 1865, Lincoln Assassination Eyewitness Accounts, N.P.S. files.

16. "The Washington Diary of Horatio Nelson Taft," 3 vols., June 1, 1864–May 30, 1865, vol. 3, entry for Apr. 30, 1865, Manuscript Division, Library of Congress, http://www.loc.gov/resource/mtaft.mtaft3/#seq-106 (accessed Apr. 2, 2012).

17. J. Ferguson, statement to investigators; Barron, "With John Wilkes Booth in His Days as an Actor."

18. "The Rathbone Tragedy: A Reminiscence of the Unfortunate Man's Life Here," *Washington Post,* Dec. 30, 1883.

19. *Terrible Tragedy at Washington,* 23; invalid pension records, June 27, 1890, application, NARA.

20. "Rathbone Tragedy."

21. Helen Du Barry, eyewitness account, in Good, *We Saw Lincoln Shot,* 52–55.

22. Invalid pension records, June 27, 1890, NARA; C. Harris, affidavit, Apr. 17, 1865.

23. J. Ferguson, statement to investigators; Barron, "With John Wilkes Booth in His Days as an Actor."

24. W. J. Ferguson, "Story of the Assassination."

25. W. J. Ferguson, "Lincoln's Death," 37.

26. Edwin Bates to Mr. and Mrs. Jacob Bates of Derby, VT (his parents), Apr. 15, 1865, Lincoln Assassination Eyewitness Accounts, N.P.S. files.

27. W. J. Ferguson, "Story of the Assassination," 37.

28. Ibid., 37.

29. "Find Actor's Story of Lincoln's Death."

30. Olszewski, *Restoration of Ford's Theatre,* 45.

31. "This Man Saw Lincoln Shot," *Good Housekeeping,* Feb. 1927, 20–21, 112, 115–16, 121–22.

32. Charles A. Leale to Benjamin Butler, July 20, 1865, Lincoln Assassination Eyewitness Accounts, N.P.S. files.

33. Good, *We Saw Lincoln Shot,* 173–74.

34. Ibid., 129; undated newspaper clipping from *Washington Post,* Assassination folder, N.P.S. files.

35. "Lucille Ball Episode," *I've Got a Secret,* Samuel J. Seymour, interview, Feb. 9, 1956, CBS, Internet Archive, https://archive.org/details/Game_Show_Lucille_Ball (accessed May 5, 2013).

36. Hawk to his father, Apr. 1865 (copy); W. J. Ferguson, "Story of the Assassination."

37. Wynkoop, letter to the editor, *Los Angeles Times,* Feb. 16, 1916; "Actress, Who Played before Lincoln on Fateful Night, Tells of Horror," unidentified 1923 newspaper clipping, N.P.S. files.

38. W. J. Ferguson file, quote from *Americana Magazine,* 1902, William Ferguson folder, N.P.S. files.

39. "Lincoln's Murder as I Saw It from the Stage."

40. Hawk to his father, Apr. 1865 (copy); W. J. Ferguson, "Story of the Assassination."

41. Lt. John J. Toffey to his grandmother, Apr. 20, 1865, courtesy of Toffey family.

42. Lt. John J. Toffey to his parents, Apr. 17, 1865, courtesy of Toffey family.

43. C. Harris, affidavit, Apr. 17, 1865.

44. "John Wilkes Booth's Other Victim."

45. Pitman, *Assassination of President Lincoln,* 421.

46. "Find Actor's Story of Lincoln's Death."

47. Testimony of Mrs. Mary Ann Turner, 1865, in "Investigation and Trial Papers Relating to the Assassination of President Abraham Lincoln."

48. Harriet R. Davis, "Civil War Recollections of a Little Yankee," 44–45, records of the Columbia Historical Society, 1942–43.

12. Thunderstruck

1. Lincoln Assassination Eyewitness Accounts, N.P.S. files.

2. Olszewski, *Restoration of Ford's Theatre,* 60.

3. "Ford's Theatre," National Park Service.

4. W. J. Ferguson, "Story of the Assassination."

5. Dr. Charles A. Leale, report on assassination, Apr. 15, 1865, Record Group 112, Office of the Surgeon General 1775–1959, entry 12, Letters Received 1818–1889, NARA.

6. Du Barry, eyewitness account, in Good, *We Saw Lincoln Shot*, 52–55.

7. "Actress, Who Played before Lincoln on Fateful Night."

8. Olszewski, *Restoration of Ford's Theatre*, 103.

9. "Lincoln's Murder as I Saw It from the Stage."

10. W. J. Ferguson, "Lincoln's Death."

11. Leale, *Lincoln's Last Hours*, 4.

12. Ibid., 5.

13. Ibid., 5; William Kent to his mother, Apr. 15, 1865, Lincoln Assassination Eyewitness Accounts, N.P.S. files.

14. Kent to his mother, Apr. 15, 1865; Leale, *Lincoln's Last Hours*, 6.

15. Daniel D. Beekman, speech delivered Feb. 11, 1915, Lincoln Assassination Eyewitness Accounts, N.P.S. files.

16. Leale, *Lincoln's Last Hours*, 6.

17. Styple, *Generals in Bronze*, 303-5; Dr. Charles A. Leale, interview with James E. Kelly, Jan. 20, 1922 (copy), courtesy of New York Historical Society.

18. Leale, *Lincoln's Last Hours*, 7.

19. "Lincoln's Assassination," *St. Louis Globe Democrat*, Dec. 3, 1891.

20. Emma Rawson (Laura Keene's daughter), letter to *Philadelphia Weekly Times*, Laura Keene Papers, Manuscript Collection, Library of Congress.

21. "Washington Diary of Horatio Nelson Taft," vol. 3, entry for Apr. 30, 1865.

22. "Lincoln's Murder as I Saw It from the Stage."

23. James P. Ferguson folder, N.P.S. files.

24. Frank Kaylor (Colonel Pren Metham's great-grandson), "80th Ohio Volunteer Infantry," Ancestry.com, http://freepages.genealogy.rootsweb.ancestry .com/~keller/ovi80/work/metham.html (accessed Aug. 8, 2013); Good, *We Saw Lincoln Shot*, 99–100.

25. Bryan, *Great American Myth*, 182; James S. Knox to family member, Apr. 15, 1865, Abraham Lincoln Papers, Library of Congress.

26. Pitman, *Assassination of President Lincoln*, 79–80.

27. *New York Day Book Caucasian*, Apr. 22, 1865.

28. "Terrible News: President Lincoln Assassinated at Ford's Theatre," *Chicago Tribune*, Apr. 17, 1865.

29. Michael W. Kauffman, *American Brutus* (New York: Random House, 2004), 12–13.

30. *Terrible Tragedy at Washington*, 87.

31. *Ohio State Archaeological & Historical Society Quarterly* 30 (1921): 3, Internet Archive, https://archive.org/stream/ohioarchologic300hio#page/n3/ mode/2up.

32. George E. Dorrance to his sister Hattie, Apr. 15, 1865, Lincoln Assassination Eyewitness Accounts, N.P.S. files.

33. Shepherd, letter, Apr. 16, 1865.

34. Kitty Brink, recollections, *Spartanburg (SC) Herald-Journal*, Feb. 17, 1935, N.P.S. files.

35. Good, *We Saw Lincoln Shot*, 52.

36. Charles Sanford, letter, Apr. 16, 1865, N.P.S. files; W. Henry Pearce, letter, Apr. 16, 1865, "A Northerner Responds to the Assassination of President Lincoln," Gilder Lehrman Institute of American History, https://www.gilderlehrman.org/collections/e7c02156-bc65–4584–8214–523998452927 (accessed Apr. 14, 2014).

37. *Trial of John H. Surratt*, 1: 571–72.

38. Peter Taltavul, statement, in Steers and Edwards, *Lincoln Assassination*, 1258–59.

39. "Det. McDevitt's Recollections Following the Assassination," *Washington Star*, Apr. 14, 1894.

40. Captain Joseph R. Findley, eyewitness account.

13. Their Precious Burden

1. Reck, *A. Lincoln: His Last 24 Hours*, 126.

2. Shanahan, interview.

3. Getzinger, "Anna Petersen"; "Charles W. Petersen, War Dept Clerk, Died of Heart Disease at His Home in Washington, D.C.," *Washington Times*, Dec. 4, 1903.

4. Kunhardt and Kunhardt, *Twenty Days*, 98.

5. Steers, *Blood on the Moon*, 122; "Man Who Bore Dying Lincoln Dead at 90," *Washington (PA) Herald*, Jan. 10, 1936.

6. Leale, *Lincoln's Last Hours*, 7.

7. "Falls Church Woman Who Saw Lincoln Shot Relives That Tragic Night Every Feb. 12," Abraham Lincoln Relics, vol. 4, Washingtoniana Division, Martin Luther King Jr. Memorial Library.

8. Al Daggett, letter, Apr. 16, 1865, in *Lincoln Lore* (Bulletin of the Lincoln National Life Foundation) (Apr. 1961), N.P.S. files.

9. "Unsung Song Prevented Panic."

10. *Boston Sunday Globe*, Apr. 11, 1915.

11. Keith Erekson, *Everybody's History: Indiana's Lincoln Inquiry and the Quest to Reclaim a President's Past* (Amherst: University of Massachusetts Press, 2012), 66–67. (The letter is listed as in the collection of the Southwestern Indiana Historical Society, but staff could find no copy there or in the Indiana Historical Society collection.)

12. "Eyewitness Recalls Scene of Lincoln's Assassination."

13. Shanahan, interview.

14. Frances Rector Fraser (granddaughter of William Petersen), interview, *Seattle Post Intelligencer*, Jan. 7, 1934, Petersen Family folder, N.P.S. files.

15. George Francis to Josephine (his niece), May 5, 1865.

16. Shanahan, interview.

17. Charles A. Leale, US passport.

18. Leale, *Lincoln's Last Hours*, 8; *Meteorological Journal 1865*, Washington City Observatory, Friday, Apr. 14.

19. *Meteorological Journal 1865,* Washington City Observatory, Friday, Apr. 14.

20. William H. DeMotte, "The Assassination of Abraham Lincoln," *Journal of the Illinois State Historical Society* 20, no. 2 (Oct. 1927): 422–28, Jstor.org, http://www.jstor.org/discover/10.2307/40186927?searchUri=%2Faction%2FdoBasicSearch%3FQuery%3Dthe%2Bassassination%2Bof%2Babraham%2Blincoln%252C%2Bwilliam%2Bdemotte%26amp%3Bacc%3Doff%26amp%3Bwc%3Don%26amp%3Bfc%3Doff&resultItemClick=true&Search=yes&searchText=the&searchText=assassination&searchText=of&searchText=abraham&searchText=lincoln%252C&searchText=william&searchText=demotte&uid=2134&uid=2&uid=70&uid=4&sid=21103863632537.

21. "Man Who Saw Abe Lincoln Assassinated," in "Accounts of the Assassination of Abraham Lincoln."

22. Shepherd, letter, Apr. 16, 1865.

23. George Francis to Josephine (his niece), May 5, 1865.

24. *Washington Star,* Jan. 24, 1909; Laughlin, *Death of Lincoln,* 100.

25. Unidentified newspaper clipping, George Alfred Townsend scrapbook, Manuscript Division, Library of Congress.

26. Unidentified newspaper clipping, Townsend scrapbook; *Washington Evening Star,* Dec. 7, 1881; *Philadelphia Press,* Dec. 4, 1881; *Chicago Tribune,* Dec. 4, 1881; Ford's Theatre files, John Mathews file, Hall Collection; "Assassin Booth."

27. "John Wilkes Booth's Other Victim."

28. "Lincoln's Murder as I Saw It from the Stage."

29. Ibid.

30. Steers and Edwards, *Lincoln Assassination,* 516.

31. Laughlin, *Death of Lincoln,* 100.

32. George Francis to Josephine (his niece), May 5, 1865.

33. "Baltimore Woman Says Lincoln Died in Her Bed in Washington," *Baltimore Sun,* Oct 3, 1921; "Lincoln Died in Her Bed, Baltimore Woman Says," *New York Times,* Oct. 3, 1921; Bain, *Lincoln's Last Battleground,* 11–17.

34. Wallpaper sample, Chicago Historical Society.

35. "Evaluation of Bed on Which Lincoln Died," July 14, 1988, conservation report, D. F. Greeley Conservation, Evanston, IL, courtesy of Chicago Historical Society.

36. Leale, *Lincoln's Last Hours,* 8.

37. "Evaluation of Bed on Which Lincoln Died"; Leale, *Lincoln's Last Hours,* 11–12.

38. Bain, *Lincoln's Last Battleground,* 11–17.

39. George Francis to Josephine (his niece), May 5, 1865.

40. Safford to Oldroyd, June 25, 1903.

41. George Francis to Josephine (his niece), May 5, 1865.

42. Gideon Welles, *The Diary of Gideon Welles,* 3 vols. (New York: Houghton Mifflin, 1911), 2: 286, entry for Apr. 14–15, 1865.

43. Grover, "Lincoln's Interest in the Theater," 948.

44. Ward Hill Lamon, *Recollections of Abraham Lincoln, 1847–1865* (Chicago:

A. C. McClurg, 1895), 231; Donald T. Phillips, *Lincoln on Leadership* (New York: Warner, 1993), 31.

45. *Louisville Daily Union Press,* Apr. 17, 1865.

46. Tanner to Walch, Apr. 17, 1865; Leale, *Lincoln's Last Hours,* 11; Welles, *Diary,* 2: 286.

47. Tour of kitchen, Petersen House; Hemphill, "Deathbed Relics"; Dr. Robert Stone, letter, Apr. 15, 1865, Shapell Manuscript Foundation, http://www.shapell .org/manuscript.aspx?doctor-of-abraham-lincoln-obervation-of-presidents-last-hours-alive-and-postmortem.

48. Maunsell Field, *Memories of Many Men and of Some Women* (London: Sampson, Low, Marston, Low & Searle, 1874), 321–27.

49. Ibid., 321–27.

50. Ishbel Ross, *President's Wife: Mary Todd Lincoln* (New York: Putnam, 1973), 242.

51. Brown, *Reminiscences of Senator William M. Stewart of Nevada,* 192.

52. C. C. Bangs, reminiscences, Lincoln Assassination Eyewitness Accounts, N.P.S. files.

53. Jason Emerson, *Giant in the Shadows: The Life of Robert T. Lincoln* (Carbondale: Southern Illinois University Press, 2012), 101; C. C. Bangs, reminiscences.

54. Betty J. Ownsbey, *Alias Paine: Lewis Thornton Powell, the Mystery Man of the Lincoln Conspiracy* (Jefferson: McFarland, 1993) 79–86; Steers and Edwards, *Lincoln Assassination,* 362; Wesley Harris, "Tools of the Assassin, Part II," paper presented at the Surratt Society Annual Lincoln Assassination Conference, 2013.

55. Alfred Cloughley, statement, N.P.S. files.

56. Good, *We Saw Lincoln Shot,* 152.

57. Brown, *Reminiscences of Senator William M. Stewart of Nevada,* 19.

58. Welles, *Diary,* 2: 290.

59. "Lincoln Assassination," *New York Herald,* Apr. 15, 1865.

60. Brockett, *Life and Times of Abraham Lincoln,* 621.

61. Edmund E. Schreiner, interview, *Washington Daily News,* Feb. 13, 1933.

62. Poore, *Conspiracy Trial for the Murder of the President,* 190.

63. Styple, *Generals in Bronze,* 285.

64. Reck, *A. Lincoln: His Last 24 Hours,* 132.

65. Petersen House file, N.P.S. files.

66. Reck, *A. Lincoln: His Last 24 Hours,* 132.

67. Clara Harris, letter, Apr. 25, 1865 (copy).

68. Shanahan, interview.

69. Ibid.; accession file: Sardo pillow, collection, Ford's Theatre Museum.

70. "One of Last to See Lincoln Succumbs," unidentified newspaper clipping, Omaha, May 13, 1929, N.P.S. files.

71. Bryan, *Great American Myth,* 202.

72. Tour of upper floors, Petersen House, May 14, 2010.

73. Bryan, *Great American Myth,* 202.

74. *The Great Impeachment and Trial of Andrew Johnson* (Philadelphia: T. B. Peterson, 1868), 782–83.

75. *Washington Evening Star,* Dec. 7, 1881; *Philadelphia Press,* Dec. 4, 1881; Weichmann, *True History of the Assassination,* 158–59.

76. *Great Impeachment and Trial of Andrew Johnson,* 782–83.

77. *Washington Evening Star,* Dec. 7, 1881; *Philadelphia Press,* Dec. 4, 1881; Weichmann, *True History of the Assassination,* 158–59.

78. *Philadelphia Press,* Dec. 4, 1881.

79. *Boyd's Washington and Georgetown Directory 1865,* 433.

80. Unidentified newspaper clipping, Townsend scrapbook.

81. Ridgate (no first name provided), letters, N.P.S. files; recounting of *New York Herald* article, June 25, 1878, N.P.S. files; Weichmann, *True History of the Assassination,* 202.

82. *Washington Evening Star,* June 9, 1893.

83. *Once a Week* 7, no. 1 (n.d.), N.P.S. files.

84. Collection, Chicago Historical Society.

85. Melissa Naulin, researcher, White House Office of the Curator, interview with the author, n.d.

86. National Park Service documents, N.P.S. files.

87. Petersen House folder, N.P.S. files.

88. Leale, *Lincoln's Last Hours,* 8; Hemphill, "Deathbed Relics"; Horatio N. Taft, "Washington during the Civil War: The Diary of Horatio Nelson Taft, 1861–1865," Manuscript Division, Library of Congress.

89. Field, *Memories of Many Men and of Some Women,* 324.

90. Dr. Charles A. Leale, quoted in an unidentified article, N.P.S. files; Kunhardt and Kunhardt, *Twenty Days,* 49.

91. Stone, letter, Apr. 15, 1865.

92. Hugh McCullough, *Men and Measures of Half a Century* (New York: Scribner's, 1889), 222–24.

93. Brockett, *Life and Times of Abraham Lincoln,* 623.

94. *Louisville Daily Union Press,* Apr. 17, 1865.

95. James Tanner, "Tanner Also Present," *Washington Post,* Apr. 16, 1905; Bain, *Lincoln's Last Battleground,* 19.

96. Pauline Petersen Wenzing, interview, unidentified newspaper, Petersen Family folder, N.P.S. files.

97. Bain, *Lincoln's Last Battleground,* 14–21.

98. Taft to Oldroyd, Oldroyd folder, N.P.S. files; Welles, *Diary,* 1: 287.

99. Bain, *Lincoln's Last Battleground,* 14–21.

100. Elizabeth Dixon, letter, May 1, 1865, courtesy of Caroline Welling Van Deusen (Dixon's great-great-granddaughter).

101. Bain, *Lincoln's Last Battleground,* 14–21.

102. Wenzing, interview.

103. Tanner, "Tanner Also Present."

104. Laughlin, *Death of Lincoln,* 112.

105. Grover, "Lincoln's Interest in the Theater," 948.

106. *Meteorological Journal 1865,* Washington City Observatory, Sunday, Apr. 9, 1865–Saturday, Apr. 15, 1865.

107. Jacob Soles, account, Lincoln Assassination Eyewitness Accounts, N.P.S. files.

108. John V. Hinkel, "St. Patrick's: Mother Church of Washington," records of the Columbia Historical Society, 1957–59.

109. "Lincoln Assassination," *New York Herald,* Apr. 15, 1865; Shepherd, letter, Apr. 16, 1865.

110. Brinkerhoff, *Recollections of a Lifetime,* 166–67.

111. David Donald, *Lincoln's Cabinet: The Civil War Diaries of Salmon P. Chase* (New York: Longmans, Green, 1954), 260.

112. Brockett, *Life and Times of Abraham Lincoln,* 650.

113. Moss, "Lincoln and Wilkes Booth."

114. Donald, *Lincoln's Cabinet,* 260; Moss, "Lincoln and Wilkes Booth," 953.

115. Kenneth G. Alfers, *Law and Order in the Capital City: A History of the Washington Police, 1800–1866* (Washington, DC: George Washington University, 1976), 27.

116. Brown, *Reminiscences of Senator William M. Stewart of Nevada,* 193.

117. Edwin Bates to Mr. and Mrs. Jacob Bates, Apr. 15, 1865.

118. *The Assassination of Abraham Lincoln, late President of the United States of America, and the Attempted Assassination of William H. Seward, Secretary of State, and Frederick W. Seward, Assistant Secretary, on the Evening of the 14th of April, 1865, Expressions of Condolence and Sympathy Inspired by These Events* (Washington, D.C.: Government Printing Office, 1867), 134.

14. Enough Evidence to Hang Booth

1. Tanner to Walch, Apr. 17, 1895.

2. Tanner, "Tanner Also Present"; Mose Sanford to John Beatty, Apr. 17, 1865 (copy), N.P.S. Files.

3. Ibid.

4. James Tanner, interview, clipping from *Journal Inquirer,* Tanner folder, N.P.S. files.

5. Tanner to Walch, Apr. 17, 1895.

6. Virta, *Archeology at the Petersen House.*

7. Tanner to Walch, Apr. 17, 1895.

8. James Tanner, letter, *Washington Post,* Apr. 16, 1905, Washingtoniana Division, Martin Luther King Jr. Memorial Library.

9. Grover, "Lincoln's Interest in the Theater."

10. Serial Division, Library of Congress, http://www.loc.gov/rr/news/circulars/nyherald.txt (accessed Aug. 9, 2014); "First Report of Assassination and Attack," University of Missouri Kansas City Law School, http://law2.umkc.edu/faculty/projects/ftrials/lincolnconspiracy/lincolnnews.html (accessed Aug. 9, 2014); "Notable Visitors: Lawrence A. Gobright (1816–1881)," Mr. Lincoln's White House,

http://www.mrlincolnswhitehouse.org/inside.asp?ID=722&subjectID=2 (accessed Aug. 9, 2014); Abott A. Abott, *The Assassination and Death of Abraham Lincoln* (New York: American News Company, 1865), 2–3, Internet Archive, https://archive.org/stream/assassinationdea00inabot#page/n0/mode/2up.

15. Waiting for History

1. "Northern News: An Account of Mr. Lincoln's Death by an Eye Witness," *Raleigh Daily Progress,* Apr. 27, 1865.

2. Geoffrey Johnson, "True Lincoln," *Chicago Magazine,* Dec. 2004, 116–52.

3. "Account of Mr. Lincoln's Death by an Eye Witness."

4. Leale, *Lincoln's Last Hours,* 9.

5. Styple, *Generals in Bronze,* 284–85.

6. *Washington Star,* Jan. 24, 1909.

7. *New York Day Book Caucasian,* Apr. 22, 1865; *Louisville Daily Union Press,* Apr. 17, 1865.

8. Welles, *Diary,* 2: 288.

9. K. Helm, *Mary, Wife of Lincoln,* 155.

10. Henry Ulke, interview, *National Tribune,* Dec. 10, 1891.

11. Hemphill, "Deathbed Relics."

12. Bain, *Lincoln's Last Battleground,* 22.

13. Styple, *Generals in Bronze,* 304.

14. Bain, *Lincoln's Last Battleground,* 24; George Rector to David Rankin Barbee, Apr. 29, 1935, David Rankin Barbee papers; "Baltimore Woman Says Lincoln Died in Her Bed in Washington."

15. Styple, *Generals in Bronze,* 287.

16. That's the Last of Him

1. Hemphill, "Deathbed Relics"; John Usher, letter, Apr. 16, 1865, Manuscript Division, Library of Congress.

2. "Account of Mr. Lincoln's Death by an Eye Witness"; Welles, *Diary,* 2: 228.

3. *Frank Leslie's Illustrated Newspaper,* Apr. 20, 1865, N.P.S. files.

4. "Account of Mr. Lincoln's Death by an Eye Witness."

5. Welles, *Diary,* 1: 228; Bain, *Lincoln's Last Battleground,* 21.

6. "Lincoln Assassination," *Washington Post,* Apr. 14, 1883.

7. Ulke, interview.

8. F. B. Carpenter, *The Inner Life of Abraham Lincoln* (Lincoln: University of Nebraska Press, 1995), 264–65. Originally published as *Six Months at the White House with Abraham Lincoln* (New York: Hurd and Houghton, 1866).

9. Grant, *Personal Memoirs,* 580.

10. Stimmel, *Personal Reminiscences of Abraham Lincoln,* 88.

11. Leale, *Lincoln's Last Hours,* 12.

12. Ibid., 12.

13. Dixon, letter, May 1, 1865.

14. C. S. Taft, *Abraham Lincoln's Last Hours,* 15–16.

15. Leale, *Lincoln's Last Hours,* 11.

16. *New York Day Book Caucasian,* Apr. 22, 1865; Reck, *A. Lincoln: His Last 24 Hours,* 139.

17. James Tanner, letter, *Litchfield County Times,* Feb. 13, 1867 (copy), William Petersen file, James O. Hall Research Center.

18. Reck, *A. Lincoln: His Last 24 Hours,* 151–53.

19. Tour of four levels and rear quarters, Petersen House, May 14, 2010.

20. Gary Ferguson, National Parks Service interpreter, Abraham Lincoln Birthplace National Historic Park, via Gloria Swift, National Parks Service curator, Ford's Theatre.

21. Field, *Memories of Many Men and of Some Women,* 324.

22. *New York Day Book Caucasian,* Apr. 22, 1865.

23. Styple, *Generals in Bronze,* 287.

24. Tanner, "Tanner Also Present."

25. C. S. Taft, *Abraham Lincoln's Last Hours,* 13.

26. "Washington Diary of Horatio Nelson Taft," vol. 3, entry for Apr. 30, 1865.

27. C. S. Taft, "The Murder of President Lincoln," *Medical and Surgical Reporter,* Apr. 22, 1865, http://history.furman.edu/benson/fyw2010/graham/grahamcharactersource3.htm.

28. "Account of Mr. Lincoln's Death by an Eye Witness."

29. Reck, *A. Lincoln: His Last 24 Hours,* 157.

30. A. F. Rockwell, "Memoranda on the Life of Lincoln," *Century Magazine* (June 1890): 311, Unz.org, http://www.unz.org/Pub/Century-1890jun-00310.

31. Leale, *Lincoln's Last Hours,* 12.

32. Reck, *A. Lincoln: His Last 24 Hours,* 157.

33. John G. Nicolay, *A Short Life of Abraham Lincoln* (New York: Century Co., 1919), 540.

34. A. F. Rockwell, drawing, Apr. 15, 1865, N.P.S. files; C. S. Taft, *Abraham Lincoln's Last Hours,* 12.

35. Tanner, "Tanner Also Present"; Nicolay and Hay, *Abraham Lincoln,* 10: 344.

36. Styple, *Generals in Bronze,* 287.

37. Reck, *A. Lincoln: His Last 24 Hours,* 151–53.

38. Tour, Dr. Mudd House Museum, 2012.

39. "Mourning: Further Details of the Terrible Tragedy at Washington."

40. Ibid.; Steers and Edwards, *Lincoln Assassination,* 181.

41. C. S. Taft, *Abraham Lincoln's Last Hours,* 14.

42. *National Tribune,* Dec. 10, 1891; Hemphill, "Deathbed Relics"; Bain, *Lincoln's Last Battleground,* 28.

43. Field, *Memories of Many Men and of Some Women*, 327.

44. Brown, *Reminiscences of Senator William M. Stewart of Nevada*, 194.

45. Good, *We Saw Lincoln Shot*, 100; Forman, *Guide to Civil War Washington*.

17. Caught in the American Nightmare

1. Bain, *Lincoln's Last Battleground*, 29.

2. Shields, interview; "Lincoln's Last Hours," *Harper's Weekly*, July 13, 1909.

3. Weichmann, *True History of the Assassination*, 158; Field, *Memories of Many Men and of Some Women*, 326, 376.

4. Kunhardt and Kunhardt, *Twenty Days*, 97; Bain, *Lincoln's Last Battleground*, 28; Weichmann, *True History of the Assassination*, 158.

5. Weichmann, *True History of the Assassination*, 158; Field, *Memories of Many Men and of Some Women*, 326, 376; Kunhardt and Kunhardt, *Twenty Days*, 97; Bain, *Lincoln's Last Battleground*, 28.

6. National Park Service excavation, Petersen House grounds.

7. Kunhardt and Kunhardt, *Twenty Days*, 97; Bain, *Lincoln's Last Battleground*, 28.

8. Office of the Quartermaster, War Department, General Consolidated Correspondence File, 1794–1915, Old Box 568, Lincolniana, NARA.

9. Steers, *Blood on the Moon*, 268–69; Leale, *Lincoln's Last Hours*, 12.

10. Leale, *Lincoln's Last Hours*, 13.

11. Moss, "Lincoln and Wilkes Booth," 950; Leale, *Lincoln's Last Hours*, 18.

12. Ernest B. Furgurson, *Freedom Rising: Washington in the Civil War* (New York: Vintage, 2004), 384; Field, *Memories of Many Men and of Some Women*, 326.

13. W. J. Ferguson, "Lincoln's Death."

14. "Lincoln Assassination," *New York Herald*, Apr. 15, 1865.

15. "National Calamity: President Lincoln Assassinated," *Dayton Extra Journal*, Apr. 15, 1865.

16. *Chicago Tribune*, Apr. 15, 1865.

17. *Meteorological Journal 1865*, Washington City Observatory, Apr. 14–15, 1865.

18. Gen. Thomas M. Vincent, "Abraham Lincoln and Edwin M. Stanton," address to Burnside Post No. 81, Apr. 25, 1889, Google Books, 25, http://books.google.com/books?id=PC9CAAAAIAAJ&pg=PA25&dq=his+mortal+wound,+from+which+his+life%27s+blood+was+oozing&hl=en&sa=X&ei=BqjmU56pE50RyASi5YDwDg&ved=0CB4Q6AEwAA#v=onepage&q=his%20mortal%20wound%2C%20from%20which%20his%20life's%20blood%20was%2000zing&f=false.

19. Daggett, letter, Apr. 16, 1865.

20. Dieterich to *New York Sun*.

21. Field, *Memories of Many Men and of Some Women*, 326.

22. Petersen House boarders, N.P.S. files.

23. "White House Coffee Cup," National Museum of American History, Smithsonian Institution, http://americanhistory.si.edu/collections/search/object/nmah_515538 (accessed Aug. 19, 2013).

24. Dixon, letter, May 1, 1865.

25. George Francis to Josephine (his niece), May 5, 1865; *Louisville Daily Union Press,* Apr. 17, 1865; Hemphill, "Deathbed Relics."

26. Steers, *Blood on the Moon,* 269; *Louisville Daily Union Press,* Apr. 17, 1865; Field, *Memories of Many Men and of Some Women,* 326.

27. C. S. Taft, *Abraham Lincoln's Last Hours,* 15; *Meteorological Journal 1865,* Washington City Observatory, Sunday, Apr. 9, 1865–Saturday, Apr. 15, 1865.

28. Mose Sanford to John Beatty, Apr. 17, 1865 (copy), courtesy of Ed Steers Jr.

29. C. S. Taft, *Abraham Lincoln's Last Hours,* 15.

30. *New York Day Book Caucasian,* Apr. 22, 1865.

31. Daggett, letter, Apr. 16, 1865; Steers and Edwards, *Lincoln Assassination,* 325–26.

32. Forman, *Guide to Civil War Washington,* 101.

33. John Richter III, Center for Civil War Photography, interview, n.d.; *Lincoln Lore* (bulletin of Louis A. Warren Lincoln Library and Museum), no. 1751 (Jan. 1984).

18. Grief and Greed

1. Willie Clark, letter, Apr. 19, 1865 (copy), N.P.S. files.

2. Dixon, letter, May 1, 1865.

3. "Closing Scenes," *New York Times,* Apr. 16, 1865.

4. Willie Clark, letter, Apr. 19, 1865.

5. Mrs. W. T. Clark, letter, Mar. 5, 1896, N.P.S. files.

6. Ibid.

7. "Mourning: Further Details of the Terrible Tragedy at Washington."

8. Charles East, ed., *Sarah Morgan: The Civil War Diary of a Southern Woman* (New York: Simon & Schuster, 1991), 608.

9. Barron, "With John Wilkes Booth in His Days as an Actor."

10. Ibid.

11. Ibid.

12. Bain, *Lincoln's Last Battleground,* 41–43.

13. Hemphill, "Deathbed Relics."

14. Bain, *Lincoln's Last Battleground,* 58.

15. *Philadelphia Inquirer,* June 26, 1865; M. R. Bennett, "Old Watch Ticks Lincoln Tragedy Anew," N.P.S. files.

16. Mose Sanford to Johnnie, Apr. 17, 1865 (copy), courtesy of Edward Steers Jr.

17. Louisa Petersen's one-page diary, N.P.S. files; Bain, *Lincoln's Last Battleground,* 46.

18. Department of the Interior, informational circular, 1966, N.P.S. files

19. Louisa Petersen's one-page diary; Bain, *Lincoln's Last Battleground,* 46.

20. Bennett, "Old Watch Ticks Lincoln Tragedy Anew."

21. Thomas A. Jones, *Wilkes Booth: An Account of his Sojourn in Southern Maryland after the Assassination of Abraham Lincoln, His Passage across the Potomac, and His Death in Virginia* (Chicago: Laird & Lee, 1893), 74–78, Internet Archive, https://archive.org/stream/jwilkesboothacc000iljone#page/n5/mode/2up.

22. Ibid., 74–78.

23. "Did John Wilkes Booth Ever Attend Georgetown?" Georgetown University Library, http://www.library.georgetown.edu/infrequently-asked-questions/did-john-wilkes-booth-ever-attend-georgetown (accessed Mar. 30, 2013).

24. "A Nation in Tears," *Chicago Tribune,* Apr. 17, 1865; "Honors to Mr. Lincoln's Memory on the Pacific Coast," *Hartford Daily Courant,* Apr. 22, 1865.

25. John T. Ford, testimony before Judiciary Committee, May 25, 1867, Box 4, Folder 212, Barbee Papers.

26. *Philadelphia Inquirer,* Apr. 15, 1865; *Newburyport Herald Extra,* Apr. 15, 1865, http://www.loc.gov/item/scsm000452/.

27. *Dubuque Daily Times,* Apr. 16, 1865, http://www.loc.gov/item/scsm001229/; *Official Records of the Civil War* (Anderson: THA New Media, 2008).

28. F. H. Pierpont to Edwin Stanton, telegram, Apr. 15, 1865, in *Official Records of the Civil War.*

19. The Most Elaborate Funeral in US History

1. Ralph G. Newman, "In This Sad World of Ours, Sorrow Comes to All: A Timetable for the Lincoln Funeral Train" (Springfield, IL, 1865), 7, N.P.S. files.

2. William Bushon, White House Historical Association, speaking at Surratt Society conference, Clinton, MD, Sept. 15, 2013; E.R. Shaw, "The Assassination of Lincoln," *McClure's Magazine,* Dec. 1908, 181, American Periodicals Series Online, https://archive.org/stream/accountsofassassefhlinc#page/n3/mode/2up.

3. Kunhardt and Kunhardt, *Twenty Days,* 120.

4. *New York Day Book Caucasian,* Apr. 22, 1865; Kunhardt and Kunhardt, *Twenty Days,* 95.

5. Newman, "In This Sad World of Ours," 7.

6. Steers, *Lincoln Assassination Encyclopedia,* 99–100.

7. "Dawn's Early Light: The First 50 Years of American Photography," Cornell University Library, http://rmc.library.cornell.edu/DawnsEarlyLight/ (accessed June 3, 2013).

8. Titone, *My Thoughts Be Bloody,* 376.

9. Dorothy Meserve Kunhardt, "What Happened to Lincoln's Body," *Life,* Feb. 15, 1963, Googlebooks.com, http://books.google.com/books?id=n0EEAAAAMBAJ&printsec=frontcover&source=gbs_ge_summary_r&cad=0#v=onepage&q&f=

false; "Abraham Lincoln's Body Exhumed and Viewed," RogerJNorton.com, http://rogerjnorton.com/Lincoln13.html (accessed Apr. 15, 2014).

10. Louisa Petersen's one-page diary.

11. John Rhodehamel and Louise Taper, *"Right or Wrong, God Judge Me"* (Urbana: University of Illinois Press, 1977), 154–55.

12. Ibid.

13. Collection, Ford's Theatre Museum.

14. Dr. Adonis, "Letter from Washington," *Chicago Tribune,* Apr. 26, 1865.

15. W. Emerson Reck, "Colonel Rathbone's Mania," *Lincoln Herald* 86, no. 4 (Winter 1984).

16. Newman, "In This Sad World of Ours," 7–9; *Terrible Tragedy at Washington,* 85.

17. Newman, "In This Sad World of Ours," 8.

18. *A Tribute of the Nations* (Old Saybrook: Konecky & Konecky, 2009), Washingtoniana Division, Martin Luther King Memorial Library, n.p.

19. "The Assassination of Abraham Lincoln, Reaction of Foreign Countries," 10, Lincoln Financial Foundation Collection, Internet Archive, http://www.lincolncollection.org/collection/categories/item/?cat=17&page=49&pagesize=48&item=44606 (accessed Feb. 6, 2013).

20. Leale, *Lincoln's Last Hours,* 1.

21. "Lincoln Received Fatal Shot at Hands of Booth in Ford's Theatre 75 Years Ago Today," *Washington Star,* Apr. 14, 1940, Box 2, Folder 137, Barbee Papers.

22. Leale, *Lincoln's Last Hours,* 1; "Charles A. Leale, M.D., the First Surgeon to Reach the Assassinated President Lincoln," compiled by Helen Leale Harper Jr., Apr. 1965, Manuscript Division, Library of Congress.

23. Newman, "In This Sad World of Ours," 7.

24. Ibid., 7, 8.

25. Pratt, *Personal Finances of Abraham Lincoln,* 119.

26. Wayne Wesolowski and Mary Cay Wesolowski, *The Lincoln Train Is Coming* (Cortaro: privately printed, 1995), 8–10.

27. Ibid., 13.

28. For the ship's location, see Steers, *Blood on the Moon,* 183.

29. "Death of the President," *Century Magazine* (Jan. 1890): 442.

30. Jones, *Wilkes Booth,* 78.

31. Rhodehamel and Taper, *"Right or Wrong, God Judge Me,"* 154–55.

32. Visit to Stuart home and tour of John Wilkes Booth's Escape Route, Surratt Society, Apr. 14, 2012.

33. Newman, "In This Sad World of Ours," 10; William T. Coggleshall, "Lincoln Memorial: The Journeys of Abraham Lincoln," *Columbus Ohio State Journal,* 1865, 153, https://archive.org/stream/lincolnmemorialj00cogg#page/n7/mode/2up.

34. A. D. Gillette, "God Seen Above All National Calamities," sermon, Apr. 23, 1865, First Baptist Church, Washington, DC, "The Martyred President: Sermons

Given on the Occasion of the Assassination of Abraham Lincoln," Emory University, http://beck.library.emory.edu/lincoln/sermon.php?id=gillette.001.

35. Steers and Edwards, *Lincoln Assassination,* 188–92, 255, 257.

36. Newman, "In This Sad World of Ours," 11.

37. Herbert Garrett Peters, address to the Rochester-Avalon Historical Society, MI, Feb. 2011, courtesy of Garrett family.

38. Ibid.

39. Pinkerton National Detective Agency 1856–1865, Box 4, Allan Pinkerton correspondence folder, Manuscript Division, Library of Congress.

40. Ibid.

41. *Philadelphia North American and United States Gazette,* Apr. 26, 1865, http://www.loc.gov/exhibits/lincoln/interactives/long-journey-home/apr_25/pdf/600f.pdf

42. "Teddy Roosevelt and Abraham Lincoln in the same photo," National Archives, http://blogs.archives.gov/prologue/?p=2445 (accessed Dec. 20, 2013).

43. Newman, "In This Sad World of Ours," 11–13.

44. Adonis, "Letter from Washington"

20. The Manhunt Closes In

1. David Taylor, address to Surratt Society, Mar. 16, 2013, based on interviews with Garrett descendant Mary Louise Hughes; tour of John Wilkes Booth's Escape Route, Surratt Society.

2. William H. Garrett, "True Story of the Capture of John Wilkes Booth," *Confederate Veteran* 29, no. 4 (Apr. 1921): 129, Internet Archive, https://archive.org/stream/confederateveter291921#page/128/mode/2up/search/garrett.

3. Newman, "In This Sad World of Ours," 11–13.

4. *Journal of American Irish Historical Society* 16 (1917): 145.

5. Clara Harris, letter, Apr. 29, 1865 (copy).

6. "Life of Philip Whitlock."

7. Edward P. Doherty, statement, M619, Reel 456, frames 273–84, NARA.

8. "Phases of the Moon, 1800–1899," National Aeronautics and Space Administration, http://eclipse.gsfc.nasa.gov/phase/phases-1899.html (accessed Sept. 14, 2013).

9. Poore, *Conspiracy Trial for the Murder of the President,* 1: 318–21.

10. Edward P. Doherty, "Pursuit and Death of John Wilkes Booth," *Century Magazine* (Jan. 1890): 448–49.

11. Poore, *Conspiracy Trial for the Murder of the President,* 1: 318–21.

12. Taylor, address to Surratt Society, Mar. 16, 2013; Steers, *Blood on the Moon,* 203.

13. Poore, *Conspiracy Trial for the Murder of the President,* 1: 318–21.

14. James L. Swanson, *Manhunt: The 12-Day Chase for Lincoln's Killer* (New York: Harper, 2007), 328–47, 351, 371; Ernest B. Furguson, "The Man Who Shot the Man Who Shot Lincoln," *American Scholar* (Spring 2009): http://

theamericanscholar.org/the-man-who-shot-the-man-who-shot-lincoln/#
.U03XiPk7t8E; "Thomas P. 'Boston' Corbett," Kansapedia, Kansas State Historical
Society, http://www.kshs.org/ (accessed Nov. 12, 2013).

15. Swanson, *Manhunt*, 328–47, 351, 371; Furgurson, "Man Who Shot the Man
Who Shot Lincoln."

16. Furgurson, "Man Who Shot the Man Who Shot Lincoln."

17. Collection, Ford's Theatre Museum; "Booth Killed," *New York Times*, Apr.
28, 1865.

18. Richard H. Garrett, petition for reimbursement for lost property, June 28,
1865, *Reports of the Committees, The House of Representatives for the First Session of
the Forty-Third Congress 1873–74*, 5 vols. (Washington, DC, Government Printing
Office, 1874), 4: Report No. 743; Taylor, address to Surratt Society, Mar. 16, 2013.

19. Poore, *Conspiracy Trial for the Murder of the President*, 1: 308–13.

20. Swanson, *Manhunt*, 344.

21. Steers and Edwards, *Lincoln Assassination*, 849–50; *Washington Star*, Apr.
27, 1865.

22. *New York Times*, Apr. 28–29, 1865; *Trial of John H. Surratt*, 1: 319.

23. Leech, *Reveille in Washington*, 422.

24. Swanson, *Manhunt*, 346–47.

25. Ronald L. Fingerson, "Books at Iowa—John Wilkes Booth in the Bollinger
Lincoln Collection," http://www.lib.uiowa.edu/scua/bai/fingerson.htm (accessed
Aug. 26, 2012).

26. Newman, "In This Sad World of Ours," 5–13.

21. Unrivaled Honors and an Unexpected Invoice

1. Newman, "In This Sad World of Ours," 13.

2. Harold Holzer, Craig L. Symonds, and Frank J. Williams, *The Lincoln Assassination: Crime and Punishment, Myth and Memory* (New York: Fordham University Press, 2010), 43–49.

3. Newman, "In This Sad World of Ours," 15, 16.

4. *Tribute of the Nations*, n.p.

5. Newman, "In This Sad World of Ours," 17, 18.

6. Frank A. Flowers, *History of the Republican Party: Embracing Its Origin,
Growth and Mission* (Springfield: Union Publishing, 1884), 470.

7. Office of the Quartermaster General, consolidated correspondence file,
1794–1915, Old Box 568, Lincolniana, NARA.

22. Paltry Meanness

1. Office of the Quartermaster General, Consolidated Correspondence File,
1794–1915, Old Box 568, Lincolniana, NARA.

2. Ibid.

3. *Alexandria Louisiana Democrat,* July 12, 1865 (copy), http://chronicling-america.loc.gov/lccn/sn82003389/1865–07–12/ed-1/; *Philadelphia Inquirer,* June 26, 1865.

4. *Philadelphia Inquirer,* June 26, 1865.

5. William Petersen, letter to the editor, *National Intelligencer,* June 29, 1865.

6. Ibid.; Bain, *Lincoln's Last Battleground,* 36.

7. Petersen, letter to the editor, *National Intelligencer,* June 29, 1865.

8. *Washington Post,* May 13, 1878. (The interviewee is described only as "young Mr. Petersen, son of William Petersen," but his youth, location, and references make it evident that this is Charles Petersen, born May 8, 1855.)

9. William Petersen, obituary, *Evening Star,* June 19, 1871, Washingtoniana Division, Martin Luther King Jr. Memorial Library.

10. George Francis to Josephine (his niece), May 5, 1865.

11. Ninth Census of the United States, 1870, District of Columbia, Ancestry.com.

12. Petersen, obituary, *Evening Star,* June 19, 1871; William Petersen, obituary, *New York Times,* June 19, 1871.

13. Petersen, obituary, *Evening Star,* June 19, 1871; Petersen, obituary, *New York Times,* June 19, 1871.

14. Jean B. Crabill, "The Immigrants and Their Cemetery," *Washington Evening Star,* June 19, 1871, Washingtoniana Division, Martin Luther King Jr. Memorial Library.

15. Author's visit to Prospect Hill Cemetery, Washington, DC, Oct. 2, 2009; Crabill, "Immigrants and Their Cemetery."

16. "Prospect Hill Cemetery: Our Nation's Capital's Historic German-American Cemetery," Prospect Hill Cemetery, www.prospecthillcemetery.org (accessed Feb. 2, 2010).

17. Author's visit to Prospect Hill Cemetery, Oct. 2, 2009; Vera Craig, *Furnishing Plan: House Where Lincoln Died* (Harpers Ferry: National Park Service, 1976), 18–21. (No 1871 death records survive at the Office of Public Records Management Archival Administration, Washington, DC, or at the National Archive and Records Administration.)

18. "Interesting People at Prospect Hill Cemetery," Prospect Hill Cemetery, http://www.prospecthillcemetery.org/Biographies.html (accessed Mar. 1, 2013).

19. Auction records, Old Series Administrative Case Files, Record Group 21, Entry 115, No. 6584, NARA; Getzinger, "Anna Petersen"; Anna Petersen, Last Will and Testament, filed Oct. 21, 1871 (four days after her death), Office of Public Records Management Archival Administration, Washington, DC.

20. Petersen Family folder, N.P.S. files; Rector to Barbee, Apr. 29, 1935.

23. History Forgot Tenth Street

1. Ford's Theatre file, N.P.S. files.

2. *Washington Star,* Feb. 24, 1883; *William A. Petersen House,* 14; *Washington Sunday Star,* Feb. 11, 1906.

3. William B. Benton, *The Life of Osborn Oldroyd* (Washington, DC: privately printed, 1927), 6–29; James T. Mathews, *History of the Lincoln Museum, the Ford Theatre and the Oldroyd Collection* (Washington, DC: National Art Service, 1935), n.p.; "The House in Which Abraham Lincoln Died," pamphlet, N.P.S. files; "Lincoln Museum Is Now Open," *New York Times,* May 23, 1936, Lincolniana Division, Martin Luther King Jr. Memorial Library.

4. Tara McClellan McAndrew, "The First Abraham Lincoln Presidential Museum," *Illinois Times,* Nov. 19, 2008, http://illinoistimes.com/article-5463-the-first-abraham-lincoln-presidential-museum.html.

5. *William A. Petersen House,* 14.

6. "Patient Guards Hear Praise and Criticism," *Washington Post,* Feb. 7, 1937.

7. *Washington Star,* Jan. 12, 1928.

24. Lincoln Would Not Be the Last to Die at Ford's

1. *Los Angeles Times,* June 10, 1893.

2. *New York Times,* June 10, 1893.

3. *Washington Evening Star,* June 9, 1943.

4. Ibid.; Hinkel, "St. Patrick's."

5. *Los Angeles Times,* June 10, 1893.

6. "Attending Ford's Theater with the Lincolns: The Tragic Lives of Clara Harris and Henry Rathbone," *From the Stacks: The N-YHS Library Blog,* July 10, 2013, http://blog.nyhistory.org/attending-fords-theater-with-the-lincolns-the-tragic-lives-of-clara-harris-and-henry-rathbone/.

7. *Washington Star,* June 25, 1926.

25. A Place to Make Him Comfortable

1. Getzinger, "Anna Petersen," 21.

2. Henry Fowler, "Character and Death of Abraham Lincoln," address delivered Apr. 23, 1865, Auburn, NY (New York: Sheldon & Co., 1865), "The Martyred President: Sermons Given on the Occasion of the Assassination of Abraham Lincoln," Emory University, http://beck.library.emory.edu/lincoln/sermon.php?id=fowler.001.

Epilogue

1. Jennifer L. Bach, "Acts of Remembrance: Mary Todd Lincoln and Her Husband's Memory," *Journal of the Abraham Lincoln Association* 25, no. 2 (Summer 2004): 47–48.

2. Senator James Nesmith to his wife, Feb. 6, 1862 (copy), courtesy of Oregon Historical Society.

3. Rev. Phineas Gurley to Hon. E. D. Brooks, May 22, 1865, Miscellaneous Collection, Library of Congress.

4. *New York Times,* Dec. 29, 1883; Reck, "Colonel Rathbone's Mania;" *New York Tribune,* Dec. 29, 1883.

5. Reck, "Colonel Rathbone's Mania."

6. Steers, *Lincoln Assassination Encyclopedia,* 81.

7. "First Physician to Tend Lincoln When Shot Dies," *Chicago Tribune,* June 14, 1932; Watson, *Physicians and Surgeons of America;* Leale, *Lincoln's Last Hours,* 1.

8. *Los Angeles Times,* May 18, 1882.

9. Caroline W. Van Deusen (great-granddaughter of Elizabeth Dixon), interview with the author, n.d.

10. W. T. Clark, obituary, *Boston Globe,* Apr. 5, 1888, N.P.S. files.

11. J. A. Walter, "The Surratt Case," *U.S. Catholic Historical Magazine* 3, no. 12 (1890): 353–61; Morris J. MacGregor, *A Parish for the Federal City* (Washington, DC: Catholic University of America Press, 1994), 168–70.

12. Paul Liston, "Suggested Reading," *Potomac Catholic Heritage* 27 (Spring 2009): 38–44; Hinkel, "St. Patrick's," 33–43.

13. Walter, "Surratt Case," 353–57.

14. Steers, *Lincoln Assassination Encyclopedia,* 460–61, 154.

15. Shanahan, interview.

16. "William J. Ferguson," IMDb, http://www.imdb.com/name/nm0272639/ (accessed Sept. 17, 2010).

17. "Find Actor's Story of Lincoln's Death"; W. J. Ferguson, "Story of the Assassination."

18. Asia Booth Clarke, *John Wilkes Booth: A Sister's Memoir* (Jackson: University Press of Mississippi, 1999), 15.

19. Joseph Hazelton, IMDb, http://www.imdb.com/name/nm0371979/ (accessed Apr. 11, 2010).

20. "Lucille Ball Episode," *I've Got a Secret;* "S. J. Seymour Dies: Last Lincoln Slaying Witness," *Washington Star,* Apr. 13, 1956.

21. Taltavul folder, Hall Collection.

22. Carrie Weiss (Ulke family member), interview with the author, n.d.

23. "The Acquisition of Presidential Portraits for the White House," White House Historical Association, http://www.whitehousehistory.org/history/documents/WHHA-History-Acquisition-Portraits-Monkman.pdf (accessed June 22, 2013).

24. Ed Folsom, "Notes on the Major Whitman Photographers," *Walt Whitman Quarterly Review* 4, no. 2 (Fall 1986): 63–71.

25. *Bulletin of Louis A. Warren Lincoln Library and Museum* (Jan. 1984): 1–3; "Funeral Services for Julius Ulke Will Be Held at Scientist's Home Today," *Washington Post,* Aug. 2, 1910.

26. James E. Smith, *A Famous Battery and Its Campaigns 1861–64: The Career of Cpl. James Tanner in War and In Peace* (Washington, DC: W. H. Lowdermilk, 1892).

27. Tanner, "Tanner Also Present."

28. "Once a Lincoln Suspect: Death of John Mathews, Who Was Booth's Room-

mate at the Time of the Assassination," *Boston Daily Globe,* Jan. 12, 1905, N.P.S. files; "Actor Who Saw Lincoln Shot Dies," Box 4, File 212, Barbee Papers; unidentified clipping from *Lincoln Log,* N.P.S. files.

29. Van De Wielle, interview; Presidential Carriage Collection, Studebaker National Museum, http://www.studebakermuseum.org/p/whats-happening/exhibits/the-presidential-carriage-collection/ (accessed Mar. 8, 2012).

30. Wynkoop, letter to the editor, *Los Angeles Times,* Feb. 16, 1916; "Veteran Actress Is Dead," *New York Times,* May 3, 1924; "Eyewitness Recalls Scene of Lincoln's Assassination"; "Actress, Who Played Before Lincoln on Fateful Night."

31. *Washington Times,* Dec. 4, 1903.

32. Petersen & Child ad, *Washington National Republican,* Nov. 8, 1884.

33. Ninth Census of the United States, 1870, Washington, DC; "More Happy Apart," *Washington Post,* July 28, 1891; "Puts the Blame on His Wife," unidentified clipping mentioning divorce proceedings for Ferdinand Petersen and Emily Petersen, N.P.S. files.

34. "Charges against Mrs. Petersen: Her Divorced Husband Wants to Stop Paying Her Alimony," *Washington Post,* Mar. 9, 1893.

35. Petersen, letter to the editor, *National Intelligencer,* June 29, 1865; "Charges against Mrs. Petersen"; "Puts the Blame on His Wife."

36. R. L. Polk & Co.'s Baltimore City Directory, 1906, 2083.

37. "Big Price for Realty," *Baltimore Sun,* Sept. 1, 1908.

38. "Mrs. Wenzing's Will Is Held Valid by Jury," *Baltimore Sun,* May 7, 1933.

39. William F. Petersen, Los Angeles City, California Voter Registers, 1866–1898, Great Registers, 1866–1898, California State Library, Ancestry.com.

40. Alfred T. Andreas, *History of Chicago,* 3 vols. (Chicago: A. T. Andreas, 1886), 3: 362; Tenth Census of the United States, 1880, Chicago; Ken Bloom, *Broadway: Its History, People, and Places: An Encyclopedia* (New York: Routledge, 2003); *New York Times,* Sept. 23, 1914; George Rector, *The Girl from Rector's* (Garden City: Doubleday, Page, 1927), 3, 6, 7, 15, 24, 25, 26, 28, 64, 67, 94, 95, 108, 198.

41. Bloom, *Broadway;* Rector, *Girl from Rector's.*

42. *Pittsburg Dispatch,* Nov. 12, 1889, N.P.S. files; "The Bloody Evidence," Chicago History Museum, http://chicagohistory.org/wetwithblood/bloody/pillow/index.htm (accessed Nov. 14, 2011).

43. "The Death Bed of Lincoln," *New York Times,* Oct. 2, 1921; Rector to Barbee, Apr. 29, 1935.

Bibliography

All journals, newspapers, magazines, and Web pages used to research this book are listed in the chapter notes. The books I consulted are listed below. I especially relied on the works of Timothy S. Good, Clara E. Laughlin, Margaret Leech, Clara Morris, W. Emerson Reck, Edward Steers Jr., and Nora Titone.

Abott, Abott A. *The Assassination and Death of Abraham Lincoln.* New York: American News Company, 1865.

Abraham Lincoln: Tributes from His Associates, Reminiscences of Soldiers, Statesmen and Citizens. New York: Thomas Y. Crowell, 1895.

Account of the Terrific and Fatal Riot at the New-York Astor Place Opera House. New York: H. M. Ranney, 1849.

Alfers, Kenneth. *Law and Order in the Capital City: A History of the Washington Police, 1800–1866.* Washington, DC: George Washington University, 1976.

Andreas, Alfred T. *History of Chicago.* 3 vols. Chicago: A. T. Andreas Co., 1886.

The Assassination of Abraham Lincoln, late President of the United States of America, and the Attempted Assassination of William H. Seward, Secretary of State, and Frederick W. Seward, Assistant Secretary, on the Evening of the 14th of April, 1865, Expressions of Condolence and Sympathy Inspired by These Events. Washington, DC: Government Printing Office, 1867.

The Assassination of President Lincoln and the Trial of the Conspirators. Cincinnati: Moore, Wilstach & Baldwin, 1865.

Bain, Robert T. *Lincoln's Last Battleground.* Bloomington: Author House, 2005.

Benton, William B. *The Life of Osborn Oldroyd.* Washington, DC: privately printed, 1927.

Bloom, Ken. *Broadway: Its History, People, and Places: An Encyclopedia.* New York: Routledge, 2003.

Bogar, Thomas A. *Backstage at the Lincoln Assassination.* Washington, DC: Regnery History, 2013.

Boyd's Directory of the District of Columbia 1870. Washington, DC: William Boyd, 1870.

Boyd's Washington and Georgetown Directory 1865. Washington, DC: Boyd's Directory Co., 1865.

Brands, H. W. *Andrew Jackson: His Life and Times.* New York: Doubleday, 2005.

Brinkerhoff, Roeliff. *Recollections of a Lifetime.* Cincinnati: Robert Clarke Co., 1904.

Brockett, L. P. *The Life and Times of Abraham Lincoln.* Philadelphia: Jones, 1865.

Brooks, Noah. *Washington in Lincoln's Time.* Washington, DC: Century Co., 1895.

Brown, George R. *Reminiscences of Sen. William M. Stewart of Nevada.* New York: Neale Publishing, 1908.

Bryan, George S. *The Great American Myth: The True Story of Lincoln's Murder.* New York: Carrick & Evans, 1940.

Buckingham, J. E., Sr. *Reminiscences and Souvenirs of the Assassination of Abraham Lincoln.* Washington, DC: Press of Rufus H. Darby, 1894.

Burlingame, Michael. *Abraham Lincoln: A Life, Vol. 2.* Baltimore: Johns Hopkins University Press, 2008.

Carpenter, F. B. *Six Months at the White House.* New York: Hurd and Houghton, 1866.

Clarke, Asia Booth. *John Wilkes Booth: A Sister's Memoir.* Jackson: University Press of Mississippi, 1999.

———. *The Unlocked Book.* New York: G. P. Putnam's Sons, 1938.

Clinton, Catherine. *Mrs. Lincoln: A Life.* New York: HarperCollins, 2009.

Craig, Vera. *Furnishing Plan: House Where Lincoln Died.* Harpers Ferry: National Park Service, 1976.

Donald, David Herbert, *Lincoln.* New York: Simon and Schuster, 1995.

———. *Lincoln's Cabinet: The Civil War Diaries of Salmon P. Chase.* New York: Longmans, Green & Co., 1954.

East, Charles, ed. *Sarah Morgan: The Civil War Diary of a Southern Woman.* New York: Simon & Schuster, 1991.

Ellis, John B. *The Sights and Secrets of the National Capital.* New York: U.S. Publishing, 1869.

Emerson, Jason. *Giant in the Shadows: The Life of Robert T. Lincoln.* Carbondale: Southern Illinois University Press, 2012.

Epstein, Daniel Mark. *The Lincolns: Portrait of a Marriage.* New York: Ballantine, 2008.

Erekson, Keith A. *Everybody's History: Indiana's Lincoln Inquiry and the Quest to Reclaim a President's Past.* Amherst: University of Massachusetts Press, 2012.

Eskew, Garnett Laidlaw. *Willard's of Washington.* New York: Coward-McCann, 1954.

Field, Maunsell. *Memories of Many Men and of Some Women.* London: Sampson, Low, Marston, Low & Searle, 1874.

Fischer, Claude S. *Made in America: A Social History of American Culture and Character.* Chicago: University of Chicago Press, 2010.

Flowers, Frank A. *History of the Republican Party: Embracing Its Origin, Growth and Mission.* Springfield: Union Publishing Co., 1884.

Forman, Stephen M. *Guide to Civil War Washington.* Washington, DC: Elliott & Clark, 1995.

Furgurson, Ernest D. *Freedom Rising: Washington in the Civil War.* New York: Vintage, 2004.

Garrett, Jim, and Richard Smyth. *The Lincoln Assassination: Where Are They Now? A Guide to the Burial Places of Individuals Connected to the Lincoln Assassination in Washington, D.C.* Gettysburg: Ten Roads Publishing, 2013.

Good, Timothy S. *We Saw Lincoln Shot: One Hundred Eyewitness Accounts.* Jackson: University Press of Mississippi, 1995.

Grant, U. S. *Personal Memoirs of U. S. Grant.* Cleveland: World Publishing Co., 1952.

The Great Impeachment and Trial of Andrew Johnson. Philadelphia: T. B. Peterson & Bros., 1868.

Green, Julia Gates. *Abraham Lincoln on the Niagara Frontier.* N.p., n.d. Library of Congress.

Haley, James L. *Sam Houston.* Norman: University of Oklahoma Press, 2004.

Hall, James O. *John Wilkes Booth Escape Route.* Clinton: Surratt Society, 2000.

Heidler, David, and Jeanne Heidler, eds. *Encyclopedia of the American Civil War.* New York: W. W. Norton and Co., 2000.

Helm, Katharine. *Mary, Wife of Lincoln.* New York: Harper & Bros., 1918.

Holzer, Harold, Craig L. Symonds, and Frank J. Williams. *The Lincoln Assassination: Crime and Punishment, Myth and Memory.* New York: Fordham University Press, 2010.

Jones, Thomas A. *Wilkes Booth: An Account of his Sojourn in Southern Maryland after the Assassination of Abraham Lincoln, His Passage across the Potomac, and His Death in Virginia.* Chicago: Laird & Lee, 1893.

Kauffman, Michael W. *American Brutus.* New York: Random House, 2004.

Keckley, Elizabeth. *Behind the Scenes.* New York: G. W. Carleton & Co., 1868.

Keneally, Thomas. *American Scoundrel: The Life of the Notorious Civil War General Dan Sickles.* New York: Doubleday, 2002.

Ketcham, John H. *The Life of Abraham Lincoln.* 1884. Rpt., London: Forgotten Books, 2008.

Kimmel, Stanley. *The Mad Booths of Maryland.* Indianapolis: Bobbs-Merrill Co., 1940.

———. *Mr. Lincoln's Washington.* New York: Bramhall House, 1957.

Kunhardt, Dorothy Meserve, and Philip B. Kunhardt. *Twenty Days.* Secaucus: Castle Books, 1965.

Lamon, Ward Hill. *Recollections of Abraham Lincoln, 1847–1865.* Chicago: A. C. McClurg & Co., 1895.

Laughlin, Clara E. *The Death of Lincoln.* New York: Doubleday, Page & Co., 1909.

Leale, Charles A. *Lincoln's Last Hours.* Address Delivered before the Commandery of the New York State Military Order of the Loyal Legion of the United States. New York: privately printed, 1909.

Leech, Margaret. *Reveille in Washington, 1860–1865.* New York: Harper & Bros., 1941.

Longacre, Edward G. *Lincoln's Cavalrymen.* Mechanicsburg: Stackpole, 2000.

Lowry, Thomas P. *The Civil War Bawdy Houses of Washington, D.C.* Fredericksburg: Sergeant Kirkland's Museum and Historical Society, 1997.

MacGregor, Morris J. *A Parish for the Federal City: St. Patrick's in Washington, 1794–1994.* Washington, DC: Catholic University of America Press, 1994.

Mathews, James T. *History of the Lincoln Museum, the Ford Theatre and the Old-royd Collection*. Washington, DC: National Art Service, 1935.

McClure, Stanley. *The Lincoln Museum and the House Where Lincoln Died*. Historical Handbook, Series No. 3. Washington, DC: National Park Service, 1949.

McCullough, Hugh. *Men and Measures of Half a Century*. New York: C. Scribner's & Sons, 1889.

Meacham, Jon. *American Lion*. New York: Random House, 2008.

Miller, Ernest C. *John Wilkes Booth, Oilman*. New York: Exposition Press, 1923.

Morris, Clara. *My Life on the Stage*. New York: McClure, Phillips and Co., 1901.

Newell, Clayton R., Charles R. Shrader, and Edward M. Coffman. *Of Duty Well and Faithfully Done: A History of the Regular Army in the Civil War*. Lincoln: University of Nebraska Press, 2011.

Nickell, Joe. *A Handbook for Photographic Investigation*. Lexington: University Press of Kentucky, 2005.

Nicolay, John G. *A Short Life of Abraham Lincoln*. New York: Century Co., 1919.

Nicolay, John G., and John Hay. *Abraham Lincoln, A History*. 10 vols. New York: Century Co., 1905.

Official Records of the Civil War. Anderson: THA New Media, 2008.

Olszewski, George J. *Restoration of Ford's Theatre: Historic Structures Report*. Washington, DC: National Park Service, 1965.

Ownsbey, Betty J. *Alias Paine: Lewis Thornton Powell, the Mystery Man of the Lincoln Conspiracy*. Jefferson: McFarland & Co., 1993.

Phillips, Donald T. *Lincoln on Leadership*. New York: Warner, 1993.

Pitman, Benn. *The Assassination of President Lincoln and the Trial of the Conspirators*. Cincinnati: Wilstach & Baldwin, 1865.

Poore, Benjamin, ed. *The Conspiracy Trial for the Murder of the President, and the Attempt to Overthrow the Government by the Assassination of its Principal Officers*. 3 vols. Boston: J. E. Tilton, 1865.

Pratt, Harry E. *The Personal Finances of Abraham Lincoln*. Springfield: Abraham Lincoln Association, 1943.

Reck, W. Emerson. *A. Lincoln: His Last 24 Hours*. Jefferson: McFarland & Co., 1987.

Rector, George. *The Girl from Rector's*. Garden City: Doubleday, Page & Co., 1927.

Reichel, William C., and William H. Bigler. *A History of the Moravian Seminary for Young Ladies*. Bethlehem: Moravian Seminary, 1901.

Rhodehamel, John, and Louise Taper. *"Right or Wrong, God Judge Me": The Writings of John Wilkes Booth*. Urbana: University of Illinois Press, 1997.

Ross, Ishbel. *President's Wife: Mary Todd Lincoln*. New York: Putnam, 1973.

Sandburg, Carl. *Mary Lincoln: Wife and Widow*. New York: Harcourt, Brace, 1932.

Smith, James E. *A Famous Battery and Its Campaigns, 1861–64: The Career of Cpl. James Tanner in War and in Peace*. Washington, DC: W. H. Lowdermilk & Co., 1892.

Steers, Edward, Jr. *Blood on the Moon*. Lexington: University Press of Kentucky, 2001.

Steers, Edward, Jr., and William C. Edwards, eds. *The Lincoln Assassination: The Evidence.* Champaign: University of Illinois Press, 2009.

———. *The Lincoln Assassination Encyclopedia.* New York: Harper Perennial, 2010.

Stewart, T. D. *An Anthropologist Looks at Lincoln.* Washington, DC: Government Printing Office, 1952.

Stimmel, Smith. *Personal Reminiscences of Abraham Lincoln.* Minneapolis: William H. M. Adams, 1928.

Stuart, G. H. *The Life of George H. Stuart.* Philadelphia: J. M. Stoddart & Co., 1890.

Styple, William B., ed. *Generals in Bronze: Interviewing the Commanders of the Civil War.* Kearny: Belle Grove, 2005.

Swanson, James L. *Manhunt: The 12-Day Chase for Lincoln's Killer.* New York: Harper Perennial, 2007.

Taft, Charles S. *Abraham Lincoln's Last Hours, from the Notebook of Charles Sabin Taft M.D., an Army Surgeon Present at the Assassination, Death and Autopsy.* Chicago: privately printed, 1934.

The Terrible Tragedy at Washington: Assassination of President Lincoln. Last Hours and Death-Bed Scenes of the President. Philadelphia: Nabu Public Domain Reprints, 2011.

Titone, Nora. *My Thoughts Be Bloody: The Bitter Rivalry That Led to the Assassination of Abraham Lincoln.* New York: Free Press, 2010.

The Trial of John H. Surratt. 2 vols. Washington, DC: French and Richardson, 1867.

A Tribute of the Nations. Old Saybrook: Konecky & Konecky, 2009.

Virta, Matthew R. *Archeology at the Petersen House.* Washington, DC: National Park Service, 1991.

The War of the Rebellion: A Compilation of the Official Records of the Union and Confederate Armies. Tamarac: Historical Archive Corp., THA New Media, 2006.

Watson, Irving A. *Physicians and Surgeons of America.* Concord: Republican Press Association, 1896.

Weichmann, Louis J. *A True History of the Assassination of Abraham Lincoln and of the Conspiracy of 1865.* New York: Alfred A. Knopf, 1975.

Welles, Gideon. *The Diary of Gideon Welles.* 3 vols. New York: Houghton Mifflin Co., 1911.

Wesolowski, Wayne, and Mary Cay Wesolowski. *The Lincoln Train Is Coming.* Cortaro: privately printed, 1995.

William A. Petersen House: The House Where Lincoln Died. Historic Structure Report. Washington, DC: National Park Service, 2001.

Wilson, Rufus Rockwell, ed. *Intimate Memories of Lincoln.* Elmira: Primavera Press, 1945.

Withers, Nan Wyatt. *The Acting Style and Career of John Wilkes Booth.* Madison: University of Wisconsin Press, 2009.

Index

CPSIA information can be obtained at www.ICGtesting.com
Printed in the USA
BVOW02*0805111115

426605BV00001B/2/P